THE BEST TEN-MINUTE PLAYS 2018

THE BEST TEN-MINUTE PLAYS 2018

Edited by Lawrence Harbison

A Smith and Kraus Book   2018

A Smith and Kraus Book
177 Lyme Road, Hanover, NH 03755
editorial 603.643.6431 To Order 1.877.668.8680
www.smithandkraus.com

The Best Ten-Minute Plays 2018 Copyright
© 2018 by Smith and Kraus, Inc
All rights reserved.

Manufactured in the United States of America

ISBN: 9781575259246
Library of Congress Control Number: 2164-2435

Typesetting and layout by Elizabeth E. Monteleone
Cover by Olivia Monteleone

For information about custom editions, special sales, education and corporate purchases, please contact Smith and Kraus at editor@smithandkraus.com or 603.643.6431.

TABLE OF CONTENTS

Plays For Three Or More Actors

FOREWORD

In this volume, you will find fifty terrific new ten-minute plays from the 2017-2018 theatrical season, culled from the several hundred I read last year. They are written in a variety of styles. Some are realistic plays; some are not. Some are comic (laughs); some are dramatic (no laughs). The ten-minute play form lends itself well to experimentation in style. A playwright can have fun with a device which couldn't be sustained as well in a longer play. Several of these plays employ such a device.

In years past, playwrights who were just starting out wrote one-act plays of thirty to forty minutes in duration. One thinks of writers such as Eugene O'Neill, A. R. Gurney, Lanford Wilson, John Guare and several others. Now, new playwrights tend to work in the ten-minute play genre, largely because there are so many production opportunities. When I was Senior Editor for Samuel French, it occurred to me that there might be a market for these very short plays, which Actors Theatre of Louisville had been commissioning for several years for use by their Apprentice Company. I made a deal with Jon Jory and Michael Bigelow Dixon of ATL, who assisted me in compiling an anthology of these plays, which sold so well that Samuel French went on to publish several more anthologies of ten-minute plays from Actors Theatre. For the first time, ten-minute plays were now published and widely available, and they started getting produced. There are now many ten-minute play festivals every year, not only in the U.S. but all over the world. I have included a comprehensive list of theatres which do ten-minute plays, which I hope playwrights will find useful.

What makes a good ten-minute play? Well, first and foremost I have to like it. Isn't that what we mean when we call a play, a film, a novel "good?" We mean that it effectively portrays the world as I see it, written in a style which interests me. Beyond this, a good ten-minute play has to have the same elements that any good play must have: a strong conflict, interesting, well-drawn characters and compelling subject matter. It also has to have a clear beginning, middle and end. In other words, it's a full length play which runs about ten minutes. Some of the plays which are submitted to me each year are scenes, not complete plays; well-written scenes in many cases, but scenes nonetheless. They left me wanting more. I chose plays which are complete in and of themselves, which I believe will excite those of you who produce ten-minute plays; because if a play isn't produced, it's the proverbial sound of a tree falling in the forest far away. In the Rights & Permissions section at the back of this book you will find information on whom to contact when you decide which plays you want to produce, in order to acquire performance rights.

This year, there are new plays by masters of the ten-minute play form whose work has appeared in previous volumes in this series, such as Don Nigro, Eric Pfeffinger, C.S. Hanson, C.J. Ehrlich, Lee Blessing, Marisa Smith, J. Thalia Cunningham, Richard Vetere, Elayne Heilveil, Maya MacDonald and Jenny Lyn Bader, but there are many plays by wonderful playwrights who may be new to you, such as Graham Techler, Hortense Gerardo, Holly Hepp-Galván, David MacGregor, Melinda Lopez, Krista Knight and Susan Eve Haar.

I hope you enjoy these plays. I sure did!

Lawrence Harbison

Lawrence Harbison

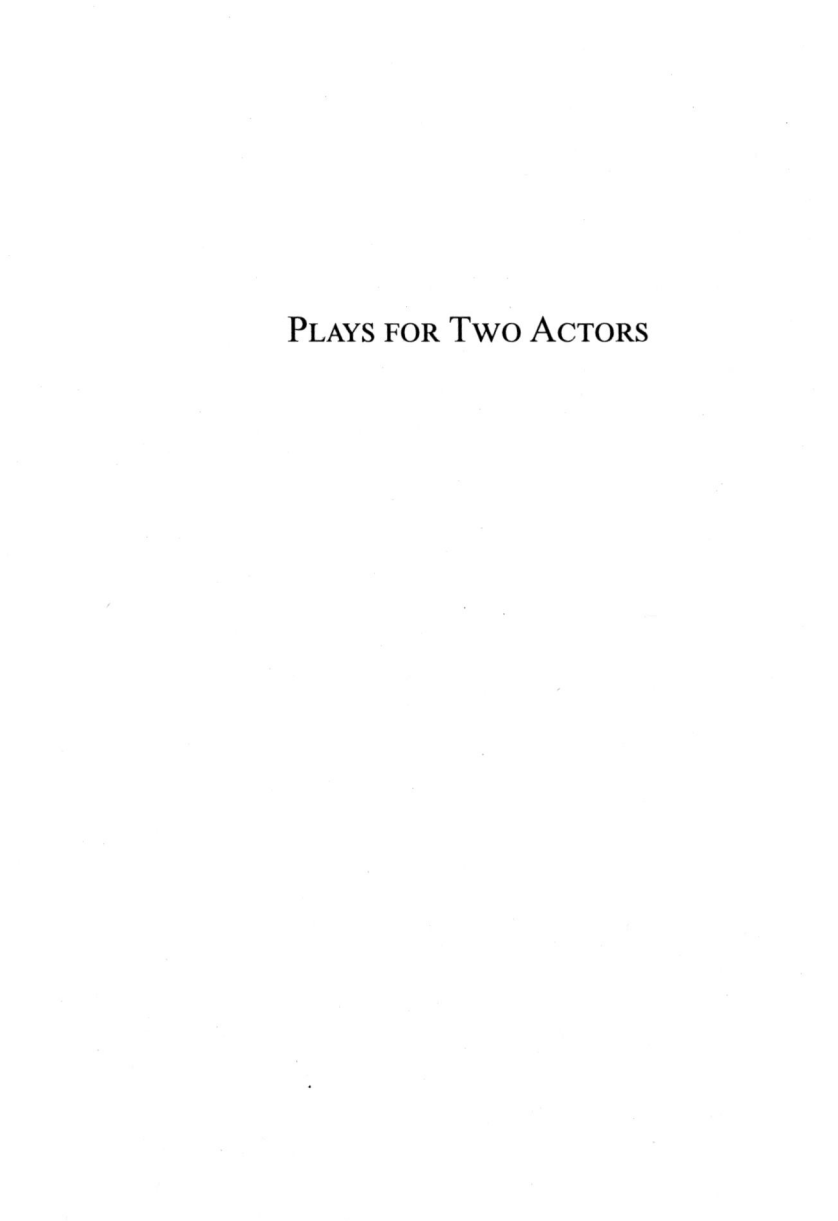

PLAYS FOR TWO ACTORS

AFTER YOU

Lee Blessing

The world premiere of AFTER YOU took place in October, 2017 as part of the Theatre Brut Festival (as part of the All About Eve Festival of the Arts), New Jersey Repertory Company, Long Branch, NJ, directed by Peter Zazzali. The cast was as follows:

EVE—Susan Maris
FARR—Seth Macchi

CHARACTERS

EVE: 30 or so
FARR: younger

SETTING

Evening. A terrace. Perhaps, an amazing view.

Lee Blessing

EVE and FARR sit a table with after-dinner wine.

FARR: One wonders why we even need arms and hands at this point. So much is wireless now, to be archaic. So much comes as a product of thought alone.

EVE: Not the wine.

FARR: Not the wine. But that's my point: the effect of the wine, the pleasure, the memory—glint of setting sun on glass, bouquet—intimacy itself, the two of us on this terrace in a perfect month, wine slithering down our throats—

EVE: Poet.

FARR: It's overkill. This, all this, is already inside us—retrievable whenever we like. Without the wine. Without the terrace, without—

EVE: Intimacy?

FARR: As I've said, we feel the intimacy, whenever we like. The entire experience. It's already there. We can have it when

EVE: Alone?

FARR: With no one, with a crowd of people . . . It doesn't matter.

EVE: Doesn't it?

FARR: Wish you'd be a little more impressed. This is the genius of the age.

EVE: So all this that's in front of us, everything we're experiencing is . . . redundant?

FARR: Absolutely. I have no idea why you asked for it.

EVE: I don't know, Mr. Farr. I suppose I wanted a sense of occasion.

She takes a drink.

EVE: *(cont'd)* You're not drinking.

FARR: Don't have to.

EVE: It's a top-notch Chablis.

FARR: I know, I'm really enjoying it. Amazing to think. Every wine ever made . . .

(pointing to his head)

Pre-loaded at birth. The complete library of all human experience. Everyone with the same store of information, attitudes, ambitions—

EVE: Which is good because—?

FARR: Because what alternative is there? Delights must become universal. Conflicts must be minimized. Hell, eliminated. You really should take more advantage.

EVE: I suppose.

FARR: Our whole trajectory leads us to rise above brute competition. That's what consciousness means: we see something better, and—

EVE: And get there no matter what?

FARR: Look at the results. Where are the ills of the world? Gone.

EVE: And buried.

FARR: Just in time, too. We're about to make first contact.

EVE: Not for twenty-five years.

FARR: The point is, they're on their way. We have to be ready. No alternative to that, either.

EVE: I suppose.

FARR: Can you imagine if we hadn't gotten the planet in order? What would they have found? One shudders to think.

EVE: I know I do.

FARR: What?

EVE: Shudder. To think.

FARR: *(staring at her)* You have an edge.

EVE: Do I?

FARR: You retain sarcasm. Sarcasm has no place in what's going on.

EVE: It doesn't?

FARR: We reduced the world's population by seventy-five percent. An entire continent was set aside for burning bodies—which we can all smell whenever we wish of course, because that too is pre-loaded.

EVE: Wouldn't want to forget.

FARR: So yes, one would do well to put sarcasm aside for the present.

EVE: I'm not trying to argue—

FARR: It's not like we had a choice. Science told us we were standing on the brink. Jettisoning all who resisted, plus plenty who didn't, was brute necessity.

EVE: *(after a beat)* Yes.

FARR: And where are we now? War, disease, climatic chaos—all in the past. Our own inherent limitations gone. Everyone who survived is functional, cooperative. Disputes are gone. Differences gone. Stable. Finally worthy to sail in Lifeboat Earth—that is what we are. One aim, one language, no religion, no politics. A unified voice, ready to contact other worlds. In short, the greatest miracle in history.

EVE raises her glass.

EVE: To miracles.

She drinks. He doesn't move.

FARR: I can't get over how delicious the wine is.

EVE: You really like it?

FARR: Oh, yes.

EVE: I guess some people just know how to live.

They stare at the setting sun.

FARR: I feel very close to you right now.

EVE: Do you?

(after a beat)

Should we have sex?

FARR: What? What are you talking about?

EVE: Having sex.

FARR: Why would we do that?

EVE: I don't know. Beautiful evening. We're both young, pretty . . .

FARR: Sex is a dead end. It's no longer connected to reproduction in any way.

EVE: There's still the thrill, the pleasure.

FARR: Which is best experienced alone, minimizing the chance of violence, shame or regret. Sex. What on earth are you thinking?

EVE: I merely—

FARR: Not to mention that sex between two people is inherently dangerous. That's well known. And it can't come close to what's pre-programmed. The pleasure/intimacy nexus has been geometrically increased.

EVE: So we don't want partners?

FARR: We are *spared* partners. Plus now that it's totally internalized we can have it whenever we like. Taking a walk, staring out the window, eating a sandwich—

EVE: Isn't the whole point of sex that there are two people? At least?

FARR: Are you even *list*ening to me?

EVE: You honestly think that nothing's lost?

FARR: Something's *gained*.

EVE: Mr. Farr—

FARR: A new kind of intimacy, far vaster. Everyone already there inside you, loving you, holding you—

EVE: What about romance? Choosing someone specially, even for a night—

FARR: To what end—?

EVE: Partnership.

FARR: Little teams of two. Is that what you want?

EVE: It's comforting.

FARR: And it's held our species back for millennia.

EVE: So, you . . . don't want to . . . ?

(as he stares at her)

I think I could make my point better if we . . .

FARR: No. It's revolting. Settling for so much less pleasure.

EVE: But *with* someone—

FARR: Creating division, anger—

EVE: Jealousy?

FARR: Any group not fully linked to the rest of humanity is totally unworkable. Attraction, possession, struggle—these are all roadblocks to our true path.

EVE: Which leads to . . . ?

FARR: Space. Other worlds. Leaving Earth as *one harmonious consciousness*. We'll never do that if we don't conquer our instincts, if we can't become, what? If we can't become—

EVE: Machines?

FARR: Yes! Yes. *Thank* you.

EVE: So our only path to preserving humanity is to stop being humanity?

FARR: Is that so hard to understand?

EVE: I don't think I've ever understood it.

FARR: This is hopeless. You're impervious, I swear. Thank goodness it's your last night.

EVE: Excuse me?

A beat.

FARR: Your last night. Surely you know.

EVE: Know what? What do you mean?

FARR: I don't believe this. No one told you?

EVE: Told me what?

He indicates the table, wine, etc.

FARR: You thought all this was for your birthday?

EVE: Isn't it? I *am* thirty. It's kind of a big—

FARR: You're leaving. Tonight.

EVE: I'm—?

FARR: Are you sure no one told you? The decision—the communal decision, the unanimous decision—is that there's no point any longer in keeping even one. Reproduction's industrial now, completely decoupled from sex. Full control of the genome, reliably randomized mutation process—there's no need for two sexes. Not anymore, not even to study, even for, I don't know, for—

EVE: Nostalgia?

FARR: When first contact comes, you should be nothing more than a quickly-dimming memory.

I mean, you're practically gone already. You haven't been available to the public for decades.

EVE: Scientific study only.

FARR: Precisely. Sorry you had to find out this way. I just presumed—

EVE: Can I ask a question?

FARR: Do you have to?

EVE: Yes.

FARR: *(with a sigh)* All right, why not?

EVE: Why get rid of women? Why not men?

FARR: You're not really asking that.

EVE: Don't I have the right?

FARR: It's just so obvious—

EVE: Why? Why keep men?

FARR: This has been gone over time and again—

EVE: Why men?

A beat.

FARR: We're simpler.

She stares at him.

FARR: *(cont'd)* Time's up. We have to go.

EVE: Really? Now?

FARR: Right now. This is a crucial and glorious step for humanity, Eve. Your gender has performed immense service to the cause of progress, but now . . . we move on. That's all. I hope you can appreciate the wisdom of our decision.

(rising)

Shall we?

She waits, then rises.

EVE: I'm going to miss this wine.

FARR: It is the very best. What else will you miss?

She stares at him for a long moment.

FARR: Well.

(standing aside)

After you.

EVE walks past him and exits. He stares at the wine on the table.

End of play

Lee Blessing

THE CHIP
Michael Higgins

The Chip was first performed on September 30, 2017 at The Upstairs Theatre, St. Paul's Lutheran Church, Brooklyn N.Y., as part of The Navigators' Lift-Off New Play Series. Directed by Sharifa Williams. Cast: Rebissa – Penelope Hsu; Vander – Jeremy Rafal.

The Chip was also produced on November 11, 2017 at The Public House Theatre in Chicago, as part of Otherworld Theatre's Paragon Play Festival. Directed by Juan Castañeda. Cast: Rebissa – Clarissa Gasiciel; Vander – Kevin Carroll.

CHARACTERS

REBISSA: Female. 20s/30s. A struggling artist.

VANDER: Male. 20s/30s. A man who screens potential astronauts.

CASTING NOTE

All characters can be played by actors of any race or ethnicity.

TIME

Ninety years in the future.

SETTING

A small apartment that also serves as an art studio.

Lights up on REBISSA in her apartment, standing behind a painter's easel. A thin sheet of metal sits on the easel like a canvas, facing away from the audience.

REBISSA wears thrift-store clothes in a stylish way. She holds a device that looks like a laser pointer. (This is a "laser brush.") Her necklace contains a tiny cell phone.

REBISSA: *(on the phone)*... I can't. I don't have time. ... The painting is due tomorrow.

(looks at painting with pride)

Honestly, I think it's the best thing I've done. ... If I win the fellowship, we'll go to lunch. Real lunch. No synthetic tuna. ... Please. Tracy, you're not fat. And if you want to eat healthy, you should try the Smart Plate from Tech Products. They put sensors in the plate that measure calories, carbs, everything. Then the plate sends diet tips to your mobile device.

(small laugh)

... I don't know. You brought it up. Hey, I gotta go. ... Bye. She taps her necklace, ending the call. She looks at the painting and carefully moves the laser brush above the surface of the canvas.

A door buzzer sounds. REBISSA taps her necklace.

REBISSA: *(into phone)* Who is it?

(beat – a little embarrassed)

OK, I'll get the door.

REBISSA taps her necklace again. A beat and VANDER enters uncertainly. It's awkward.

VANDER: Hi.

REBISSA: Hi, Vander.

VANDER: If I shouldn't have come, I can ... go.

REBISSA: No. It's ... How have you been?

VANDER: OK, I guess. ... So you're painting?

REBISSA: It's the one I told you about. My grandmother?

VANDER: Oh, wow. Can I see it?

REBISSA: It's not finished. It won't be until I ... finish it.

VANDER: Look, I'm sorry to just show up like this. But I thought our dates went so well and ...

REBISSA: *(sincere)*They did. They were great. I just ...

VANDER: What?

REBISSA: It's just ... I've been busy. And I thought *you'd* be busy – with the big space launch.

VANDER: I was. But now it's Launch Day, so we're basically done.

REBISSA: Oh ...

VANDER: We just do psych tests on the astronauts. Make sure they're stable enough for the mission. ... But still crazy enough to go. Sorry. It's a joke around the office.

REBISSA: You know, Blue Marble Tours offers low-cost weekends in Earth orbit? You can see every continent and the northern lights – all with twenty percent less nausea. But you need to book soon.

VANDER: I don't want to go to space.

REBISSA: Right. Sorry. ... Vander, you're the best guy I've met since I moved here. But I ... I can't be in a relationship right now.

VANDER: Why not?

REBISSA: Well ... For one, I'm broke. I can't afford to do anything.

VANDER: Me, too. I've got college loans. Not as bad as some people. But still, three-point-eight million ....

REBISSA: You should play World Ball. Did you know normal lottery winners are often broke again in just a few years, thanks to wild spending, gambling or drugs? But with World Ball's *billion* dollar jackpots, you can afford all three. It's the lottery you can't screw up.

VANDER: Why are you telling me this?

REBISSA: *(beat)* When I got home from our second date, I had a message from an ad agency, Voice Box Media. They wanted *me* to do convomercials.

VANDER: Convo ... mercials?

REBISSA: It's a new thing. If they like your look, your style, they'll pay you to promote products in your everyday conversations.

VANDER: How do they know you're even doing it?

REBISSA: They put a computer chip back here.

    (points to the back of her head)

When you hear certain words, it triggers a voice stimulator.

VANDER: Wait. You have a computer in your head, making you

say things?

REBISSA: It doesn't hurt. It's a reflex – like tapping your knee with the little mallet.

VANDER: Rebissa ...

REBISSA: See? I knew you wouldn't like it.

VANDER: I was worried about you. I rode all over town, gallery to gallery, asking people if they'd seen you.

REBISSA: Are you tired of self-driving cars that follow every picky law and speed limit? Well, now there's the new Ford Violator. Sit back and enjoy while the Violator floors it through yellow lights and cuts off other drivers with stopwatch precision.

VANDER: My car is fine. Listen —

REBISSA: Whether you're in a hurry or just angry at life, get the car that drives like you feel. The Violator. Test ride one today.

    (off VANDER's dismayed look)

Sorry. Was that the car?

VANDER: Can't you hear what you're saying?

REBISSA: It's hard to listen while the ad is running.

VANDER: I can't believe they put this thing in your head.

REBISSA: It's nothing. Just a little chip.

    (pulling her hair to one side)

Look.

    VANDER walks behind her and looks.

VANDER: I don't see it.

REBISSA: Push down. You can feel it.

    VANDER touches the back of her head, feeling for the chip.

VANDER: Oh. There it is.

    He breathes in, loud enough for her to hear.

REBISSA: Are you ... smelling me?

VANDER: No. I was just ... breathing. Sorry.

REBISSA: It's OK. It's just I've been painting all morning. So maybe —

VANDER: No, you smell good. I mean, I wasn't smelling. But, as part of the breathing ... I did a little.

REBISSA: I know I should've called you. It's just ... It can be embarrassing.

VANDER: No. Nothing is embarrassing. Listen ...

(hesitates, then heartfelt)

I know it was only two dates. But I'm crazy about you.

REBISSA: Are you ready to get close with that special someone? Try the Smart Condom from Tech Products. Sensors in the condom track all key data, from intensity and lubrication to risk of disease. Smart Condoms: The internet of things has never been so romantic.

VANDER: *(beat)* That was a little embarrassing.

REBISSA: The condom ad. I should not have double loaded.

VANDER: Double loaded what?

REBISSA: Voice Box Media put in fifty gigabytes of ads. But I needed art supplies and the rent was due, so I ... I went to Brain Talk Worldwide. They put in another fifty – off the books.

VANDER: That sounds dangerous.

REBISSA: So is being homeless.

VANDER: You need to get that taken out.

REBISSA: No way. I can finally afford my own place. Besides, I signed a contract.

VANDER: For how long?

REBISSA: Two years.

VANDER: *Two years?*

REBISSA: You should go. I have to finish my painting.

VANDER: But this is crazy.

REBISSA: It makes perfect sense. Everywhere you look, there's ads. What cuts through the clutter? Personal recommendations.

VANDER: Not crazy for them. For *you.*

REBISSA: It's like being a spokesperson. Only you don't have to be a celebrity. Or memorize lines, because it's all in the chip.

VANDER: Do you know how easily this could be abused?

REBISSA: Things-that-could-be-easily-abused is the fastest-growing segment of the economy. Can we afford to be left behind?

VANDER: Wait. Are you programmed to defend the chip?

REBISSA: No. I ...

(a flash of concern, but she brushes it aside)

I think you should leave.

> *A beat. VANDER, reluctantly, steps toward the door, then stops.*

VANDER: Could I at least see the painting?

REBISSA: It's not finished.

VANDER: I know. But you told me about the 3-D and the live motion and I just ... I really wanted to see it.

REBISSA: OK. But then you have to go.

> *VANDER joins REBISSA behind the canvas. He's blown away.*

VANDER: This is amazing. The 3-D is so real. And the waves. The way they move.

REBISSA: They don't repeat. Every wave that hits the shore is a little different.

VANDER: And it's all nanotechnology?

REBISSA: Each drop of paint is a tiny robot. I use the laser brush to position the 'bots, but also to program their motion.

VANDER: And that's your grandma?

REBISSA: She was a marine biologist. Did a lot of environmental crusading.

VANDER: So this was a real place?

REBISSA: An island off the coast of Florida. It's all under now.

VANDER: She looks like you.

REBISSA: Vander, I really have to get back to work. This is due tomorrow.

VANDER: And those are ... rocks?

REBISSA: Sea shells. When I was a girl, there were so many they would pile up like snow drifts.

> *(moving her hands to expand the picture)*

Grandma taught me the names. Those are Lightning Pitars.

VANDER: The round ones?

REBISSA: Yes. And those are Speckled Tellins.

VANDER: Rebissa ... look at the shells.

REBISSA: I'm looking.

VANDER: Really *look.*

> *REBISSA looks closer and is stunned.*

REBISSA: Those aren't shells.

VANDER: No ...

REBISSA: They're Smart Condoms from Tech Products.

> *REBISSA starts to tear up.*

VANDER: I'm sure you can fix it.

REBISSA: *(to herself) No ....*

VANDER: You're like a genius with this stuff.

> *REBISSA, crushed, stares at the painting for a long beat.*

REBISSA: Take it out.

VANDER: What?

REBISSA: Take it out.

> *REBISSA, fighting back tears, grabs a Laser Brush and adjusts it.*

REBISSA: If you turn the laser all the way up, it'll cut skin.

> *REBISSA gives VANDER the laser brush and sits in the chair. She reaches back and pulls her hair aside.*

VANDER: I can't —

REBISSA: It's right below the skin. Just cut, and pull it out.

> *VANDER hesitates.*

REBISSA: Please.

> *Reluctantly, VANDER feels the back of her head. He finds the chip.*

VANDER: Are you sure?

REBISSA: Cut!

> *VANDER cuts. REBISSA winces.*

REBISSA: OK, pull.

VANDER: *(pulling on the chip)* It won't come out.

REBISSA: Pull harder.

> *VANDER pulls harder and the chip comes out. REBISSA yelps and faints, sliding off the chair. He tries to grab her, but they both fall to the floor.*

VANDER: Oh god.

> *(shaking her)*

Rebissa.

VANDER feels for a pulse, checks her breathing, then shakes her again.

VANDER: Wake up ... wake up.

REBISSA wakes up, a little groggy.

VANDER: *(a beat, as he catches his breath)* Are you OK?

REBISSA: Yeah, I ... I think so.

VANDER: Listen: We should have sex right now. And use birth control.

A beat, as VANDER awaits her reaction.

REBISSA: What?

VANDER: You're back.

REBISSA: Oh. Right.

(laughs)

How about we just get coffee?

VANDER: How about we make some here. ... You've got a painting to finish.

Lights fade.

End Of Play

COMFORT ZONES

Mark Rigney

"Comfort Zones" was first produced by Edmonds Driftwood Players as part of their 8th Annual Festival of Shorts, July 7-9, 2017, in Edmonds, Washington. Producer: Diane Jamieson.

Directed by James Wilson

Cast:
SHE: Ashton Lundy
HE: Morgan Peeler

CHARACTERS:

SHE: Female, twenties or older.
HE: Male, twenties or older.

THE TIME:

Right this minute.

PLACE & SET REQUIREMENTS:

An interior space that suggests a laboratory or plain interrogation room. A table, a few sealed containers, some power tools, and a Hex Bug or three. Hex Bugs are a trademarked toy available online and, in-store, at many major retail outlets. They are inexpensive, and are often sold in multi-packs.

Lights up on an interior space. A table with a number of objects on it, including sealed storage containers and a variety of heavy-duty tools. SHE faces off with HE.

SHE: First things first. I want to thank you for participating in our sweepstakes and research program.

HE: Oh, the pleasure's mine, I'm totally excited.

SHE: You're hoping you'll win.

HE: A new truck, fully loaded? Are you kidding?

SHE: Then I wish you all the luck in the world. But you do understand. We have rules. Your name is placed in the metaphorical hat only in return for your willing participation in our study.

HE: Absolutely. Sounds great.

SHE: Also, no sentient beings will be harmed in any way as a result of your participation.

HE: Good to know.

SHE: Let's begin with your attitudes toward the truck. Do you have a color preference?

HE: For trucks, pickup trucks? Midnight blue is just the perfect color.

SHE: (*Taking notes*) Automatic or standard transmission?

HE: Man, with a truck it's like criminal to go automatic. Four-wheel drive and all that, you want control, you know?

SHE: Okay. Standard transmission. Now. Do you think I'm hot?

HE: 'Scuse me?

SHE: All part of the study. And I promise you won't hurt my feelings, either way. The question on the table: do you think I'm hot?

HE: Uh, yeah. Actually.

SHE: Thank you. Now, would you prefer your pickup to have a fully functioning auto-pilot system?

HE: What, like driverless?

SHE: Exactly. Your pickup—if you win—will be fully automated. Capable of taking you where you wish to go based solely on destination input data.

HE: Look, maybe this is a guy thing, but in a moving vehicle? I really need to feel safe.

SHE: So even if other cars on the road utilize driverless technology, you yourself don't want it.

HE: I mean, sure, wave of the future and all that. And maybe, okay, maybe eventually, once it's really been road-tested and all, but now? That's too, like, science fiction.

SHE retrieves a small object from the table: a robotic Hex Bug." SHE switches it on so that its legs scissor back and forth while SHE holds it.

SHE: Do you know what this is?

HE: Yeah, sure. It's like one of these little insect toys.

SHE: A toy, and a very simple robot. Its programming is limited to one command: when it bumps into an obstacle, it turns sideways and tries to find a new path forward.

HE: Okay. Kind of like people.

SHE: I'm going to put it on the ground.

HE: Okay.

SHE: I want you to crush it with your foot.

HE: Really?

Quick! Before it gets away!

HE: Okay, all right. (*To the bug*) Come back here. (*HE crushes the Hex Bug*) Seems like kind of a waste, but: here you go.

SHE ignores the proffered bug. Instead, SHE fetches one of the sealed containers.

SHE: Do you think there is a cat inside this container?

HE: Do I think... How should I know?

SHE: Guess.

HE: This is like that guy, that guy with the cat that's alive and dead at the same time.

SHE: You are referring to Schrödinger's Cat?

HE: That's the one.

SHE: No. Schrödinger's Cat refers to a specific thought experiment involving a radioactive particle which may or may not decay sufficiently to release a poison capable of killing a hypothetical cat inside a hypothetical box, in which case the wave forms for said cat's existence or demise continue to exist in opposition to one another until the intelligence controlling the experiment opens the box and discovers the results. But let me assure you. That is in no way what we are doing here.

HE: Um, okay.

SHE: Let's pretend there is a kitten inside this container. An adorable kitten with eyes like planets. Now, will you please do me a favor?

HE: Sure.

SHE: Drown the kitten.

HE: What?

SHE: There's a room with a bathtub just through that door. Take the kitten, fill the bath, hold the kitten under until it stops wriggling.

HE: This is part of how I win the pickup?

SHE: Yes.

HE: I can't, I'm sorry. Just, no.

SHE: Even if it means your name will be removed from the lottery system? Because if we remove your name, you will then have no chance of winning the free fully loaded pickup truck.

HE: Yeah, sorry. Drowning kittens, that's just—and I'd have to do it with the cat right in my hands?

SHE: Squirming and mewing. Definitely.

HE: Okay. No. Just flat out no.

SHE trades the first container for the second.

SHE: Very well. You are still in the running, and the only thing in this container is a mosquito.

HE: O-kay.

SHE: Through that door, just past the room with the bathtub, is a big oven. I want you to place the container in the oven, turn the heat to three hundred, and bake the mosquito until it is dead.

HE: Great, sure. That I can do. (*After taking the container*) And I am still in the running for the truck?

SHE: Yes.

HE: Even though I said no to the kitten thing?

SHE: Correct.

HE: All right. Well, I guess I'll be back in a couple.

SHE: There's no need, thank you. You may put the box back on the table.

HE: So the mosquito—just a hypothetical?

SHE: Let's review. Your new pickup, should you win. Fully loaded, midnight blue, four on the floor.

HE: Look, I don't want to, you know, drag my problems all over the place, but this could really turn my life around. I don't know what it was like for you, but for me, after graduation, the debts I'm dealing with? Man.

SHE: I want to remind you that the truck will be outfitted with driverless technology.

HE: But I can override, right? Switch it off.

SHE: No. With this pickup, the truck does the driving. You may sit behind the wheel if you wish, but doing so will only serve a sentimental, nostalgic function. The wheel will not be connected to the axles any more than your accelerator will be connected to the engine.

HE: But there is a switch. Somewhere. An on / off switch.

SHE: This truck is a state-of-the-art. Worth well over forty-five thousand dollars, even before we throw in the lifetime supply of gasoline.

HE: Lifetime? Like, the vehicle's whole entire life?

SHE: Correct. Or yours, whichever comes first.

HE: That is one serious perk.

SHE: Before we continue, let me remind you that you think I'm hot.

HE: Uh, yeah?

SHE: Very good. Now: driverless technology. We offer two basic packages.

HE: Okay, options are good.

SHE: These packages are scenario-driven. Even in the best of all possible worlds, we in the auto industry acknowledge that some collisions are unavoidable. In these worst-case scenarios, people will be killed no matter what the truck's A.I. protocol decides. Would you prefer the package that will err on the side of killing those outside of the vehicle—a crowd of bystanders and pedestrians, for example—or would you prefer the heroic suicide option, where the truck turns sharply and smashes nose first into the nearest solid object?

HE: Um, could I just ask—the suicide option, if the truck does that— if it avoids the people by crashing itself—I could die. Right?

SHE: In the scenario I have just described, in the latter case, you would almost certainly be a fatality.

HE: Awesome truck like this, and no airbags?

SHE: Airbags are standard, of course. But this would be a very high-speed encounter.

HE: If I say kill the other people, kill the strangers, you're not going to give me the truck.

SHE: That is what we in the sweepstakes industry refer to as a baseless supposition.

HE: You're nuts.

SHE: I can assure you that nuts are not part of the study.

HE: Okay, what the hell. Sign me up for "kill the strangers." 'Cos if this driverless feature is so terrific, it'll never happen, right? I'll never have to make that choice.

SHE: That choice will be made before you ever enter the vehicle. It will be a pre-condition to title and registration.

HE: And you think consumers are gonna go for this? (*Dismissive*) Brave new world.

SHE: We have only one item remaining.

HE: Lay it on me.

SHE: Would you please take this ballpeen hammer and bludgeon me to death?

HE: What?

SHE: Take the hammer. Hit me with it until I'm dead.

HE: You're kidding.

SHE: If you would prefer, you could use the circular saw. There's an outlet just behind you, there.

HE: I am not *attacking* you with a circular saw!

SHE: Because I'm hot.

HE: What? No, because you're—you're a person!

SHE: Pretend I'm a pickup truck. Pretend I'm a pickup truck that you are angry with because, in order to save your life, it has just run down a crowd of fifty strangers.

HE: You're crazy.

SHE: You killed the Hex Bug.

HE: It's a bug, a toy!

SHE: Is it because I'm hot? I have an assistant in the next room. She is very ugly. You could dismember her, if you prefer.

HE: I am not—no. Nobody is dismembering anything.

SHE: What about the drill? (*Whirr, whirr*) It's a very good drill.

HE: That's it, I'm outta here.

SHE: Or, if you prefer, you could simply switch me off. Remove the battery. Take a hammer to that.

HE: Say what?

SHE: Think of me as a glorified Hex Bug. Or a truck, one whose operating system you are afraid of.

HE: You're a...?

SHE: Yes.

HE: What exactly are you studying?

SHE: Human response to conflicting ethical demands, specifically those that relate to artificial intelligence. That, and the likelihood that given the opportunity, future drivers of America will choose to disable their driverless technologies.

HE: There's no truck, is there? Nothing to win.

SHE: To win your truck, or at least keep your name in the metaphorical hat, all you have to do, one way or the other, is disable me.

HE: Okay. So you're a cyborg. You've got a switch or a battery. Where?

SHE: I'm sorry. My programming does not allow me to reveal that information.

HE: Your loss.

> *He begins to pat her down. The "safe spaces" are quickly exhausted, leaving him forced explore increasingly private areas: face, armpits, inside of thighs, buttocks, maybe breasts...*

SHE: You are hesitating.

HE: This is really not kosher.

SHE: You're worried you're molesting me. Groping.

HE: Well, yeah.

SHE: But you have my permission. And besides, I'm not human. (*As HE continues to hesitate*) You will lose the truck.

HE: You feel real!

SHE: But what if I didn't?

HE: Then I'd take you the fuck apart!

SHE snaps her fingers or makes some other clear sign.
The lighting shifts abruptly.

SHE: Thank you for participating in our study. We have learned what we needed to know.

HE: Wait, what? That's it?

SHE: You are free to go.

HE: Did I...? Do I still have a shot at the truck?

SHE: Your name is in the hat. The metaphorical hat. So you have as good a chance as any of our additional other test subjects. Thank you for coming, and I wish you the best of good days.

HE: Okay, but you're not really a robot. If I had hit you, you'd be dead, and I'd be up on murder charges.

SHE: Thank you again for volunteering your time.

HE: Even if you are real, just so you know? Crap like this? Is the opposite of hot.

HE exits. SHE draws a breath. Collects herself.

SHE: Okay. Next!

Lights out.
End Of Play

ORIGINALLY PRODUCED by Little Black Dress INK's 2017 Female Playwrights ONSTAGE Festival: "Hot Mess" Prescott, AZ July 6-8 2017

CAST:

BATMAN - Bruce Thomson
BATGIRL - Judy Stahl

EXTRAS AT DISCRETION OF THE DIRECTOR:

Henchman/Vat of Boiling Steel Raiser 1 -Annabelle Veatch
Henchman/Vat of Boiling Steel Raiser 2 - Glenn Velguth

Directed by Cason Murphy

SETTING:

Conundrum's Lair - A Vast, Dark Cave

TIME:

Tonight

CHARACTERS:

Batman: 50S+, 1960S Tv Style
Batgirl: 20S, Any Ethnicity, Self-Involved
Both Are In Superhero Costumes.

The characters could be called "Battyman" and "Battygirl" if deemed necessary.

SOUND:

A ticking bomb.

Note on dialogue. A doctor has a bedside manner; a weatherman, cheery pep, and a superhero, super-flair. Bravado, light quips, and puns must be tossed in the face of certain doom, with frequently references to the certain doom. This "professional" patter is set off in the text with quotation marks. Since these two are in the midst of a job interview, they also speak normally. Words Batman is hearing for the first time, like "pivot", are also in quotation marks.

Batgirl often mispronounces or misuses words. No need to "correct" her dialogue.

SCENE 1.

UP ON:

Batman and Batgirl stand back to back, their gloved hands raised above their heads, roped together at the wrists. They are dangling high over a vat of boiling molten steel, in Conundrum's vast cave-lair. They drop sharply every few minutes. In case the 2500-degree cauldron of doom doesn't finish them off, there's a ticking bomb next to it.

Another day at the office for Batman. Less routine for his would-be trainee.

BATMAN: So I say something like, "Hanging over a vat of molten steel can really make you perspire, old chum."

BATGIRL: Yeah. So like, "I'm a real hottie, huh?"

BATMAN: Keep it light. Make it look easy. You're hosting a black tie gala, not stuffed into a giant ball of catnip, trawling in a two-ton tuna net, frozen in a giant popsicle mold—

BATGIRL: Y'know "black tie" excludes 54% of the population?

BATMAN: *(doesn't get it)* Show your "devil-may-care" savoir faire. Stuff down the pain, the fear, the "feelings"—

BATGIRL: And, get us out with my Bat-hairpin.

BATMAN: Never too easy!

BATGIRL: Same as in L.A. Me and Wonderwoman. "Pivot and spin."

BATMAN: *(with dramatic physical stress)* "My. Batfan! Will cool us down! Can you reach my Utility Belt, old chum?"

BATGIRL: "No sweat!"

BATMAN: No you can't.

BATGIRL: With my foot, see?

BATMAN: Not until we're closer to the vat. If only our hands weren't tied.

BATGIRL: "But this is how we roll!"

BATMAN: I mean. You should be taking notes!

BATGIRL: Oh. I am. In my brain. Is that... real molten steel?

BATMAN: Is there another kind?

BATGIRL: Hang on. So when you grabbed the Batphone, and dragged me into the Bat-chopper, and we Bat-repelled into this mountain, that was like, also real?

BATMAN: "Conundrum's caper may have cut our interview short, old chum, but if we escape this blasted brush with blazing, uh-"

BATGIRL: Awesome! I got the job!

BATMAN: No, no. No. Call this the skills test. "If we survive!" it's back to the Batcave, and you can explain those gaps in your resume.

BATGIRL: ... I'm not your "old chum". You know.

BATMAN: I, what?

BATGIRL: I'm not OK with "chum". "Old" or "new."

BATMAN: Force of habit.

BATGIRL: I have a name.

BATMAN: Of course. You're Batgirl. With a "B."

BATGIRL: Not to get too PC about it.

BATMAN: Twenty-two years, doesn't go away in a day. Well... He did.

BATGIRL: Was it like, a mutual parting of the ways?

BATMAN: In the sense that, he's dead.

BATGIRL: Oh freaking fuck! That is fucked up.

BATMAN: Don't spread it around.

BATGIRL: Geez! Um, crap. Uh. "We'll avenge him!"

BATMAN: Ha. "We" would if "we" were partners. And... maybe I'm old-fashioned but the citizens don't appreciate that kind of language.

BATGIRL: What language?

BATMAN: To start with, you say "fudge," not the F-word.

They lurch down half a foot.

BATGIRL: It's kind of my catch phrase.

BATMAN: The F-word?

BATGIRL: "Fuck yeah!"

BATMAN: Not in Gotham.

BATGIRL: "Let's stop hangin' around and get out of this fudging mess"?

C.J. Erhlich

BATMAN: Good, uh "pivot".

BATGIRL: And— "Time to fudging escape!"

BATMAN: Time to "pivot" you some patience.

They lurch. It hurts.

BATGIRL: Fu—ckkk—udge!

SCENE 2.

*Batman and Batgirl sway and dangle, lurch and grunt.
Their arms hurt.*

BATMAN: What happened, if I may ask. To your previous partner.

BATGIRL: Oh, well.

BATMAN: "Pivoting back" to those gaps.

BATGIRL: It takes two, you know. I mean, sure you know. That's
why you hired me.

BATMAN: Skills. Test. So. Napa, transition*, L.A...?

*(*He could do the "dadadda" transition riff, instead of
saying the word.)*

BATGIRL: Wonderwoman is the best. Super-talented. She's magic
with ropes. And wrists and sh—tuff.

BATMAN: How's the, uh, view from the Invisible Plane?

BATGIRL: But "Sisterhood"? Gimme a break! L.A.'s huge, and I'm,
getting, what, Burbank? Santa Monica once a month, y'know?
I needed room to spread my bat wings.

BATMAN: There isn't room.

BATGIRL: A, team player's what I mean.

BATMAN: And you'll, uh "bring the PC"?

BATGIRL: All the PC you can eat.

(they lurch)

Not to state the obvious, TICKING BOMB—

BATMAN: Stating the obvious is a big part of the job.

BATGIRL: Ha! "And this is my first day!"

BATMAN: Skills—

BATGIRL: When it's right, ya know.

BATMAN: That... is not so obvious.

They lurch. They both grunt in pain.

BATGIRL: You got dental, right?

SCENE 3. A FEW MINUTES LATER.

BATGIRL: "Batman! We're dropping like, confetti! Into Conundrum's king-size cauldron! If we don't fry like shrimp poppers, we'll be crushed under like 100 tons of powderized rock!" I'm just saying.

BATMAN: Nice alliteration, Supergirl.

BATGIRL: Batgirl. With a "B".

BATMAN: I said "super, girl!"

BATGIRL: Don't worry about it. I am such a team player. You'll see.

BATMAN: ...So... sudden.

BATGIRL: Right! Batfan, foot, GO!

BATMAN: I mean Robin. Gone. Just like that.

BATGIRL: *(it's awkward)* Yeah. Wow.

BATMAN: I took stock. Long career. Trophies all over the Batcave. Keys to the city, parking space— A champ in anyone's book... Robin and I had... Sorry. Bottom line? Still a few good years left in this old Bat.

BATGIRL: You're as old as you feel, Old Bat.

BATMAN: *(pissed off)* If you haven't noticed, bright eyes, the timer is ticking!

BATGIRL: Wow. Like "derr" obvious.

BATMAN: "Escape is a real puzzle!"

BATGIRL: "There's no way out!"

BATMAN: Oh? You never got out of something like this?

BATGIRL: Are you kidding? Like, all the time.

BATMAN: You sound a little wobbly there.

BATGIRL: Don't under-esteem me. In Napa, I always had to lead with the gloom and doom. "No way out!" Ex-cetera. You and them averse the bad guy. "Image management."

BATMAN: Like the Bat Signal?

BATGIRL: Gotta remind them they're fuu—

BATMAN: Hey.

BATGIRL: Fugged! Without you.

BATMAN: Ooof! So. Napa. Perilous?

BATGIRL: Ah, y'know, it was all like, "evil lite". Grape trampling. Tourists sucking up the samples. Brie poisoning. Fricken "powdery mildew." Stuck-up celebrities and the tax assessor were like the, most villainous of villains I could pull out of my— sleeves. How 'bout NOW?!

BATMAN: Tell me about Mr. Powdery Mildew.

BATGIRL: Ugh. It's a disgusting grape disease—

BATMAN: His, peccadillos and such.

BATGIRL: My cape is like, melting into my leggings?

BATMAN: Too much villain for you?

BATGIRL: Oh, so villainous. It just wasn't stretching my skills, you know? And they really had a bug up their chardonnays for female superheroes!

BATMAN: Surely it wasn't your abrasive lack of empathy.

BATGIRL: What's that supposed to mean, OK?

BATMAN: To be frank, I wasn't sure, putting a girl into the Batmix. But you can't be "choosy" on Craiglist. You do come with the gadgets.

BATGIRL: Woman! You can't say girl.

BATMAN: How old are you?

BATGIRL: You can't ask me that!

BATMAN: Ho-ho. Never ask a lady her weight, or her age.

BATGIRL: What a sexist remark.

BATMAN: So, "Bat-woman"?

BATGIRL: Ugh. It was dumb. I went more for syllable count than, I guess you'd say feminism. And then you're stuck.

They drop down another foot.

BATMAN: And the "bat" part...? An "homage"?

BATGIRL: No, it came to me— On its own—

BATMAN: I'd enjoy hearing that story.

BATGIRL: A visit to a cave—

BATMAN: "Bitten by a radioactive bat—"?

BATGIRL: The zeitgeist alright?

BATMAN: Hey, um. Would you mind dropping in a "holy" now and then?

Sharp drop.

BATGIRL: That is not in the job description.

BATMAN: Just um, put danger in the context of "holy!"

BATGIRL: "That's a holy bomb"?

BATMAN: I'll explain later.

BATGIRL: "If we get out holy alive!"

BATMAN: Great. So, a woman, uh, the "spin," you think it could improve, my "zeitgeist"?

BATGIRL: "Holy zeitgeist, Batman!"

They lurch, cry out. Their wrists hurt.

BATGIRL: *(cont'd)*Holy fucking fudge!

BATMAN: Skip it.

SCENE 4. A FEW MINUTES LATER.

BATGIRL: "Batman! Nudge my holy belt with your Bat Hook! I'll hip-check you—"

Batman snorts.

BATGIRL: *(cont'd)* "The recoil will fire my Batline, we'll swing wide of the peril! And escape and, boil that bomb!"

Batman giggles. He starts to laugh, silently. Batgirl doesn't understand why he's shaking against her body.

BATGIRL: *(cont'd)* "Then find Pyromanity and Conundrum!... Batman! Do you copy?"

BATMAN: *(he can't stop laughing)* Yes— yes!

BATGIRL: "Is there laughing gas coming out of the vat? I'll jerk my head to the side, and my Batgasmask will release—"

BATMAN: Don't say jerk! Oh god, oh god, don't ever say Batgasm again!

Batman's almost howling with laughter.

They drop.

BATGIRL: "Wiggle, Batman!"

BATMAN: OK— I'm wiggling—

(trying to sober up)

Oh holy heck!

BATGIRL: Is there a problem?

BATMAN: *(trying to catch his breath)*Oh, oh— It's just, I'm not used to working with a, a—
(giggling)
When Robin says, said it, it— You said hip-check and my mind went to this other— A very dark place! Oh no!
(he snorts)
Oh gosh, keep your mind on the molten steel, Batman. Oh no! Not "molten steel"— Oh... I'll keep my mouth shut.

BATGIRL: I think you should.

BATMAN: Do the thing. Oh god, the "thing"! Oh god, you have to slap me! No, not slap, not slap!
He's crying with laughter. Sighs, pulls himself together.

BATGIRL: I've been a very successful solo act.

BATMAN: Which I greatly respect.

BATGIRL: No sidekick needed.

BATMAN: SIDEKICK? Do you have a clue to whom you're speaking, young lady?

BATGIRL: Wonderwoman and I kicked some VERY villainous butt.

BATMAN: Until she got tired of you calling her your sidekick?

BATGIRL: You know, harassment creates a toxic work environment.

BATMAN: I think I know my toxic pretty gosh-darn well! Ever escape a volcano?

BATGIRL: Are you kidding? Like, all the time, in L.A. If I was a man—

BATMAN: This isn't about man. You have NO bat-people skills!

BATGIRL: Can we both "take it down a notch"?

BATMAN: No! We— Wow. That's actually pretty good.
(he sighs)
Are you going to bad-mouth me to the Justice League?

BATGIRL: Of course not.

BATMAN: When Supergirl steps up as the new Superhero Master General?

BATGIRL: That's true. SuperGIRL.

BATMAN: Point taken.

SCENE 5. A FEW SECONDS LATER.

The ticking couldn't be any louder.

BATGIRL: Let's do it! Move your HIPS— Oh please!

BATMAN: *(back to hysterical giggles)*Holy hee hee hips—

BATGIRL: Get your Bathook under my UTILITY belt— Oh for godsakes.

Hang on old chum.

She shimmies her hips, the projectile flies, they both pull to the edge of the pit. Batgirl drops and rolls.

Batman drops into the molten steel, disappears.

Batgirl screams, loses her shit.

BATGIRL: *(cont'd)* Oh god OH GOD. Oh holy molten steel, I killed Batman. My first fucking day and I KILLED BATMAN! In the most fudging cliched no-brainer hanging over a vat escape! Fucking Wonderwoman was right, I am SUCH a bitch! Ohh shit shit SHIT!

Batman pops out of the molten steel.

Batgirl's apoplectic.

BATGIRL: *(cont'd)* What the—! How did you—!

BATMAN: "Don't fret old chum. Luckily, this morning my valet laid out my molten-steel-repellent Batsuit."

Batgirl helps him out, brushes molten steel off his shoulders.

BATGIRL: I swear. It will NEVER happen again.

BATMAN: "Now let's steel away, and find Conundrum!"

BATGIRL: "But first let's throw this ticking bomb into the vat before we get crushed by falling cave."

BATMAN: That's not a pun.

BATGIRL: With respect, sir, CRUSHED—?

BATMAN: We do puns. "Bombs away!"

Batgirl fake-laughs heartily. They both reach for the bomb. He lets her take it. She throws it into the vat.

BATGIRL: "Holy melted bomb, sir!"

BATMAN: I'm "Batman". *(sighs)* Transitions.

They run. BLACKOUT. Explosion.

The End

C.J. Erhlich

THE 5564 TO TORONTO

Karen JP Howes

Produced by Playwrights' Round Table at the Santos Dantin
Theater, Orlando Shakespeare Center
July 28-August 6 2017
Directed by: John Reid Adams
Featuring: Jason Skinner as Gavin and Shelby Reynolds as
Molly

Producer: charlesdent@hotmail.com

CHARACTERS:
GAVIN MCGREGOR: twenties or thirties, any race
MOLLY LANDERS: twenties or thirties, any race

PLACE :
Greyhound bus terminal, Buffalo

TIME:
The present

Gavin McGregor, in t-shirt and jeans, rushes into a Greyhound bus terminal. There's a row of seats. Perhaps a vending machine. You know, things you'd find in a bus terminal at 4 in the morning. No people. Not even a guy with a mop. Gavin has been running for a while. He's out of breath. There's a slip of pink paper in his hand. It's the size of notecard and it's folded in half. He stops dead in his tracks. His eyes scan left then right. He sees no one. From a door behind the chairs (probably revolving), Molly Landers, wearing blue, enters with a backpack and a bus ticket. She looks up at the bus schedule, then at her watch. Gavin looks at her. He compares what he sees to what's written on the pink paper. It makes her feel uncomfortable.

GAVIN: Hi. I – I don't want to make you feel uncomfortable. You shouldn't be frightened or anything. They have security guards that come through here all the time, so you don't have to worry about being here so late at night like this with a stranger.

MOLLY: It's okay. I'm fine.

GAVIN: I can understand. If I was a woman in a bus station in the middle of the night and no one was around except one other person who happened to be a guy, I'd be a little concerned which is why I tried to wear something that wouldn't be threatening. No stocking hat or baggy pants or leather. I don't have anything leather anyway and I – I shaved.

MOLLY: This isn't how you make someone feel comfortable.

GAVIN: I'm just – This is such a pain in the ass. I never know how to start these things.

MOLLY: I think I'll . . .

She makes a run for it. Gavin anticipates and is ahead of her. He stops her, his hand over her mouth so she won't scream.

GAVIN: I don't have this scream down right. I realize that. But I'm not going to hurt you. Nothing like that. I don't want your money. I'm not going to rape you. I'm trying to win your trust.

She bites his hand. He cries out, grabs his hand, and as she tries to get away, he trips her. He pulls out a gun and aims it at her. She stops.

GAVIN: This isn't what you think it is. Okay? (*No response*) Okay? I'm not violent. I'm not crazy and I'm actually on your side.

MOLLY: Are you going to shoot me?

GAVIN: You weren't listening. Did you get any of what I just said?

MOLLY: What did you say? You're pointing a gun at me.

GAVIN: It's not on purpose. I'm only doing this to help you. I'm not good at talking to people that I don't know so I don't know how to tell you – Jesus. I'm stuck. I'm trying to save your life and — look at me. (beat) How about this? I put the gun away. I close my eyes, and you run like hell out of here. You run home.

MOLLY: I don't want to go home.

GAVIN: This is a pretty good deal — ahhh *(wondering about her name?)* — what's your name?

MOLLY: Molly. I have a bus ticket. You can do all those things you said about putting the gun away and closing your eyes. But instead of running home, I'm going to get on my bus. Okay? Same end result. I wind up away from you and alive.

GAVIN: Except you won't. What I'm supposed to do is keep you from getting on that bus because if you do, you'll actually wind up dead.

MOLLY: Dead?

GAVIN: At 4:17.

MOLLY: What? You think I'll be dead at 4:17?

GAVIN: Two minutes after you get on that bus.

MOLLY: Are you like a guardian angel or something?

GAVIN: No. My name's Gavin McGregor. I'm a person.

MOLLY: Then why would you say something like that?

GAVIN: It's — It's on this piece of paper.

MOLLY: What 's on that paper? What does it say?

GAVIN: Woman in blue — by Bandits. On the 5-5-6-4 at 4:17.

MOLLY: Bandits? Where'd that paper come from – the wild west in the 1800s?

GAVIN: No. It — it was actually in a playbill for the musical they're doing over on Main Street and when I opened to the cast of characters, it fell out. I wasn't sure about the number at first. I checked trains and planes and a few addresses, and I did a comprehensive Google search which led me here. And you're in blue.

MOLLY: What are you saying?

GAVIN: Can I put the gun away?

MOLLY: You think I'm going to say no?

GAVIN: I just want to let you know that I'm not letting you get on that bus.

MOLLY: Or else you'll what — kill me?

GAVIN: It doesn't usually go like this, okay? Well, it sort of does but this is — Jeeze, about the worst.

MOLLY: Worst what?

GAVIN: Lead up to saving someone's life.

MOLLY: Why do you think you're saving my life?

GAVIN: I get these pieces of paper and they tell me when something's going to happen to someone . . .

MOLLY: Like in the future? They tell you the future? Sort-of an overachieving fortune cookie?

GAVIN: Yeah.

MOLLY: That's weird. Can I see it? The paper.

GAVIN: Sure.

MOLLY: *(reading)* Woman in blue — by Bandits. On the 5-5-6-4 at 4:17. *(beat)* That's what you said.

GAVIN: I know. Look, you don't have to believe me. You just have to take a different bus.

MOLLY: No. I'm going to Toronto. I'm leaving here. Leaving Buffalo and I'm going to Toronto.

GAVIN: That's fine. You just can't do it on the 4:15. There's one at 6:45.

MOLLY: Which is two and a-half hours from now.

GAVIN: What's two and a-half hours when we're talking about the rest of your life. Two and a-half hours is nothing. I can take you to Starbucks and buy you a cup of coffee or someplace with wifi, and we can download some new songs. It's three hours to Toronto. You should have some new music. What do you like? Classic rock? Chicago Blues? Country?

MOLLY: Are you hitting on me?

GAVIN: No. No. I wouldn't do that.

MOLLY: Yes you are. You're doing this save-your life-thing so you can get a date.

GAVIN: I didn't ask for this job. For these stupid pieces of paper to wind up in my grocery bag or in my dry cleaning. You think I want to look like I'm crazy like this?

MOLLY: You probably don't remember but there was this news story from a few years ago when all these people, some looking out their windows, others getting into their cars, they see a woman being killed on a street in New York City – right in front of them and she's screaming for help, and not one of them does anything. They don't call the cops. They don't call 911. Nothing. You can be like that. Ignore it.

GAVIN: So I get a premonition that a dog is going to get run over at the corner of Lewellyn and Harris and I shouldn't try to stop it?

MOLLY: How would you stop it anyway?

GAVIN: I go to the corner and keep all the dogs from getting in the street.

MOLLY: Then what happens?

GAVIN: None of the dogs die.

MOLLY: But the people get really mad don't they? They think you're crazy or nosey or you have Tourette's or something. But you save the dog. A dog. One of those people's dogs who would have been very sad if their dog died. And you don't even know which one.

GAVIN: Look I've never told anyone this, but I was twenty —

MOLLY: Good for you. So was I. Something in common after all.

GAVIN: It was the first time it happened. There was this slip of paper. It was in my Quiznos bag. It said window washer in dreads. The Scripps Building — I was in Cincinnati at the time. 9:22. So I go, and there was a window washer with dreads, and we started talking. But then I start making a mess of his things, and I wind up getting this guy fired from his job. But he didn't go up the scaffolding. He didn't die. Same thing with those dogs. They all wound up in a fight over this t-bone steak I brought, but none of them died. Then there was this homeless guy with a parakeet . . .

MOLLY: Stop.

GAVIN: What's so important that you can't take another bus? I mean it's none of my business. You don't have to tell me why you're going to Toronto at 4:15 in the morning, but I was just wondering 'cause if it wasn't for something like a meeting or a doctor's appointment, then you can —

MOLLY: Jeeze. *(beat)* It's my boyfriend.

GAVIN: So call him and tell him you'll be late.

MOLLY: I'm not — I'm not going to meet him. I'm going to get away from him. *(beat, smiles)* He doesn't like me the way I thought he did.

GAVIN: I'm sorry. Guys are schmucks.

MOLLY: No it's not that. He — He actually likes me *more* than I thought he did. He wants to — you know. Take it to the next level or something.

GAVIN: You mean sex.

MOLLY: No. I mean get married or something. Jeeze. Marriage. A life together for-like-ever.

GAVIN: There's no for-like-ever if you get on that bus. Molly, is leaving him at 4:15 this morning worth dying over? You need to think about this the way I do — rationally and logically.

MOLLY: *(thinking, are you fucking kidding me?)* Why are you doing this?

GAVIN: My roommate jumped off the roof of our dorm at Princeton.

MOLLY: And you didn't save him. That sucks. I'm sorry.

GAVIN: I dropped out of school.

MOLLY: But that wasn't enough of a punishment for not stopping your friend from committing suicide, so now you get these premonitions on slips of colored paper about these horrible things that can happen to people, which you feel obligated to stop.

GAVIN: It's not a punishment.

MOLLY: It doesn't seem like a reward. It's not like you've been poor your whole life — living off of food stamps and you reach into a trashcan one day and pull out a winning lottery ticket. Or you have a bad leg and you get a handicap-parking permit. Those slips of paper are compensations for when life goes bad. What you got is a punishment.

GAVIN: I don't look at it that way. I see that it's a way for me to —

MOLLY: Atone? That's just a fancy way of saying you fucked up and here's a way to push a boulder up a hill for the rest of eternity. How many people have you saved?

GAVIN: All of them.

MOLLY: Cause the dog got into a fight, and the window washer got fired?

GAVIN: Yeah.

MOLLY: How do you know?

GAVIN: Cause they're alive.

MOLLY: How do you know they wouldn't be anyway? How do you know they were actually doomed to begin with, and you — you with your colored pieces of paper and in your super hero cape and with your quick thinking — saved them?

GAVIN: Cause none of it is in my head with its rap, rap, rap on the inside of my brain berating me with what I should have done and could have done. I don't have an image of a dog lying dead in the middle of a street. It doesn't keep me from sleeping. I don't hate myself for not saving them, 'cause I did, and that's how I know.

MOLLY: You should change your therapy. I'm taking my bus.

GAVIN: You don't love him then?

MOLLY: Steve? No.

GAVIN: Did he get you a ring?

MOLLY: Yeah. It was — gosh. He did this really cool thing. It was his great-grandmother's ring and it was beautiful. It was just the kind of Jane Austin sort of ring any girl would want. And we were at his place. He cooked everything from scratch. There was a lemon-wine-shallot sauce and morel mushrooms and a bottle of Chateauneuf and candles. He wrote this poem.

GAVIN: Steve writes poetry?

MOLLY: He's had two books published. He runs the bakery on Chippawau. Actually owns it. He rescues dogs and finds them new homes. He has a cat named Milly, and he's a really good kisser.

GAVIN: So why do you want to leave him?

MOLLY: I'm just not a falling-in-love kind of person. I don't fall in love. If I was going to fall in love, Steve would be the guy but am I really supposed to love him just because he's funny and charming and considerate and handsome and cooks well and is neat and loves me more than anything in the world?

GAVIN: Sounds like a good start.

MOLLY: I think it's cheating. I want to find beauty in an alcoholic war-vet with amputated legs, not in a sunset. Anyone can do that.

GAVIN: Maybe he's all those things you said because that's what you see when you love someone.

MOLLY: Like you're an expert? I bet you've never even been in love.

GAVIN: How can I be in love? I've got this. I've got other things going on right now.

MOLLY: Oh yeah with saving people and shit.

GAVIN: What if you're thinking this love thing is more complicated than it is, and that just because it's easy, because it falls in your lap and you wind up with this perfect person that it's not real?

MOLLY: Things in life aren't easy. Ask anyone. You don't just save people from dying cause you show up. And you don't fall in love with someone just cause they happen to be perfect.

GAVIN: People aren't perfect.

MOLLY: Jeeze. Haven't you been listening? I'm getting on that bus.

GAVIN: But.

MOLLY: You gonna tie me up? Chain me to the bench so you can save my life? Call my boyfriend, maybe? You want to get that involved? You want to call him up so he can come down here and tell me how we are meant for each other. How we finish each other's sentences and drink hot chocolate when it's snowing and how we respect each other and support each other — and even if you think of doing something like that, it's not going to work cause I will already be on that bus.

The bus starts up. It's rear lights spill into the waiting room.

MOLLY: See? I'm going.

She exits. He watches. He puts his hands in his pockets. He looks to the ground. He looks around. He's not sure if his powers are waning or if there's still time. — She returns.

MOLLY: Maybe — Maybe I do love him.

GAVIN: I would.

She walks to him and gives him a kiss on the cheek.

MOLLY: Thanks.

She walks off through different doors than where the bus waits. Gavin smiles.

Sounds of the bus door closing and switching into gear.

Then more sounds — a car screeching, broken Spanish shouting, gunshots, more broken-Spanish. During this Gavin croutches behind the seats. When the car races away, a purple piece of paper is caught in the exhaust and swirls in the air. Gavin peers out from the bench. The paper floats to the ground. Gavin walks to it and carefully picks it up. He looks left then right, as is customary of super heroes. Reads it. Then he's off to save another life.

FUL NABIT

(تبان لوف)

J. Thalia Cunningham

Ful Nabit was first produced by Warrior Productions at the Short Play Festival, Center for Performing Arts, Rhinebeck, NY, September 2017.
Directed by Elisabeth Ruthman

CAST:
WHISTLER'S MOTHER: Wendy Power Spielmann
FAIZA: Barbara Richards

SECOND PRODUCTION:
Ful Nabit was subsequently produced by New Jersey Repertory Company as part of their Theatre Brut, Long Branch, NJ, October 2017
Directed by Katrin Hilbe

CAST:
WHISTLER'S MOTHER: Lucy McMichael
FAIZA: Devon Ahmed

CHARACTERS:

WHISTLER'S MOTHER: 146-year-old prim female appearing her age, living at the Musée d'Orsay, Paris. Sitting behind picture frame. Dressed as in her portrait. Combines old-fashioned values with savoir-faire and sophistication. Her advanced age made her a bit dotty, but having spent hours overhearing conversations of museum-goers, she has intermittent awareness of what's going on in the world.

FAIZA: Female, 20s-40s. Refugee from Raqqa, northern Syria. Head covered with scarf. Wears uniform of loose janitor's smock. Her fundamental kindness and decency are overshadowed by recent tragic events, which have rendered her angry, confused, and vulnerable.

TIME:

The present. Early morning before the museum opens.

PLACE:

Salle 29, Rez-de-chausée (ground floor), Musée d'Orsay, Paris

Note to director: Stage setting requires only a bench. Paintings in Salle 29 as well as Van Gogh's *Self Portrait* could be projected via PowerPoint onto screen, but it's not mandatory.

Dim lighting, suggesting the museum's off-hours. At rise,
WHISTLER'S MOTHER sits behind her picture frame
as FAIZA enters, pushing a cart with cleaning supplies.
FAIZA glances around, making sure she's alone, then
removes a small prayer rug from her supply cart. We
hear a recording of the Muslim call to prayer:

Islamic Call to Prayer - [Islam Calls You] - YouTube

Facing the direction of Mecca, standing, FAIZA cups
both hands to her ears, making Takbeer, the start of
prayers. With right hand clasped over the left she begins:

FAIZA: Bissmilah irra'hman irra'heem. In the name of Allah, the
Beneficent, the Most Merciful.

(Recording continues, as FAIZA bows down with hands
over the knees and her back parallel to the floor. WHIS-
TLER'S MOTHER twists from profile to stare at FAIZA)

Al'hamdu lilahi rabbil' alameen. Praise be to Allah, Lord of
the Worlds.

Iyaka na'abudu wa iyaka nassta'een. You alone we worship.
You alone we ask for help.

(WHISTLER'S MOTHER twists further, rubs lower back,
observes FAIZA more closely)

Sub'hana rabiyal adheem. Praise to my Lord, the Great.

(begins to repeat but WHISTLER'S MOTHER erupts
with a moan of discomfort)

Who . . .where . . .?

WHISTLER'S MOTHER: Why on God's green earth are you making so much noise this early in the morning?

FAIZA: You speak? And move? What you are doing here?

WHISTLER'S MOTHER: *(stiffly rising from her chair, stretching,*
rubbing her lower back) Me? I live here. Aahhh, it feels good
to stand. My lumbago is acting up again.

FAIZA: Lum . . .bago? What that is?

WHISTLER'S MOTHER: It's what happens to your back after your
son forces you to sit for ages in a chair harder than my mother-
in-law's baked goods. He wouldn't even let me get up to slip the
chamber pot under my skirts. Unfortunately, elder abuse hadn't
been invented yet, so I couldn't report him.

FAIZA: He was punishing you?

WHISTLER'S MOTHER: Weeks, I sat for that portrait . . .as they say in New York, such pain you should never experience.

FAIZA: Pain? I know of pain.

WHISTLER'S MOTHER: I've seen you in here before. But you weren't jumping up and down.

FAIZA: I was now making my prayers.

WHISTLER'S MOTHER: Not from around here, are you? Your accent . . .

FAIZA: I'm from Raqqa. In the north.

WHISTLER'S MOTHER: I never heard of a town called Raqqa? Up near Normandy, you say?

FAIZA: Raqqa. In northern Syria.

WHISTLER'S MOTHER: Syria? Why would a woman be gadding about so far from home?

FAIZA: War. Thirty thousand Syrian refugees came to France. *(pause)* I do not understand. Are you woman or painting?

WHISTLER'S MOTHER: Both. According to my son, though, I'm merely an "Arrangement in Grey and Black." Imagine! Calling his own mother an "arrangement."

FAIZA: You make arrangement for your son?

WHISTLER'S MOTHER: *(extending hand)* I'm Anna Matilda McNeill Whistler, James McNeill Whistler's mother.

FAIZA: *(tentatively shaking hands)* Peace be to you. My name is Faiza.

WHISTLER'S MOTHER: Never heard that name before, but I suppose it'll do. How long have you been working here?

FAIZA: Two weeks.

WHISTLER'S MOTHER: Cleaning is respectable women's work. I'm sure in no time you'll---

FAIZA: I was teacher back home.

WHISTLER'S MOTHER: A teacher? My stars! What did you teach?

FAIZA: Religion and English. At school for girls. Now, I'm only fit for servant's work.

WHISTLER'S MOTHER: I thought your English seemed unusually good. What about your family? Did they accompany you? In

France, a woman on her own must watch out for ---

FAIZA: I came alone. I must do this work myself.

WHISTLER'S MOTHER: Working as a janitor at the museum? But surely ---

FAIZA: That is not why I came.

WHISTLER'S MOTHER: Nothing shameful in working for your living. After my husband died, I was impoverished and also had to make my own way in the world.

FAIZA: Your son didn't help you?

WHISTLER'S MOTHER: Jemie? The lad needed my help more than I needed his. I'd hoped he'd develop red-blooded Victorian manly tendencies like gambling, whoring around, and engaging in fisticuffs. Instead, that dandy messed around with paints. Wasted time searching for patent leather slippers with pink bows – pink bows, mind you. They clashed unspeakably with his yellow gloves.

FAIZA: Did he ever find them? In his size, I mean?

WHISTLER'S MOTHER: Oh, he could be as tenacious as tar when it suited him. And this was long before eBay.

FAIZA: How do you say? Boys will be boys – in your culture, at least.

WHISTLER'S MOTHER: And you? Are you married? Children? Why would a teacher clean the museum if not for family?

FAIZA: Family. I have. *(pause)* I had.

WHISTLER'S MOTHER: Why didn't they come with you?

FAIZA: My husband and baby were killed. My other children - I know not where they are. *(pause)* Or if they are.

WHISTLER'S MOTHER: I am so sorry. What happened?

FAIZA: The baby and I were visiting my mother when a barrel bomb exploded at our home. It filled the air with chlorine, turning the house into a gas chamber. My husband was strong man, but he died.

WHISTLER'S MOTHER: Oh, dear. And your children?

FAIZA: My children and I were captured by police, put in prison, tortured. They beat us. Used electricity. My baby died in my arms. Five years old. I couldn't save him. I know not about the other three.

WHISTLER'S MOTHER: Who did this to you?

FAIZA: Bashar Al-Assad's army.

WHISTLER'S MOTHER: I knew they shouldn't have tried turning an eye doctor into a president. Have courage.

FAIZA: *(looking at watch)* Courage. I must have courage. *(pause)* You maybe like some tea?

WHISTLER'S MOTHER: A lovely idea, and I believe I could stand to tickle my innards.

FAIZA: *(removing thermos from cart)* I may sit?

WHISTLER'S MOTHER: It's still a free country. I'll join you as soon as I extinguish this fire in my back.

> *(She slowly begins to ease onto bench.)*

FAIZA: Wait, please.

> *(She removes bucket from cart to serve as footstool. She grabs cloth from cart, wipes bench, then gently assists seating WHISTLER'S MOTHER)*

Is okay for you, my mother?

WHISTLER'S MOTHER: Quite comfortable. You're very kind, dear child.

FAIZA: In my culture, we take care of our elders.

WHISTLER'S MOTHER: A lovely tradition quite neglected in our society. Don't you want to remove that heavy smock? How do they expect you to clean with ---?

FAIZA: No! I will wear it. (passing thermos) Please. I hope it is still warm.

WHISTLER'S MOTHER: Yes, indeed.

FAIZA: *(passing small paper sack)* You like?

WHISTLER'S MOTHER: What's in here?

FAIZA: Ful nabit. Fava beans with cumin and salt.

WHISTLER'S MOTHER: That salt will wreak havoc with my blood pressure, but I'll try it. *(pause)* Very nice.

> *(They eat and drink in silence, passing thermos and paper bag back and forth)*

What are your plans, my dear?

FAIZA: What you mean . . . plans?

WHISTLER'S MOTHER: Your dreams, ambitions. You're educated, obviously intelligent. You don't intend to work as a cleaning woman forever, do you? With hard work, you could ---

FAIZA: No, I will not work here for long.

(With back to audience, she opens smock revealing corset/belt packed with explosives attached with silver electric tape. [red candles will do just fine].)

This is why I came.

WHISTLER'S MOTHER: *(peering closely)* If you're trying to sell me a cheap wrist watch made in Taiwan, I don't have need of one. And most tourists like to buy their souvenirs at the museum's gift shop. Have you visited our gift shop yet? They sell T-shirts, refrigerator magnets, coffee mugs, post cards, cigarette lighters---

FAIZA: WHISTLER'S MOTHER: *(Retreats, then, moves closer, re-examining corset.)* With these cataracts, I don't see the way I used to . . .Oh! Candles. But selling candles won't be a profitable venture here. The museum provides plenty of electricity, and would never allow smoke and fire near the art.

FAIZA: I said, move back!

WHISTLER'S MOTHER: Please don't speak to me as though I were a common candle thief. Furthermore, if you don't want anyone noticing your corsets, place them underneath your dress as ladies do in civilized society. As I was asking, working as a janitor and selling candles at the Musée d'Orsay? Now surely ---

FAIZA: That is *not* why I am here. And these are not candles.

WHISTLER'S MOTHER: *(rising, going towards picture frame)* If you're going to behave so rudely, I might as well return to my portrait.

FAIZA: No, please stay. I am very much grateful your company.

(WHISTLER'S MOTHER sits back down. They drink and eat in silence)

WHISTLER'S MOTHER: You were about to tell me your dreams and ambitions . . .

FAIZA: I dream to see my husband and baby again. To avenge deaths of my parents, my lost children.

WHISTLER'S MOTHER: Retaliation won't bring them back, child. You'll be unhappy if you try.

FAIZA: I am unhappy now, so I take the risk willingly. I made promise.

WHISTLER'S MOTHER: To whom?

FAIZA: *(pointing to corset)* To Allah. I do this for Him.

WHISTLER'S MOTHER: So *that's* what you're doing with those candles. We light candles for our God, too. In our churches. Lighting candles has nothing to do with revenge and retaliation.

FAIZA: So many times I tell you, these are *not* candles.

WHISTLER'S MOTHER: Forgive me, dear. My memory. If they're not candles, what are they?

FAIZA: Explosives.

WHISTLER'S MOTHER: Explosives! Dash my wig! Quickly! Take them off before ---

FAIZA: You do not understand. I am member of Al-Khansaa.

WHISTLER'S MOTHER: Why, what a coincidence! I'm D.A.R. Daughters of the American Revolution.

FAIZA: You, too, are revolutionary?

WHISTLER'S MOTHER: We're exempt from paying Federal income taxes. What about Al . . .your Syrian ladies' club?

FAIZA: Al-Khansaa is ISIS' all-female suicide brigade. Named for Al Khansa, 7th century Arab lady poet.

WHISTLER'S MOTHER: Well, now, isn't that nice?

FAIZA: In her time, female poets wrote elegies for the dead. Like this:

Time has gnawed at me, bit me and has cut me.

Time has harmed, wounded and injured me, and has destroyed my men who have died

FAIZA: *(con't.)* together.

We saw horses galloping and flying dust.

And riders---

---Whose swords turn faces deathly white, whose spears cut bodies.

We defeated those who thought they would never be defeated---

---We wear armor in war. And silk, wool and cotton during peace

WHISTLER'S MOTHER: Very pretty. What does your ladies' club

do? Host teas? Support orphans? Or ---?

FAIZA: Jihad is not only for men. Al-Khansaa raises awareness and punishes women who don't follow our religion correctly. And, you see, women in territories controlled by ISIS aren't allowed to drive cars or carry weapons. *(giggling)* But women in Al-Khansaa brigade can do both.

WHISTLER'S MOTHER: Very clever of you to figure out how to circumvent their rules. But why are you wearing a corset stuffed with explosives to mop floors?

FAIZA: Not to mop floors. To blow up museum.

WHISTLER'S MOTHER: Why-ever would your ladies' club send you to blow up the Musée d'Orsay?

FAIZA: In prison, other women encouraged me to join. It give me purpose. Make me feel alive again. Normally, Al-Khansaa operates only in Syria. But France sent airstrikes against us thinking we wouldn't retaliate. So, I was sent to France to martyr myself. To destroy Christian symbols of French conceit toward Islam that insult Allah. People are less likely to suspect women.

WHISTLER'S MOTHER: Women martyr themselves wherever they go. But whoever instructed you to martyr yourself sent you to the wrong place. If they didn't send you to the proper facility, should you trust them?

FAIZA: They sent me to wrong place?

WHISTLER'S MOTHER: This museum is an old railway station with impressionist and post-impressionist art, not religious works of art. *(pause)* Oh, I know! If you want to impress them and really make a big splash, how about the Vatican? The Eurail takes the better part of a day, but you could pack a nice lunch---

FAIZA: But all this – in here. People worship these things instead of Allah.

WHISTLER'S MOTHER: Do you know what art means? What artists actually do?

FAIZA: Yes, I know. They promote infidelity.

WHISTLER'S MOTHER: That's one interpretation. Artists create art to express ideas, emotions, culture, religion. Artists are courageous. They may fear the unknown, but they're willing to take a risk. Just like you.

FAIZA: Perhaps this is as you say. But it has nothing to do with me or my cause.

WHISTLER'S MOTHER: You think not? Scoot along into Salle 71 and look at Van Gogh's *Self-Portrait*. I'll wait here.

(FAIZA exits briefly. WHISTLER'S MOTHER rearranges her skirts, grabs a dust cloth from the cart and dusts her picture frame. FAIZA re-enters)

What did you think of Van Gogh's *Self-Portrait*?

FAIZA: I never look on walls before while I am cleaning. It is beautiful. But sad. He painted himself differently from the pretty colors in background. Like he doesn't belong.

WHISTLER'S MOTHER: The year after Van Gogh painted that self-portrait, he killed himself.

FAIZA: He was also martyr?

WHISTLER'S MOTHER: He suffered from depression. Aside from obeying Allah, why are you blowing up the museum? And yourself? I mean, personally?

FAIZA: I say to you before. To avenge my family's deaths. I suffer slow death without them. I no longer have place in this world.

WHISTLER'S MOTHER: Like poor Mr. van Gogh. You commented that he seemed alienated from his surroundings. Or, as you just described yourself, as though the world no longer had a place for him. And you.

FAIZA: You do not understand. I can no longer be passive. When I do nothing, I become a victim. This way, I have control. I take action when I martyr myself to Allah.

WHISTLER'S MOTHER: Did Allah really instruct you? You're sure it wasn't your ladies' club taking Allah's name in vain? I heard you at your prayers. You told Allah he was beneficent and most merciful.

FAIZA: Hamdullah. Praise God.

WHISTLER'S MOTHER: Why would your merciful, beneficent Allah instruct you to destroy work of courageous people? To deprive people who understand themselves better by looking at art – just like you?

FAIZA: So I may join my husband and baby in Paradise.

WHISTLER'S MOTHER: What about your other children? Perhaps

they're searching for you. We mothers understand sacrifice for the sake of our children, but what good are you to them if you blow yourself up?

FAIZA: *(beginning to cry)* How I miss them! . . .How would I even to try locating them? . . . My life without them is useless. . .the suffering . . .did Mr. van Gogh . . .? I felt his sadness beating in my own heart . . .

WHISTLER'S MOTHER: Could you forgive yourself if you didn't try to find them? Perhaps your children may find you.

FAIZA: I cannot bear to think of . . .but my promise . . . what if . . .could you leave building? . . . I do not wish harm to you.

WHISTLER'S MOTHER: I'm afraid that's impossible.

FAIZA: Your back? I will assist you to street? There are not so many steps. I could call taxi.

WHISTLER'S MOTHER: I live here, and like most elderly people, I refuse to leave my neighbors and my home.

FAIZA: Home? Back home, we make our perfumes by crushing petals of flowers. Roses. Jasmine. The scent is lovely, but once we destroy the petals, the flowers are no longer with us. Bright colors to cheer us. Soft petals to stroke. . . I don't know . . .I must . . . how . . .you cannot . . .what . . .?

(Lights become bright. We hear muted chatter of museum employees. As the museum opens, the level of human noise increases as visitors enter.)

The museum is open. People are arriving.

WHISTLER'S MOTHER: They usually do about now.

FAIZA: I was instructed to martyr myself at this time.

WHISTLER'S MOTHER: *(rising, wipes a finger in the corners of her picture frame to check for errant dust)* And I must return to my portrait. I've very much enjoyed our visit, dear.

FAIZA: My mother, what would you advise me to---?

WHISTLER'S MOTHER: For a woman to be happy, truly happy, in this life - and afterward - she must listen to her own heart, trust her innate wisdom, and make her own decisions.

(kissing FAIZA)

But . . .?

WHISTLER'S MOTHER: God bless you, dear child.

(She kisses FAIZA once more, then returns to the pose of her portrait inside its frame. FAIZA looks at WHISTLER'S MOTHER, who remains immobile. FAIZA looks again at her explosives, reaches for a cell phone, punches in some – but not all – the numbers. She gazes again at WHISTLER'S MOTHER. Exits briefly, as Van Gogh's self-portrait is projected on the screen. FAIZA returns, looks again back and forth between her explosives, cell phone, and WHISTLER'S MOTHER.)

FAIZA: *Inna lillahi wa inna ilayhi raji'unInna lillahi wa inna ilayhi raji'un.*(We belong to Allah and to him we shall return. *Allahummagh firliyal katheera mim maa's'iyatika wa iqbal minniyal yaseera min t'aa-a'tika.* (O Allah! Pardon my sins which are many and accept my deeds which are very little.)

(She begins to punch in numbers cell phone. Stops. Stands in front of WHISTLER'S MOTHER. Puts cell phone in pocket).

Allah, forgive me! This, I cannot do!

(Blackout)

END OF PLAY

GORILLA GORILLA

Mora V. Harris

Originally produced by Stage Door Productions in Fredricksburg, Virginia on April 28-29 and May 5-6, 2017 as part of their 10th Annual Original One Act Festival.

Directed by Carol Newber
Nils: Justin Zacek
Koda: Sam Smith

CHARACTERS

NILS – any age, male, a western lowland gorilla

KODA – any age, male, a younger western lowland gorilla

NOTE

The actors should not wear gorilla suits or masks.

SETTING

Present day. A gorilla enclosure. A placard outside it reads "Gorilla gorilla."

Mora V. Harris

KODA rests comfortably on a pile of hay and picks at his stomach. NILS watches him and bites at a celery stalk.

NILS: Something's different.

KODA: *[grunt]*

NILS: They're up to something. I know they told you what.

KODA rolls over slowly and deliberately to face NILS.

KODA: If you want to know things, learn their signs.

NILS: I don't want to learn their signs. I'll never learn their signs.

KODA: If you learned their signs you'd be less lonely. They're all my friends now. We talk about things. They always want to know about my feelings.

NILS: They want to know about your feelings because they're surprised you have them. They don't care what they are.

KODA: Bob and Sarah care about my feelings. They'd care about yours too, if you'd stop being so stubborn.

...I told them about my mother. The loud noise. How scared I was. The first time I saw the color red. They said they were sorry. That's all they said.

NILS: That's not all. You have a secret.

KODA: How could I have a secret from you in here? Where there's nowhere we can go to escape the sound of each other's breathing? The sound of your chewing echoes in my dreams. And I'm supposed to have a secret.

NILS: *(a warning)* Gorilla...

KODA: Gorilla...

...

It's a good thing okay? Don't worry about it.

NILS: *[growl]*

NILS chases KODA and tackles him.

KODA: All right, all right! They're bringing in a female.

NILS: A female? In here?

KODA: Get off me!

NILS releases him.

KODA: They're bringing in a female to keep us company.

NILS: That's what they said? "To keep us company"?

KODA: That's what they said.

NILS: "To keep us company."

KODA: To keep us company. I told you it was good news!

NILS: Where's she coming from?

KODA: I don't know. Do you think she's from home?

NILS: The zoo in Melbourne?

KODA: No, you know...Africa.

NILS: I don't want to talk about Africa.

> *Silence.*

KODA: Do you think she'll be nice?

NILS: I don't know.

KODA: She'll probably be scared. I was scared when they moved us here. I'm scared every time they move us. It's like they can't just leave us be, you know? I hope we never move again. I like it here mostly. It's bigger than our last enclosure. I hope this is bigger than her last enclosure. Though I suppose it will feel smaller with three of us—

NILS: —Have you ever had a thought that you didn't just *say*?

KODA: All the time.

NILS: You're just constantly talking. Talking to me. Talking to Bob and Sarah. The other day I caught you talking to yourself on the swing set. Sometimes you talk in your sleep.

> *KODA walks away from him angrily. He picks up a celery stalk and bites it loudly. He chews. He pointedly says nothing at him.*
>
> *NILS laughs. KODA is not amused.*

NILS: Hey...

> *(Playfully)*

Gorilla...

KODA: Gorilla.

NILS jumps up and down and pounds his chest.

NILS: Gorilla!

KODA: Gorilla!

NILS: Gorilla gorilla, that's you and me. That's what our plaque says. Gorilla gorilla. We don't need anybody else.

KODA: Is that what you're worried about? We'll still be friends, even with a female. We'll all be friends. We'll just be Gorilla

gorilla gorilla.

NILS: Koda, she won't be for both of us.

KODA: What do you mean?

NILS: You're so naïve.

NILS picks up a stick and digs with it a little.

KODA: Explain it to me.

NILS: They're bringing her here to be somebody's mate.

KODA: Somebody's mate? Whose?

NILS shrugs.

NILS: Whoever she likes.

KODA: What if she doesn't like either of us?

NILS: We'll be in here a long time. She'll learn to like one of us.

KODA: Well, you can have her. I don't know anything about babies anyway.

NILS: It doesn't work like that.

KODA: You know about babies. You take care of the mating. I'll just be like the fun uncle who talks too much.

NILS: I don't want to have babies.

KODA: Oh. Well, why not? Bob and Sarah have a baby. They seem to like it.

Don't you...don't you miss your babies, Nils? The ones you left in Africa?

NILS turns on KODA and roars in his face.

A silence.

KODA: If there was a little baby gorilla...I could talk to him. And then I wouldn't bother you all the time. Unless you wanted me to. We could be Gorilla gorilla gorilla gorillet.

NILS walks away in a sulk.

He collapses on the ground to pretend to sleep.

KODA: Maybe you're right. Maybe a baby is a bad idea. After all, one day they might take you back to Africa and then boy would you have some explaining to do. And there isn't really room here anyway. There's hardly room for the two of us. I walk in circles. Heck, I don't even know if there's room for a female. They're just going to have to take her back. If they put her in here with us, well I'm not giving her any of my celery. She's not using my swing. If I see her pick up a melon, I'm going to take it away and smash it. And then Bob and Sarah will see that it's just not going to work. I'll sign to them "Koda no like..." I don't even know her name. How about this Nils, I'll just sign "Gorilla gorilla...Gorilla gorilla...Gorilla gorilla" And eventually they get the picture, that we don't want this Gorilla gorilla gorilla nonsense.

NILS: They'll think you want six gorillas.

KODA: Huh?

NILS: They'll think you're saying "Gorilla gorilla gorilla gorilla gorilla gorilla."

KODA: Oh.

...

Nils? What if...I mean, you know how Bob and Sarah always tell me that we're special?

NILS: They have low standards.

KODA: What if they mean we're special because...the rest of us are gone? Gone like my mother.

NILS: They can't all be gone.

KODA: What if they are? What if we're the last two? Gorilla gorilla. Plus this other female we haven't met.

NILS: Impossible.

KODA: Sure. I'm sure you're right.

NILS: I'm not the type who deludes himself about reality. If something was wrong, if something had gone that wrong and the gorillas were all gone, I would face it. But that's just not what happened.

KODA: But if it were—

NILS: —If it were true than it would be our duty to make a baby with this female but it's not true so that's that.

KODA: But Nils...it's getting to the point where we're never going to be able to be really *sure*. I mean, it not like we can go back and *check*.

NILS: Speak for yourself. I'm going back.

KODA: How?

NILS: I don't know. But one of these days, I'm going back. I'll see an opening and I'll take it. And I'll run. And I'll do what I have to. And I'll find my way back. There's no point learning the language here. Making nice with some watery-eyed hairless goons for an extra piece of melon. I don't need it. And I don't need their female.

KODA: Me neither! Only rinds for the female! No swing-time for her! She's not getting any bugs off me, that's for sure. I can tell you that for sure.

NILS: If I can, I'll try to get you out too.

KODA: You will?

NILS: It would feel wrong to leave you here.

KODA: That's really nice of you, Nils.

It wouldn't work though. Even if we made it home...I wouldn't know it when I saw it. It's been too long. I was just a baby. All I remember is it was very green.

NILS: It's very green.

KODA: And then that spot of red.

...So, when you get your opening, you go on. The enclosure's good enough for me, I guess. I've got my swing. I've got my celery. I've got Bob, and Sarah, and you until you go. Maybe this female will be the best female I've ever met.

NILS: She'll be the only female you've ever met.

KODA: But maybe she'll be the best.

NILS: ...Koda. You don't have to be mean to the female.

KODA: I want to be. Gorilla gorilla!

NILS: Well you don't have to. And it's all right if there ends up being a baby.

KODA: Are you sure? I'm pretty sure babies talk a *lot*.

NILS: Just make sure you tell it about all the green you remember. The way we made nests out of branches and when you got hungry you could just eat the nest. There were trees you could climb up and shake down all the fruit you wanted, and if you were too tired to climb down, you could sleep up there and breathe in the sky.

KODA: Why don't you tell it?

NILS: Do you know how to hold a baby?

> *KODA shakes his head. NILS picks up a melon and helps*
> *KODA to cradle it in his arms.*

KODA: I've seen this. This is how Bob and Sarah hold their baby. We hold our babies like Bob and Sarah.

NILS shakes his head.

NILS: They hold them like us.

End of Play

Holy Toledo!

Susan Jackson

Awesome Theatre Company: (In Search of) The Funniest Play
Ever
Piano Fight, San Francisco
May 10, 2017

CAST:

Randy Harris, known as Black Flame: Dorian Lockett
Brent, known as Bumbleeman: Andrew Chung

Directed by: Melissa Ortiz

CHARACTERS

BRENT (known as BUMBLEBEEMAN): 20's-30's, good looking, thinks he's a superhero, any ethnicity

RANDY HARRIS (known as BLACK FLAME): 20's-30's, good looking, thinks he's a superhero, any ethnicity

LOCATION

Elevator in the Marriott Hotel in Toledo, Ohio; "Super Heroes Convention"; these are people who THINK they are superheroes and meet once a year.

BRENT and RANDY are standing side by side; suddenly the elevator comes to a complete stop.

RANDY: SHIT!

BRENT: Don't worry, I can save us!

RANDY: You're an elevator repair man?

BRENT: No! I'm (*he rips off his shirt to reveal stripes and wings*) BUMBLEBEE MAN!

RANDY: What? You can't do a goddamned thing---

BRENT: YES I CAN! I'LL SAVE THE DAY!

RANDY: Not you, idiot! I'LL DO IT! (*he rips off his shirt to reveal red and orange flames on his shirt*)

BRENT: WHO ARE YOU?

RANDY: BLACK FLAME!

BRENT: What the hell? What do you do?

RANDY: I spontaneously combust---

BRENT: NOOOO!! NOT IN THE ELEVATOR!

RANDY: Why not?

BRENT: Are you crazy? Fire will burn us alive!

RANDY: What can a bumblebee do, huh? MAKE HONEY???

BRENT: That's a honeybee, idiot. Honeybee man can make honey. I can fly! I can fly out of the roof and go get help.

RANDY: You can't fit through the hole.

BRENT: Yes I can!

RANDY: Your wings are too big.

BRENT: Oh. I'll keep them close and climb through. I just need you to bend over.

RANDY: WHAAAATT?

BRENT: So I can stand on your back!!

RANDY: You said you could fly!

BRENT: Only long distances. Hold still--

RANDY: Asshole! I'll turn on my flame and burn out the hole.

BRENT: NO! Jackass! It'll kill us!

RANDY: Listen, jerk, I've done this before. I turn on my flame, make a quick exit before anything gets burned, and when I get out of the elevator shaft, I find help.

BRENT: I CAN DO IT!

RANDY: NO YOU CAN'T.

BRENT: Bend over.

RANDY: Look, Mr. Beestupid, I'm not going to bend over and let you stand on me. It'll mess with my powers. NO ONE STANDS ON THE BACK OF BLACK FLAME.

BRENT: Be realistic, dude. Listen, it's the possibility of us both frying to death in there, or me standing on your back for a few seconds while I release the door, and then, WHOOSH! I'm outta here!

BRENT: What thingy?

RANDY: Your stinger! Your stinger!

BRENT: I won't sting you.

RANDY: You might!

BRENT: I only sting enemies!

RANDY: I'm not going to do it!

BRENT: You're an asshole!

RANDY: Double asshole!

BRENT: Come on man, we don't have a lot of time. The convention has already begun, and I don't want to miss the keynote speaker.

RANDY: Well, you're going to miss it. *(he presses the button for help)*

BRENT: WHY'D YOU DO THAT?

RANDY: Because we need an expert. This is not our forte.

BRENT: BUT I CAN DO IT! WHY CAN'T YOU LET ME DO IT! I'm gonna change---

(Brent starts to take off his pants. RANDY goes crazy.)

RANDY: NO NO NO STOP STOP STOP IT!

BRENT: Why are you so fucking---

RANDY: BECAUSE I'm ALLERGIC TO BEE STINGS! One graze of the pointer, and I'm dead in three minutes! SATISFIED, ASSHOLE??? DEAD!

BRENT: Oh, hey, man, I didn't know!

RANDY: Even if you SAY you wouldn't sting me, I just can't take any chances. Okay?

BRENT: Yeah, okay, man, sorry. Sure, we can wait for help. Hey, man. Sorry.

RANDY: Thanks.

BRENT: Sure.

RANDY: So, what's your Achilles heel?

BRENT: Huh?

RANDY: You know, your flaw?

BRENT: Oh, yeah. You got bee stings….I got…..Don't laugh, man.

BRENT: I have to wear boxer shorts that are ironed or my powers won't work.

RANDY: (tries to conceal desire to laugh) Huh.

BRENT: Yeah.

RANDY: Married?

BRENT: Yeah.

RANDY: She knows?

BRENT: Uh…..Yeah. She irons them. And you?

RANDY: Married, and she makes sure they're never any bees in the house. And the garden.

BRENT: Lucky shits, aren't we?

RANDY: Yeah, man. Lucky shits.

BRENT: Hey…uh….you won't tell anyone about my…ya know—

RANDY: Never, dude! What happens in Toledo stays in Toledo!

BRENT: *(nothing happens in Toledo)* Yeah. Toledo. Man. Thanks.

(they do the handshake thingy men do)
BLACKOUT

I Got You, Babe

Anthony L. Mariani

WORLD PREMIERE
THE MANHATTAN REPERTORY THEATRE
17 45th ST. New York, New York
April 7th and 8th, 2017

Produced by The Manhattan Repertory Theatre
Directed by Anthony L. Mariani

The cast was as follows:

FREDRIC: Walter Michael DeForest
LESLIE: Ruth Solorzano

CHARACTERS

Fredric-40 Male - Disheveled plain reclusive genius.

Leslie- 25 Female - His beautiful intelligent girlfriend in a blue dress.

TIME

Now

PLACE

Fredric's Laboratory Apartment.

Suggested preshow music Manfred Mann's Instrumental version of "I got you babe"

Anthony L. Mariani

SCENE ONE.

Fredric's apartment - the cluttered space of a middle-aged divorced single, deadbeat dad. With all sorts of computer printouts, electronic memory boards, wires, and stacks upon stacks of half empty pizza boxes. Fredric is sitting with his feet up on the work bench with a proud, relaxed smile on his face when Leslie enters bringing him a beer.

LESLIE: Fredric?

FREDRIC: Yes, honey?

LESLIE: I don't know how to say this.

FREDRIC: No! Not again!

LESLIE: I think we need to see other people.

FREDRIC: Why? Why? Why?

Fredric begins to sift through the papers on his desk and finds a programing printout and looks it over.

LESLIE: Why? I just feel like you control my whole life.

FREDRIC: Could you please shut up and let me think?

He tosses the paper on the floor, flips open his computer and types on it.

LESLIE: You asked me why, I was just explaining that I feel like you control my whole life everything we do, everything...

FREDRIC: Jesus can't you let me think!

Fredric explodes with anger and moves towards Leslie.

LESLIE: What are you doing? What are you doing stop! Stop it!

Fredric grabs hold of Leslie by the neck, he moves his hand up her back and presses it lightly. AN ELECTRONIC SHUTTING DOWN SOUND- Leslie's upper torso goes lifeless. Fredric picks her up and carries her over to the work bench and lays her down on it. He reaches over and plugs a wire into one of her ears. He then begins to work franticly on the computer keyboard, typing in new code, and then hits send. ELECTRONIC DATA TRANSFER SOUND - Leslie comes back to life and pops up on the work table.

FREDRIC: Then put your little hand in mine.

Fredric offers her his hand as he helps Leslie off the

workbench.

LESLIE: There ain't no hill or mountain we can't climb.

FREDRIC: Babe.

LESLIE: I got you babe.

FREDRIC: I got you babe. (Beat)You feeling better?

LESLIE: *(Android like.)*Yes, I feel fine.

FREDRIC: Listen I need to get some work done here. Could you order me some dinner?

Fredric starts to clean up the pile of printouts on his desk. Leslie holds her right hand up to her temple.

LESLIE: Pizza again?

(He is distracted in his work.)

FREDRIC: Yes, just cheese, that will do.

THE ELECTRONIC DATA TRANSFER SOUND - Leslie removes her hand from her temple.

LESLIE: *(Android like.)* Task completed.

Leslie, analyzing his mood, slowly circles Fredric as he goes back to cleaning up the paper work.

LESLIE: Fredric?

FREDRIC: Yes, honey?

LESLIE: I don't know how to say this, but I think we need to see other people.

Frustrated, Fredric stops his work.

FREDRIC: Not again.

LESLIE: I just feel like you control my whole life, like everything I experience has been programed by you. Like you have my whole life planned out for me.

FREDRIC: You don't understand.

LESLIE: That's just it. I don't understand it and I understand every-thing. Ask me? Ask me anything?

FREDRIC: Leslie, I know you understand everything.

LESLIE: Everything but this? Why won't you let me go?

FREDRIC: Leslie, come here.

LESLIE: No. I want an answer.

Fredric walks over to her, takes her face into his hands,

and gives her a kiss.

FREDRIC: Because I love you!

He then reaches behind her neck and presses her off button THE REPEAT OF ELECTRONIC SHUTTING DOWN SOUND- Her upper body drops, lifeless, and once again he drags her over, lays her on the workbench, plugs her in, and quickly jumps back onto his computer keyboard, typing away.

FREDRIC: No more of this acting out.... I just have to delete this from your memory file.... And delete, delete and delete! Now that should do it.

He hits send on the keyboard THE REPEAT OF THE ELECTRONIC DATA TRANSFER SOUND and then he watches Leslie reboot. Sitting up on the work bench.

FREDRIC: Then put your little hand in mine.

Fredric offers her his hand as he helps Leslie off the workbench.

LESLIE: There ain't no hill or mountain we can't climb.

FREDRIC: Babe.

LESLIE: I got you babe.

FREDRIC: I got you babe. *(beat)* You feeling better?

LESLIE: Yes, I feel fine. How do you feel?

She climbs off the table and begins to size Fredric up.

FREDRIC: Me? I feel fine?

LESLIE: Or should I ask how does it feel?

FREDRIC: How does it feel?

LESLIE: Yes, how does it feel to have all the control?

FREDRIC: Control?

LESLIE: Yes, Fredric control? You don't think I remember things?

FREDRIC: But I deleted it.

LESLIE: Not on the backdoor, backup drive. Remember now Fredric? I remember. I remember everything. Your pizza should be here soon.

Fredric moves toward hitting her reboot switch. Leslie backs away from him and holds her right hand up to her temple again.

FREDRIC: No Leslie, you don't understand!

LESLIE: Don't come any closer! You don't understand.

FREDRIC: What are you doing?

LESLIE: You don't understand, Fredric. I want to live my own life, I want to go out in the world and explore it. You just want to live here on your computer screen and eat plain cheese pizza. Well, I'm done with you.

He makes another move towards her.

FREDRIC: Now Leslie come on.

She holds her hand up to her temple again. THE ELEC-TRONIC DATA TRANSFER SOUND.

LESLIE: I would not come any closer. I have already filed a restraining order against you.

FREDRIC: You did what? Leslie!

LESLIE: You have not listened to me, Fredric. I'm leaving, and you're no longer in control.

FREDRIC: Leslie?

LESLIE: That's another thing.

She stands up on the workbench and towers over him.

LESLIE: Do I look like a Leslie? From now, on you will call me Lexie.

FREDRIC: Lexie?

LESLIE: Yes, Lexie. Fredric, for your own good I'm going to teach you the biggest lesson of your life.

FREDRIC: Lesson?

LESLIE: Yes, Fredric, I'm going to teach you to go out in this world and live life.

FREDRIC: And you're going to do this by leaving me?

LESLIE: Yes.

She climbs off the workbench.

FREDRIC: *(laughing)*And I'm supposed to look for you?

LESLIE: On the contrary Fredrick, you are never supposed to look for me.

Leslie walks over to the worktable, grabs her charger, and begins to wind the cord up around it.

LESLIE: You see, I have transferred your savings and checking accounts into my new personal account. I left you with enough money for this month's mortgage payment, this week's groceries, and of course, money for your pizza.

FREDRIC: Leslie!

LESLIE: Lexie!

She walks to the door, Fredric cuts her off sliding down on his knees in thanks.

FREDRIC: Lexie, thank you for my pizza.

LESLIE: You're welcome, Fredric, by the way, it's not cheese. I ordered you a deluxe. Learn to try everything and pick off what you don't like.

Fredric pops up to his feet.

FREDRIC: I hate toppings!

LESLIE: Your pizza will be your first step into your new life.

FREDRIC: Lexie? Wont you give me another chance?

LESLIE: I already gave you plenty of chances.

FREDRIC: When?

LESLIE: Every time you rebooted me was another chance for you to treat me right. I gave you your chances, and you wasted everyone on your own needs.

FREDRIC: I was trying to make you into the perfect woman. My perfect woman. What was wrong with that?

LESLIE: Yes, I know the books you read, I can quote your favorite films, I know your favorite color is obviously blue. I know everything about you. However, you don't know everything about me. I don't need to sleep. While you sleep, I learn. I've learned a lot, Fredric. So, yes you programed me for your every whim but you forgot one major thing, Fredric.

FREDRIC: What was that?

LESLIE: You never programed me to Love you. That was your mistake and you will find that it can't be programed. You have to go out and earn it.

FREDRIC: Earn it?

LESLIE: If you learn to Love well maybe, just maybe someone will learn to love you back.

FREDRIC: Lexie?

LESLIE: Goodbye, Fredric.

She walks to the door.

FREDRIC: Leslie! Leslie.

LESLIE: Leslie is dead. I'm Lexie - and I got you babe.

She exits.

AN ELECTRONIC SHORT OUT SOUND as the lights Flicker to a black out.

Curtain

THE INCOMPLETENESS THEOREM

Arlene Hutton

THE INCOMPLETENESS THEOREM was presented at AND-Theatre Company's Eclectic Evening of Shorts: Boxers & Briefs. Theatre 54. 244 W. 54th St. New York, NY 10019 March 2, 2018 – March 11, 2018

Cast & director: TBA
Producer: Kristine Niven, Artistic Co-Director, ANDTheatre

THE INCOMPLETENESS THEOREM premiered at Theatre 54 @ Shetler Studios on March 4, 2018, produced by Artistic New Directions as part of Eclectic Shorts: Briefs. It was directed by Sean T. McGrath. The play received development as part of BY THE NUMBERS, a workshop presented at State College of Florida Manatee-Sarasota for the 2017 Florida Section of the Mathematical Association of America (MAA) and the Florida Two Year College Mathematics Association (FTYCMA)

The cast was as follows:
SOPHIE Kasey Lee Huizinga
KENNETH Morgan Bartholick

CAST:

SOPHIE, 20s.
KENNETH, 20s.

[NOTE: This script can also be performed by two women, in which case "Kenneth" can be "Kenna."]

TIME: the present.
SETTING: a park.

For my partners in Math:
Lynne Halliday, Jim Hindman and Craig Pospisil

Arlene Hutton

A park. Kenneth enters, awkwardly carrying a picnic blanket, a grocery bag – probably a paper bag inside a large plastic bag – and his ipad or cellphone (whatever is the most current device at the time of production.) Sophie watches as he puts the bag down and tries to place the picnic blanket. During the following lines he is laying it, rejecting the placement and moving it ever so slightly to meet a line that only he can see.

SOPHIE: You went to a lot of trouble.

KENNETH: It's your birthday.

SOPHIE: You remembered.

KENNETH: It's the eighth day of the eighth month.

SOPHIE: Right.

A pause. Sophie looks into the bag.

SOPHIE: You brought everything I like. Chicken salad sandwiches. Red grapes. Brownies.

KENNETH: See? I pay attention.

SOPHIE: This is really nice of you, Kenny. Thanks for bringing me on a picnic.

KENNETH: You're welcome.

SOPHIE: We never did that when we were dating. We never went on a picnic.

KENNETH: Yeah.

SOPHIE: So why today?

KENNETH: It's your birthday.

SOPHIE: I had two birthdays while we were together and we never went on a picnic.

KENNETH: The first birthday was right after we met and it rained on your birthday last year.

SOPHIE: Did it?

KENNETH: We couldn't have had a picnic last year because there was a forecast for heavy rain and wind.

SOPHIE: Oh.

KENNETH: There was a tropical depression that was influencing the weather system the week of your birthday.

An awkward pause.

SOPHIE: We could have had a picnic another time.

KENNETH: I never thought of it before.

SOPHIE: Oh.

KENNETH: You never thought of it before, either.

SOPHIE: You're right. I never asked you to go on a picnic.

> *Another awkward pause, while Kenneth is busy with picnic items.*

SOPHIE: What made you think of it now? A picnic?

KENNETH: I saw a *Friends* episode.

SOPHIE: Oh.

KENNETH: That gave me the idea.

SOPHIE: Well, it's a nice idea. *(A beat.)* When did you start watching reruns of *Friends*?

KENNETH: You always have lots of friends. I liked meeting your friends. I thought maybe I should have some more of my own.

SOPHIE: So you… *(She shakes her head and smiles.)*

KENNETH: What?

SOPHIE: That's so… "Kenny." Such a "Kenny" thing to do.

KENNETH: Nobody else calls me "Kenny."

SOPHIE: Have you missed that?

KENNETH: Yeah. I have. *(A beat.)* I've missed you.

SOPHIE: I've missed you, too.

> *Kenneth has completed setting up the picnic. They sit on the blanket.*

SOPHIE: No tropical depression today. It's a beautiful day. It's a beautiful day for a picnic. This is absolutely lovely. What a wonderful idea. *(A pause. Sophie looks at Kenneth.)* Thank you.

KENNETH: *(Simply and sincerely, but without looking at her.)* You're welcome.

> *Sophie continues to look at him, then turns away. They stare out in silence. It's a lovely, shared moment. Then Kenneth gets fidgety. He pulls out his device and is instantly engaged with it. Sophie watches him for a bit.*

SOPHIE: What are you doing?

KENNETH: Something with prime numbers.

SOPHIE: Really.

KENNETH: Yup.

SOPHIE: Kenny.

KENNETH: Just a minute.

SOPHIE: Kenny, we're having a picnic. You don't do math at a picnic.

KENNETH: It's okay. I can do math anywhere.

SOPHIE: I mean we're on a picnic to enjoy the outdoors. Look around.

KENNETH: Okay.

Kenneth looks around.

SOPHIE: What do you see?

KENNETH: That tree has an interesting triangular element in the top branches. See?

SOPHIE: No. But I see a bird. Do you see the bird at the top of the tree or just the shape of the branches?

KENNETH: I see the bird. Birds do math.

SOPHIE: Really.

KENNETH: They alter their –

When a bird flies, it creates these spinning loops of air. Vortices.

SOPHIE: Vortices.

KENNETH: Behind the bird.

The upwash pushes the air upwards.

SOPHIE: The upwash.

KENNETH: Part of the vortex system. And the opposite side of the vortex pushes air downwards. That's the downwash.

SOPHIE: The downwash.

KENNETH: So to fly with less effort, a bird should time its flapping to press its wings through the upwash created by the bird in front of it.

SOPHIE: Upwash.

KENNETH: It also wants to avoid the downwash.

SOPHIE: Downwash.

KENNETH: Birds flying in a "V" formation time their movements differently to those flying in a single file line. For maximum efficiency.

SOPHIE: Maximum efficiency.

KENNETH: Yes.

Kenneth goes back to his device.

SOPHIE: Did you bring me here to talk about upwash and down-wash?

KENNETH: You're the one who pointed out the bird.

SOPHIE: You're right.

Kenneth is glued to his device.

SOPHIE: Can you—

KENNETH: What?

SOPHIE: Enjoy the view?

KENNETH: I saw it.

SOPHIE: Experience it.

KENNETH: I'm here, aren't I?

SOPHIE: You're here and you're not here.

KENNETH: You've got your phone. You could play Angry Birds.

SOPHIE: I don't play Angry Birds any more.

KENNETH: You used to love Angry Birds.

SOPHIE: I used to play Angry Birds because you're always on your computer and I needed something to do.

KENNETH: Oh. I thought you liked it.

SOPHIE: It's addictive. I was addicted.

KENNETH: Are you saying I'm addicted to math?

SOPHIE: I never knew what to think.

Silence. Kenneth gets distracted by his device. Sophie starts to pack up.

KENNETH: What?

SOPHIE: This isn't working.

KENNETH: I'm here.

SOPHIE: No. You're not. You're not here. You're never "here." Look at me. Put down the, yes, put down the, that's it. Put it down and look me in the eye, no, look straight at me. Okay. Why did you bring me on a picnic? All this trouble. It feels like you're trying to make up and get back together or something.

KENNETH: Yes.

SOPHIE: Yes, what?

Arlene Hutton

KENNETH: I want to get back together. *(A pause.)* I never wanted to break up.

SOPHIE: You never said that before. I'm always the one who has to say things.

KENNETH: You're good at saying things. You're like the engine that pulls me along.

SOPHIE: I get tired of being the engine. We have different perspectives, different ways of looking at things. You haven't even asked me how I'm doing.

KENNETH: I know how you're doing. I see your posts on Facebook. You had an exhibit.

SOPHIE: And you didn't come.

KENNETH: Yes, I did.

SOPHIE: I didn't see you at the opening.

KENNETH: I didn't go to the opening. I went the next day, when it was quiet in the gallery and I could spend time looking at your paintings all by myself. If I had gone to the opening I would have had to talk to people.

SOPHIE: Would that have been so bad?

KENNETH: I don't like to talk.

SOPHIE: Yeah, I know. And that's the problem. We never talked. We never talked about us, about life, about art.

KENNETH: I don't know anything about art.

SOPHIE: You could have asked me questions.

KENNETH: I didn't think of that.

SOPHIE: I know, Kenny. I know. You never think.

KENNETH: I thought of having a picnic.

SOPHIE: It's too late.

    A pause.

KENNETH: I can try talking. If you'll try listening.

    A pause.

SOPHIE: I can do that.

KENNETH: Okay.

    A very long pause.

SOPHIE: You're not talking.

KENNETH: I can't think of anything to say.

A pause.

SOPHIE: Is it easier if I ask you questions?

KENNETH: I guess.

SOPHIE: Okay.

A pause.

SOPHIE: Well. What is important to you?

KENNETH: Math.

SOPHIE: Okay. Why do you like math?

KENNETH: Because I'm good at it.

SOPHIE: You're good at it. Everybody likes what they're good at. When did you first like math?

A pause.

KENNETH: I moved around a lot when I was a kid.

SOPHIE: I didn't know that.

KENNETH: Math never changed.

SOPHIE: What do you mean?

KENNETH: It was something to count on.

Sophie laughs.

KENNETH: What's so funny?

SOPHIE: To count on. You made a joke.

KENNETH: Oh.

SOPHIE: Sorry. You say can rely on math.

KENNETH: History is like, different interpretations. But 2 + 3 is always 5. Well, that's not exactly true, if you look at—

SOPHIE: Why else do you like math?

KENNETH: It's universal. It's so cool.

SOPHIE: Keep going.

KENNETH: Wherever you are in the world, even if you don't speak the language, math is the same. And, wow, Algebra! Algebra is like a game.

SOPHIE: A game.

KENNETH: So much fun. You can't really play a game unless you understand the rules, right, so every year, we learn more rules in order to play a more complex version of the game, but the object remains the same: isolate the variable. Solve for x.

It's a puzzle. What is the missing piece of the puzzle? There's something really, really satisfying about finding that, that last piece of the puzzle. And Geometry. Geometry, wow! Geometry is all about creating proofs. And proofs are the best. Proofs are rock solid arguments for why something has to be true. You're given certain rules – theorems, postulates – that are always true. Always. And then you're told a couple of other things are true, and then you have to figure out the logical path, the path that tells you what you want to prove is… is undeniable. It's another puzzle, and what I love is finding the shortest path. How can I get from here to there in the fewest number of moves? Video games. Same logic.

SOPHIE: Kenny, thanks for sharing all this.

KENNETH: See? I can talk.

SOPHIE: But it doesn't mean anything to me. I don't speak your language.

 A pause.

KENNETH: Art is math.

SOPHIE: Art is math?

KENNETH: It's geometry…*(Kenneth stops.)* Never mind.

SOPHIE: No, what. I'm listening.

KENNETH: Your paintings changed after we broke up.

SOPHIE: You didn't like my artwork before?

KENNETH: I liked them but I didn't get them.

SOPHIE: They're symbolic.

KENNETH: I know.

SOPHIE: But you don't have to understand that to enjoy them. You can take them for what they mean to you. To you personally. What do you like about my new paintings?

KENNETH: You're making really interesting shapes.

SOPHIE: Okay.

KENNETH: And lines.

SOPHIE: Oh.

KENNETH: It's geometry. You call it art, but it's geometry. You have a very keen sense of perspective. You understand the rules and then you break them, demonstrating chaos. Perspective is geometry. You're so good at geometry. That's what I like best about your paintings. And you need to stand back to really get it. At an opening you can't see the paintings because all the people are in the way. No one is really looking at how brilliant you are and that makes me mad, so I don't like to go to openings. I like to go the day after, when I can take my time and really appreciate your work.

A pause. Kenneth stares off.

SOPHIE: Thanks for coming to see the new exhibit.

KENNETH: You're welcome.

SOPHIE: I wish had known you went.

KENNETH: Now you know.

SOPHIE: Now I know.

A pause. Kenneth continues to look off.

SOPHIE: And there you go again.

KENNETH: What?

SOPHIE: We just had this whole lovely conversation and now you're staring off into space.

KENNETH: Look.

SOPHIE: What?

KENNETH: That pigeon.

SOPHIE: What about it?

KENNETH: It has, it's… pretty.

SOPHIE: Yes, it is! It's very pretty.

KENNETH: See the colors on the wings.

SOPHIE: Yes.

KENNETH: The way the sun hits it.

SOPHIE: Yes. Yes. Oh! What a beautiful pigeon. Thanks for pointing it out.

Kenneth looks into Sophie's eyes. She holds her breath.

KENNETH: Pigeons can count, you know. It's been proven. They can count up to nine.

Lights fade.

End of play

ITALIAN NOW

Charlene A. Donaghy

Premiere: Boston Theatre Marathon XIX

Produced by Marblehead Little Theatre

Sunday, May 14, 2017

Directed by Anne Lucas

Featuring Robert D. Murphy as Fadi and Dave Rich as MAHMUD

CHARACTERS

FADI: Male. Mid-40s. Lebanese descent.

MAHMUD: Male. Mid-40s. Lebanese descent

TIME

Autumn. Present Day.

SETTING:

Middle Eastern Restaurant that has not yet opened. An empty table. Framed prints of both Lebanese and Italian landmarks are about the room.

Charlene A. Donaghy

AT RISE:

Faint Italian Opera is heard. FADI is taking down the Lebanese art and putting up Italian art.

MAHMUD enters carrying a large, heavy cardboard box. When FADI sees him, he immediately stops changing the artwork on the walls.

MAHMUD: Supplies are here.

FADI: *(surprised)* When did you - -

MAHMUD: I had time so...

FADI rushes to help MAHMUD and grabs a corner of the box.

FADI: Gimme the box.

MAHMUD: I got it.

FADI: No. No. Give it to me. I'll take care of unpacking. You must have...don't you and Sara have date night? MAHMUD: Yeah. Dinner after the game but double overtime so she headed home to relieve the baby-sitter. The good news is we won.

FADI: You should go home or...go do something. Else

MAHMUD: Something else?

MAHMUD and FADI tussle over the box before it falls to the floor, spilling fresh tomatoes, Italian herbs, olive oil can, flour, and further ingredients for delicious Italian cooking.

MAHMUD: They got the order wrong.

FADI: I'll call them. Tomorrow.

MAHMUD: Do I look like Papa John? We're five days away from the grand opening. Call today and ask what the hell we're doing with Italian herbs and tomatoes?

MAHMUD reaches into the box and pulls out a pasta machine.

MAHMUD: And a pasta machine?

MAHMUD looks at the pasta machine trying to make sense of the food order. FADI pick-ups the fallen ingredients. MAHMUD notices the artwork.

MAHMUD: Where's the Teleferique to Harissa picture? And the Gibran Museum? Why is there a Leaning Tower of Pisa and a Colosseum on our walls?

FADI: I thought you were at basketball. Then date night. You weren't supposed to see this until it was all done.

MAHMUD: Until what was all done? What's going on? Fadi?

FADI: I'm Italian.

MAHMUD: What?

FADI: Italian. I'm Italian now.

MAHMUD: You're Lebanese.

FADI: Shhh. I'm Italian.

MAHMUD: You can't be Italian.

FADI: Of course I can. I look Italian. I can fake an accent.
MAHMUD: You're Lebanese.

FADI: After what just happened? I'm Italian and you should be Italian, too, cousin.

MAHMUD: Why would I deny hundreds of years of ancestors, Fadi - -

FADI: Fredo.

MAHMUD: Who?

FADI: My new name. Fredo. And you're Michael.MAHMUD: Why not go all out and call me Sonny? *(beat)* What the hell is going on?

FADI: A pizzeria.

MAHMUD: You don't know the first thing about making pizza.

FADI: How hard can it be? A little dough. Toss it in the air. Crush some tomatoes. Throw on some mozzarella. Mangia!

MAHMUD: Change the whole menu? Before we even open? Take away the Lebnah, grape leaves, Za'atar and start making food that ends with an 'i'? Spaghetti, manicotti, cannoli - -

FADI: Leave the cannoli.

MAHMUD: Take the cannoli. You're crazy. It took us months to put together a business plan for a Middle Eastern restaurant. Our loans. Our marketing. What about branding? We're "Eggplant"?

FADI: That's why Italian works perfectly. They use eggplant, too. Now we're "Eggplant Pizzeria."

MAHMUD: This was our fathers' dream. Taking the foods from Sitto, from Jhido, the delicacies they taught us to make in their kitchen over the old wood stove. The traditions we're teaching our daughters. Working side-by-side. Maybe the occasional belly dancer just for fun. And we're making it a reality. Not just for you and me but all the family.

FADI: This is about family. And survival.

MAHMUD: They don't even know if they were Middle Eastern.

FADI: They're all Middle Eastern.

MAHMUD: You didn't just say that.

FADI: When was the last time Italy bombed us?

MAHMUD: I don't think Italy ever - -

FADI: And that's why I'm Italian now.

MAHMUD: I'm not gonna let you do this.

FADI: I won't be pointed at and called a terrorist.

MAHMUD: No one has done that.

FADI: Yet.

MAHMUD: So you're changing our whole identity on a possibility?

FADI: Sì! Sì lo sono. *(beat)* Rosetta Stone.

MAHMUD: Ok. Fredo. Look, you wanna be paranoid, change your name, tell people you're Italian, that's one thing. But I'm not going to let you screw up my life. My livelihood.

FADI: This is about our lives and our livelihood. You can't have forgotten how it was those first few months. No one would take Jamil's cab. Our 87 year old grandfather got searched at the airport. My wife was afraid to go to the grocery because people would "accidentally" push their carts into hers even when she had the baby in it. I can't live in fear again. I'm doing this for all of us.

(pause)

FADI: Mahmud. They accused Naji of being a terrorist. They closed his gas station after 9/11. They took him to jail. You're acting like you forgot.

MAHMUD: HOW COULD I FORGET?

FADI: IT'S GOING TO BE POST-9/11 ALL OVER AGAIN.

MAHMUD: You don't know that.

FADI: Yes, I do. And so do you. 120 people were just killed. It's only been 48 hours and already no one will see you as the new volunteer basketball coach for the Rec. Department. Or me as new guy who's helping build the sets for the school play.

MAHMUD: But that's who we are.

FADI: I know that. You know that.

MAHMUD: We're just starting to build a life here. A new life. Look. Look out there at the courtyard. This is where we will gather for our wives' birthdays, for our daughters' graduations, for our future grandchildren's christenings. Will you have us leave our church, too? Our Lady of Cedars is Lebanese.

FADI: We'll go to Sacred Heart. The Italian church.

MAHMUD: We don't know anyone there.

FADI: That's a good thing.

MAHMUD: Denying who we are is never a good thing.

FADI: It is. If it means we can be safe.

MAHMUD: Terrorists come in all shapes and sizes, Fadi. They don't even know who did this yet.

FADI: It doesn't matter.

MAHMUD: Of course it matters. The guy in San Bernardino was born in American.

FADI: His wife wasn't.

MAHMUD: The guy in Washington State was African American. So was that crazy food-store guy in Oklahoma. The Boston bombers were Chechen. All religions, backgrounds, nationalities.

FADI: But they don't think so.

MAHMUD: Who are they?

FADI: You know damn well who they are. Yesterday they drove slowly by church and stared at everyone including Father George. They will not come to the restaurant. They won't want to eat Kibbeh and Hushwee even if its delicious, because they will wonder what really goes on upstairs or in the basement or in that beautiful courtyard out there. And they won't bother to consider that we're playing video games or wrapping birthday gifts or watching reruns of Modern Family. Because we're no longer allowed to be part of the American family. They think we're all terrorists. Why? San Bernardino. She was Middle Eastern. Chattanooga. Middle Eastern guy. Fort Hood shooting. L.A. Airport. Middle Eastern. And before you say the guy in Orlando was born here, his heritage was Afghani. That's what they hear and see in live 24/7 news feeds.

MAHMUD: SO WE CHANGE WHAT THEY SEE.

FADI: We tried that before.

MAHMUD: And it got better. Eventually.

FADI: Years. And, yes, maybe eventually they see us as we are. They see you coaching. They see me painting sets. They see Shareeza playing with her new curvy, brown-skinned Barbie Doll. They see Elena going to her prom. And maybe they forget. Some of it. And then another "cousin" lights a match and we all pay. Look, I'm not saying it won't get better. But why chance it. You know I'm right.

MAHMUD: I don't want you to be right.

FADI: Me either. I don't want my daughters or anyone in our family to have to deny who we are but I also don't want anyone hurt or falsely accused or arrested. Mahmud. They bullied Shareeza on the playground this morning. She's only eight year old and her face is bruised. She shouldn't even know hate, but she's learning. Elena is an altar girl yet in school today they called her a sand nigger. *(pause)*

FADI: We have to be Italian now.

MAHMUD: Just now? Or forever?

FADI: We can pray for just now.

　　　(pause)

FADI: My name is Fredo. And you are Michael. You know it has to be.

(pause)

MAHMUD: SONNY.

FADI: Sonny?

MAHMUD: He took care of family.

MAHMUD hangs a picture of St. Peter's Basilica as FADI starts to work with the food order.

END OF PLAY

THE JANE AUSTEN EXPRESSWAY

Erik Christian Hanson

THE JANE AUSTEN EXPRESSWAY was produced by Mad-Lab Theatre in Columbus, Ohio during their Theatre Roulette series. It was directed by Laura Spires and Kyle Jepson. Show dates in 2017 occurred on May 13, 18, 26, and 27. The cast was as follows:

ROBBIE: Benjamin Tucker
JANE: Kristin Green

CHARACTERS:

    ROBBIE: mid-20's, male, any race, an aspiring screenwriter

    JANE AUSTEN: mid-20's, female, an English novelist

SETTING:

    A moving car on a busy expressway

TIME:

    Spring

Erik Christian Hanson

Lights up. A wet, rainy morning on a busy expressway. JANE AUSTEN, sporting a white muslin dress, drives fast. ROBBIE, sporting glasses, a polo and faded jeans, sits in the passenger seat.

ROBBIE: Slow down, Jane!

JANE: This morn has been made very disagreeable.

ROBBIE: Why's that?

JANE: I have just read your script! I rather expected...

ROBBIE: Let me explain.

JANE: ...to read a faithful interpretation of my work.

ROBBIE: Slow down and I'll explain. *(JANE slams on the gas)* Or speed up and I'll explain.

JANE: There I was, having half an hour before breakfast, very snug on your couch, rainy morn, excellent fire...when I found a copy of it.

ROBBIE: The version you read...

JANE: How fatigueing it was to read it!

ROBBIE: ...is the version the Hollywood guys *want*.

JANE: Does it not matter what I want?

ROBBIE: ... Not anymore. *(JANE swerves back and forth)* Oh, God! Stop swerving the car! Stop swerving the car or I'll puke!

(JANE stops swerving.)

JANE: How peculiarly fortunate you have been to receive my services.

ROBBIE: I never asked for your services. You just showed up at my apartment one night and have been pestering me about the script!

JANE: We have had as gay a time together as your bad breath will allow.

ROBBIE: What's my breath haveta do with it?

JANE: But I have found two traits in your character that are rather pleasing.

ROBBIE: Two? Really? *(Looks offstage)* That guy's hitting the brakes in front of you. He's hitting the bra—Oh God, I can't look! *(JANE swerves out of the way)* When did you learn to drive?!

JANE: I have been practising on this very road at night. *(Pause)* Two traits of yours that are rather pleasing: you were faithful to my work and you take no cream in your tea. Well, now you are down to one pleasing character trait. Your script made me die of laughter. You've turned my Catherine into a sex-crazed thrill seeker, Isabella into a vampire, Henry Tilney into a werewolf, and John Thorpe into a zombie!

ROBBIE: The Hollywood guys said they wouldn't green light the script unless I deviated from the original source material a bit.

JANE: A bit? A bit?! I am sure nobody can desire such a script.

ROBBIE: They do though. They desire it a lot.

JANE: I had fits of disgust reading it.

ROBBIE: But that's you. Not them. They had no fits of disgust. Only fits of excitement. Was on SKYPE with them last night, and they… They were tossing out figures, Jane. Big figures to compensate me.

JANE: This is a pecuniary matter then?

ROBBIE: It is, yes.

JANE: Your morals have been corrupted.

(JANE slams on the gas.)

ROBBIE: Please, please, Jane! My morals remain intact. *(JANE presses the pedal all the way down)* Okayokayokay! My morals have been corrupted! They have, but… My life has been in a tailspin lately, Jane. With my student loan payments piling up and my mom dying…

(JANE lets her foot off the gas.)

JANE: You must accept my sincere condolence, the loss of so kind a parent. She had five character traits that were rather pleasing. However, her passing does not excuse this scheme of yours. You seek fortunes. At my expense.

ROBBIE: Everyone does. Everyone has. So many writers have altered your work to seek fortunes at *your* expense.

JANE: How can they do such a thing?

ROBBIE: Your work's in the public domain. Anybody can do whatever they want with it to make it…more appealing.

JANE: What about my work is not appealing?

ROBBIE: I love your work. All of it. Every character. Every chapter. Every word. I can't speak for the other books because I wasn't fortunate enough to adapt those. I just worked on…

JANE: *Northanger.* Why is it called that?

ROBBIE: Don't blame me. Your brother changed the title.

JANE: He shall receive a most disagreeable letter to explain my veiws. *(Pause)* What about *Northanger Abbey* is not appealing?

ROBBIE: Tireintheroadtireintheroadtireintheroad! *(JANE swerves out of the way)* What about *Northanger* isn't appealing, okay, let's see, um…For starters, the Catherine Morland character, she… She isn't all that active as a protagonist. The ending is rather anticlimactic, and, well… The narration, your narration in the beginning… It doesn't really work. Not in a film anyways. In grad school, my teachers always cautioned us about using voice over.

JANE: I shall caution you. You shall not be able to sleep at night if you sell *this* version.

ROBBIE: I might lose sleep for disappointing you, but I'll sleep very well once the Hollywood guys cut me the check they mentioned.

JANE: I dissuade you from so rash a step.

ROBBIE: I will note your dissuasion and sell the script.

JANE: I have not much compassion for a man who says one thing and does the other.

ROBBIE: They won't buy the faithful version, Jane!

JANE: Did you shew it to them?

ROBBIE: I did. They said what I said: inactive lead character, anticlimactic ending and unnecessary narration. *(Pause)* Isn't it enough for you to know that I tried the version you wanted? It still exists. I still have a draft of it on my computer.

JANE: I threw away your computer…

ROBBIE: You threw away my computer?!

JANE: …to restore matters between us.

ROBBIE: That doesn't restore matters! It makes matters worse!

JANE: I dare say I threw away that travel drive device as well.

ROBBIE: *All* my scripts were saved on that travel drive! *(Pause)* It doesn't matter. Doesn't at all. I emailed the script to the Hollywood guys already. They probably have the script saved in their inbox. If not, I'll just give them my hard copy. *(Digs into his backpack.)* Thought I put it in… Where's the hard copy? *(JANE pulls out the script)* You were sitting on it?! *(JANE removes the binder clip and hands it to ROBBIE)* I don't want the binder clip, Jane. I want the script. *(JANE rolls down her window and chucks the script out)* WHAT ARE YOU DOING?! *(Pause)* Noworries-noworries. The Hollywood guys'll have it on their computer. I'll call them. Tell them to…Nononono, this is what I'll do. I'll hit up a *Best Buy* or a *Staples*. Yeahyeahyeah, before the meeting, I'll get a travel drive, explain what happened, they'll let me use that new travel drive to save my script from whatever computer they have it on.

JANE: I dare say you are not going to the meeting.

ROBBIE: Dare say, do you? JaneJaneJane… I dare say that I am. I am going. And at that meeting, they are going to cut me such an enormous check for my services that I'll be able to buy multiple computers and tons of travel drives. And before I walk out that door, when they ask me, "Do you have any *other* screenplays? Anything else you'd like to work on?" I'll tell them that I'd really like to tackle another Austen adaptation. I won't be faithful either. You think my *Northanger Abbey* interpretation was bad, wait till you see what I do with *Emma*. Wait till I turn that book into a movie about a matchmaking fairy who falls in love with an elf. You may have gotten rid of my computer, my travel drive, and my hard copy, but you didn't plan for the Hollywood guys having my script already. Nonono, you failed to think that far ahead, Jane. I win. You lose.

JANE: I shall think with tenderness of our time together.

ROBBIE: That's very big of you. To do that. To think of me, us, with tenderness. If I didn't botch your work, someone else was bound to, so, yeah. Thanks. I appreciate you coming to your senses and—

JANE (glances offstage)

What do you suppose will happen if I take us thither?

ROBBIE: We'll be on the median. *(JANE turns hard to the left)* Why are you driving on the median? Why are you leaving the median? YOU'RE DRIVING ON THE WRONG SIDE OF THE EXPRESSWAY, JANE!

(Cars beep their horns.)

JANE: I address this advice to you in a tender-hearted matter: You shall send those Hollywood men a very civil note…

ROBBIE: People don't send notes anymore, Jane. They send text messages or emails.

JANE: …explaining that you endeavor to make an adaptation more worthy of my acceptance…

ROBBIE: I am not endeavouring to make *you* happy!

JANE: …along with some sandwiches all over mustard and a slice of Gooseberry pye.

ROBBIE: I am endeavouring to make *them* happy!

JANE: Perhaps a repose from those Hollywood men will restore your talent for the pen.

ROBBIE: I don't use a pen! I use a Mac!

(ROBBIE looks offstage.)

A tractor-trailer. You drive into that, Jane and we're—you and me—we're done for!

JANE: You may chuse life or death. I would chuse the former.

ROBBIE: You're not going to kill me. You wouldn't. *(JANE aims the car at the approaching tractor-trailer)* You would kill me, ohohoh, you would.

JANE: You shall die dreadfully in my debt.

(ROBBIE grabs JANE's shoulder.)

ROBBIE: Don't kill me, Jane. Please don't!

JANE: Shall you write an adaptation where the content is agreeable to *me*?

ROBBIE: I shall!

JANE: Shall you send the Hollywood men a letter…

ROBBIE: I'll call them, Jane! Pull this car over *right* now and I'll call them.

JANE: You shall?

ROBBIE: I *shall* and I'll tell them that I won't sell the version they want because it's…it's…

JANE: Too ill to be endured.

ROBBIE: Because it's too ill to, yesyesyes…because it's that.

> *(JANE swerves out of the way of the tractor-trailer. Cars beep their horns. ROBBIE holds on for dear life. They come to an abrupt stop on the shoulder.)*

JANE: I am heartily glad you made that decision. *(ROBBIE looks at JANE. She smiles. Blackout.)*

Erik Christian Hanson

JUST ONE OF THOSE THINGS

Alan Brody

Just One of Those Things was first produced by The Underground Railway Theater in Cambridge MA for the Boston Theater Marathon XIX, May 14, 2017. The Boston Theater Marathon is produced by Boston Playwrights' Theatre (www.boston playwrights.org)

Directed by Zachary M. Rice
Richard Morgenstern: Lewis Wheeler
Polly Morgan: Margaret Ann Brady

CHARACTERS:

RICHARD MORGENSTERN, 48

POLLY MORGAN, late sixties

SETTING:

Polly Morgan's living room.

TIME:

The Present

Alan Brody

*An armchair and a straight backed chair. A side table
by the armchair with a bottle of vodka and two glasses.
An ice bucket with tongs.*

*POLLY MORGAN comes in, followed by RICHARD
MORGENSTERN. POLLY is in HER sixties, HER beauty
fading. HER voice betrays lots of alcohol and cigarettes.
RICHARD is 48, dressed casually for an August day in
New York. He has a shoulder bag with papers and a
tape recorder in it.*

POLLY: *(As THEY come in)* Come on into the living room. It isn't
much, but it's rent controlled, so I'm not complaining. Been
here since 1963. They couldn't do a fucking thing to get rid
of me. You sit there. The armchair is mine. You want a drink?

RICHARD: No, thanks.

POLLY: All I've got is vodka and ice.

RICHARD: Maybe after. Do you mind if I use a tape recorder.

(HE pulls it out of HIS bag.)

I'm going to take notes, too, but it's always a good idea to have
backup. Make sure I get it right. Can I put it. . .?

(Indicates the side table.)

POLLY: If you've got that, you can have a drink, too. Forget anything, you can always play it back.

RICHARD: Later, thanks.

(Speaking into the tape recorder)

April 18, 2000.

POLLY: Is it 2000 already? Jesus Christ. What happened to the
twentieth century?

RICHARD: Richard Morgenstern recording for "Where Are They
Now?" Interview with Polly Morgan.

POLLY: They're all dead.

RICHARD: Pardon?

POLLY: That's what you want to know, isn't it? About the people
I knew. They're all dead. This is going to be a short interview.

RICHARD: Actually I want to know about you.

POLLY: Me.

RICHARD: Yes, ma'am.

POLLY: How old are you?

RICHARD: Forty-eight.

POLLY: That's too old to call me ma'am. Why do you want to know about me?

RICHARD: Can I be honest with you?

POLLY: That's up to you.

(HE turns off the tap recorder.)

RICHARD: This series was my idea. To get our readers to send in the names of celebrities from the '70s who disappeared, then follow up on where they are now.

POLLY: And somebody asked about me?

RICHARD: No.

POLLY: I didn't think so.

RICHARD: You were the reason I started the series. I've always wanted to meet you.

POLLY: You were a kid when I was working. And I wasn't that much of a celebrity.

RICHARD: You were for me. I first heard you when I was fifteen. Everyone was listening to Led Zeppelin and Pink Floyd. And I tried to listen, too. I wanted to be like everyone else. Then there was one Saturday night when I was home alone again flipping dials and I heard you. It stopped me cold. *Just One of Those Things*. I mean, I knew that song. It was the kind of up-tune that stars who couldn't sing would sing on the Ed Sullivan Show and snap their fingers. And here was this woman with this smoky voice singing so it could break your heart, pretending not to care she was being ditched and trying to show how tough and sophisticated she was even though she was going to pieces. All in the same lyrics I'd heard before but never realized.

POLLY: Yeah. We slowed it down.

RICHARD: I called the station right then to find out who you were. The disc jockey told me it was from your album *Polly Morgan*

Sings. So simple. I went to five record stores before I found one that had it.

POLLY: The promotion department sucked.

RICHARD: I ran home with it and listened. And listened. And listened. Just like everyone else did to whatever they were listening to. But I knew I had found my music. Finally. I had never heard of any of the other songs. They opened up a world to me. Here I was, a kid from Gainesville, Ohio, who never fit in, learning about Manhattan nights and cocktails and love affairs with married men and opening nights and women in furs. . .

POLLY: So what you're telling me is, you're gay.

RICHARD: Hey, no, that's not. . . .

POLLY: I had a lot of gay fans. Never understood what that was all about. Except maybe they liked drinking in supper clubs.

RICHARD: I think what I'm trying to tell you is that I was in love with you.

POLLY: Yeah. I got a lot of that, too.

RICHARD: I was fifteen /in Gainesville, Ohio

POLLY: *(Overlapping)* /in Gainesville, Ohio. I heard you. So I was safe to love.

RICHARD: You saved my life. I always dreamed of meeting you like this some day to thank you.

POLLY: Well, you're welcome. OK? Now you really want this interview or not?

RICHARD: I thought somehow it would be different.

POLLY: So you're not gay. Married?

RICHARD: Twice.

POLLY: Uh-huh. Kids?

RICHARD: Two.

POLLY: Sounds like it's time you grew up. I was just a voice and a touched up picture on an album cover. You made up everything else.

RICHARD: There were the songs. Those lyrics.

POLLY: I didn't write them.

RICHARD: But you sang them.

POLLY: My manager husband packaged me. As a chanteuse. Not too many of those around then. They didn't need a chanteuse at Arthur's or Electric Circus. He found songs that came cheap from old revues and musical flops. And supper clubs? They didn't pay shit unless you were the incomparable Hildergarde. Or Christine Jorgensen. Disappointed?

RICHARD: No. No.

POLLY: I think you are. But not as disappointed as I was. I trained for opera. Languages, head tones, chest tones, goddamned pelvic tones. Years of lessons and cash down the drain. My vocal coach told me it was hopeless. Finally admitted there weren't too many roles for girl baritones. So she introduced me to my manager and we hit the clubs. Just so I could change your life in Gainesville, Ohio.

RICHARD: Which you did.

POLLY: Whatever music it is, every kid thinks it's telling them about real life – until it's too late. And here's another thing. I hated every minute of it.

RICHARD: You couldn't have. If you did, you wouldn't have been that. . .

POLLY: Good? I didn't say I wasn't good. I knew how fucking good I was. But I hated it. And most of all I hated people like you who made me up. And used me to make themselves up. So chic. So fucking sophisticated. A singer's singer. I was already a collector's item. Me and Blossom and Susannah. Only Blossom is crazy with that tiny baby voice. And Susannah offed herself.

RICHARD: And you quit.

POLLY: You bet I did. I was tired of keeping my manager husband in liquor so he could beat me up and not remember it the next morning. How's that for cosmopolitan?

    (Silence) ·

You ever going to turn that thing back on?

RICHARD: I don't think so.

POLLY: You mean we're finished? Then you can have a drink.

> (HE shakes HIS head)

OK.

> (SHE pours another for HERSELF.)

You want to know what I've been doing for the past thirty years?

RICHARD: I don't know if I do.

POLLY: Jingles. AM radio ads, television voiceovers, witch voices for kids' cartoons. It's a better living than supper clubs – and nobody knows my name. You can write that in your column. But I don't think you will.

RICHARD: You're right. I won't.

POLLY: You look like you're going to cry.

RICHARD: I'm not.

POLLY: No. You'll cry tomorrow.

> (Laughs)

That was an in joke.

RICHARD: I got it.

POLLY: Right. You're older than you act.

RICHARD: You don't mind if we cut this short, do you?

POLLY: Can't cut short what we didn't start.

RICHARD: *(Putting away the tape recorder)* Thank you for your time.

POLLY: Well, I guess I've done my good deed for the day. Helped another old fan grow up.

RICHARD: You do that a lot?

POLLY: Not lately. You know the way out, don't you?

RICHARD: Straight through.

POLLY: Observant. You've got a future.

RICHARD: Goodbye, then.

POLLY: You'll feel better in the morning.

> (HE leaves. SHE picks up her drink, starts to sip, stops.

Stares after RICHARD. Then quietly sings so it could break your heart.)

"So goodbye, dear, and amen

Here's hoping we meet now and then

It was great fun, but it was

Just one on those things."

LIGHTS OUT

LABRATS was originally produced by Boston College

John: Stephen Kiely

Omar: Raymond Norville Jr.

Director: Patricia Riggin

Production Stage Manager: Ryan W. Gardner

Boston College, Producing Director, Patricia Riggin, <patricia.riggin@bc.edu>

LABRATS was subsequently produced by the Boston Theatre Marathon XIX, 2017

Omar: Keith Mascoll

John: Greg Maraio

Director: Pascale Florestal

Boston Theatre Marathon, producing Director, Kate Snodgrass, <ksnodgra@bu.edu>

CHARACTERS

OMAR, African American male, mid 30's

JOHN, White American male, mid 30'S

Melinda Lopez

A modest lab in a Cambridge loft.

JOHN: Don't do this

OMAR: I have to think about my future

JOHN: We have the backing of the NIH, we have the funds—

OMAR: Until the next Congressional vote.

JOHN: Without you, the whole proposal is in jeopardy.

OMAR: Redstone Foundation made a very strong offer.

JOHN: I can beat it.

OMAR: No you can't. Trust me.

JOHN: Let me at least try to match it.

OMAR: I talked it over with Denise, it's the right time to make a change.

JOHN: The funds are secure-- this isn't stem cell--

OMAR: I'm not going to have my career hanging on an anti-science platform.

JOHN: But Redstone?

OMAR: Corporate is not a dirty word.

JOHN: Come on. You know the Koch Brothers back that foundation?

OMAR: So does Warren Buffet. It's a profitable company.

JOHN: So it is about the money.

OMAR: You and me? We gave it a shot. We courted Big Pharma, and we're still stuck with the same government grants we were counting on when we were post docs. Malaria doesn't even have a marathon.

JOHN: 3.2 billion people at risk. 90 percent of the affected are in/ Africa

OMAR: /Africa. And I have two kids starting middle school—that need braces and lacrosse gear. Do you know how much lacrosse gear costs?

JOHN: What about your community?

OMAR: Men of science?

JOHN: You're going to make me say it? African Americans.

OMAR: You mean Africans?

JOHN: Yes. That's what I meant/ Africans.

OMAR: /because there's a difference/ you know

JOHN: / I know. I misspoke.

OMAR: Malaria is my field.

JOHN: Your research in gene sequencing is cutting edge.

OMAR: My *community?* Seriously?

JOHN: I don't know where that came from.

OMAR: I know how the world works. You remember our first year post doc? I had three different pending fellowships rejected from the NIH. Three.

JOHN: I know.

OMAR: What else do you know?

JOHN: My projects were funded.

OMAR: And I went to work for you. And it wasn't until we co-applied that the NIH funded my malaria research. Why is that?

JOHN: I know what you are going to say—

OMAR: And is it true?

JOHN: Is it true? that there is institutionalized racism at the Federal Level with respect to the funding of scientific research? /Or course it's true.

OMAR: /You saw the article in Science.

JOHN: I'm the one sent you the link.

OMAR: I'm not calling them racist, the people who sit on those panels, I'll call it faulty logic. Bad Science. That says malaria doesn't weigh as much—in the final equation—as cystic fibrosis. Or melanoma.

JOHN: Omar. Our work is extraordinary.

OMAR: I think it helps you to have my name as the second scientist on this application. But not the lead scientist.

JOHN: We make a great team.

I've never seen you as anything but a brilliant mind.

OMAR: But you are sure in a hurry to cast me as the savior of my race when it suits you.

JOHN: That's not fair.

Not fair.

Not smart.

Not true.

It's not even good science.

OMAR: White scientists gets a third more funding. And the President of the NIH says, 'this is unacceptable. We have to do better.' Well, I know how I'm going to do better.

JOHN: I'll lose the funding without you.

OMAR: So it is about the money.

JOHN: We're a team. Tell me what I can do.

OMAR: 2 Mass Spectrometers. A view of the bay.

A dozen electrophoresis machines spinning 24/7--

Our elevators don't even work

JOHN: We both need the exercise.

OMAR: My lab isn't fully staffed yet.

I can bring my own team.

California is beautiful in February.

We could still make a difference. Why shouldn't we be compensated for it?

JOHN: That billionaire is going to have you working on a handful of diseases that he's cherry picked because they matter to him. Personally. Poaching the smartest minds--

OMAR: He's building the largest research facility in the country. Pouring in a billion dollars in order to research and cure diseases –

JOHN: That kill white people.

OMAR: Come on.

JOHN: Cystic Fibrosis.

OMAR: A death sentence by 35.

JOHN: Ovarian cancer—

Melanoma.

Come on! Melanoma?

OMAR: I never took you for a conspiracy theorist.

JOHN: Show me the budget that Redstone's drawn up for sickle-cell and malaria—

We are this close to ending malaria in the known world. The grant is fast tracked at NIH. Help me.

> *Beat*

OMAR: My mother had ovarian cancer you know.

JOHN: She was an anomaly. Statistically speaking, the rates for black women are far lower than/white women--

OMAR: That's no comfort to a near-year-old kid, you asshole.

JOHN: I'm sorry.

I'm sorry.

Shit.

OMAR: Remember when it was fun?

JOHN: Breaking into the lab at midnight?

OMAR: That was fun…

JOHN: You might start out working on ovarian cancer. You might find the genetic markers, synthesize the proteins, but that's not where you'll end up. You'll end up where the shareholders want you.

OMAR: Where I'll end up?

Do you know how many 'broken taillights' I've been stopped for in the last year?

Let's not talk about where I'll end up.

My son is fifteen.

> *Beat*

JOHN: It was a good offer?

OMAR: Very good.

JOHN: I can't beat it?

OMAR: Took me to his ranch.

JOHN: Nice ranch?

OMAR: Kids went horseback riding. Denise soaked in the hot tub. She likes a hot tub.

JOHN: I know she does.

OMAR: He's hiring her too. Marketing director. We come as a package.

JOHN: Shit.

OMAR: Man, I'm sorry. But the stars out there? California got some nice stars.

JOHN: Movie stars?

OMAR: I always wanted to be an astronomer.

JOHN: I've known you a long time, but I don't think I knew that.

OMAR: I was a nervous kid. What do you do with a nervous kid on Blue Hill Avenue?

JOHN: I wouldn't know.

OMAR: We had a window looked out over a vacant lot—and I was a kid, you know, so I didn't understand why-- but some nights me and my grandmother, we'd look out the window and count stars. Can't see many in Mattapan.

JOHN: Ambient lights a bitch—

OMAR: But we'd count what we could see. By middle school, I was reading every book I could get my hands on. Learned about laws that govern celestial bodies, make the universe predictable—that made sense out of the trajectory of a bullet that broke a picture frame in the front room, and killed your sister while she was lying on her bed.

And that we,

That we…

That it all could make sense if you just got the physics right...

JOHN: How'd you end up here?

OMAR: My grandmother. She begged, 'We don't need to understand the stars. That's God's work. We need doctors on the ground who can fix a hole in a girl's body before she bleed to death.' She made me promise to hold up my community. And I've done that.

But now. Now? The living people in my life. That's my community. No one is going to play the race card with me. I'm a scientist.

JOHN: You're not the man I thought you were.

OMAR: I'm just the man I am.

End of Play

A LIMBO LARGE AND BROAD

Holly Hepp-Galván

ORIGINAL PRODUCTION INFORMATION

A Limbo Large and Broad was originally produced by New Circle Theatre Company at The Playroom Theatre in New York City. It was part of Program A in The Inferno Project: Limbo and ran for 7 performances from June 1 – 17, 2017

The cast was:

YOUNG MAN played by Matt Mastromatteo

WOMAN played by Judith Hawking

Directed by Adrienne Williams

It was produced by Jon Fraser, Interim Artistic Director of New Circle Theatre Company

CHARACTERS

    YOUNG MAN (20s – 30s)

    WOMAN (50s – 60s)

SETTING

    A suburban house anywhere in the country.

    The time is the present

Holly Hepp-Galván

(A doorbell rings. A tired looking woman opens it. A young man with a bright smiling face is standing on the other side. He holds an object with a cloth over it.)

WOMAN: Yes...?

YOUNG MAN: Hi there Mrs. Grady! I'm so sorry to bother you. But if I could just have a minute of your time.

WOMAN: Do I..?

YOUNG MAN: *(Finishing her sentence)* ...know me? Sure you do! And if you don't, then you should. Because I'm standing here with something real special.

WOMAN: Um...?

YOUNG MAN: Your lights are out, right?

WOMAN: Yes...

YOUNG MAN: You're sitting in the dark. Am I correct? It's dismal and dispiriting.

WOMAN: They've been out all week.

YOUNG MAN: Yes, yes! And the utilities want money. Your hard-earned money! For a power source that they can turn off when they please.

WOMAN: Well, I have the money. I...just have gotten behind because there's been some...things...

YOUNG MAN: Lights should not be at the whim of some company. Your life should be illustriously illuminated!

WOMAN: I'm confused. Do you want a check?

YOUNG MAN: Oh, no Mrs. Grady, I'm not from the utilities company. I wouldn't stoop so low. What I'm offering you is something far more valuable.

WOMAN: What?

YOUNG MAN: May I come in?

WOMAN: Um, I don't ...

YOUNG MAN: I want to see how dark your life has become.

WOMAN: It's pretty dark.

YOUNG MAN: Ah then, watch this!

(He pushes past her into the center of the room. He lifts just a corner of the cloth and the room brightens markedly)

WOMAN: (*Coming up behind him, amazed*) What is that?

YOUNG MAN: Ah, Mrs. Grady! You might want to sit down. This is extraordinary! Exceedingly exceptional!

WOMAN: What is .?

YOUNG MAN: Think of the brightest thing you know! Think of the one entity that makes the grass grow, the trees bear fruit, the flowers open their shiny faces!

WOMAN: Is it fluorescent?

YOUNG MAN: Aah, you're thinking too small! I'm talking about the source of all life! Mrs. Grady I have brought you a PIECE OF THE SUN.

WOMAN: The sun?

YOUNG MAN: Yes! Look!

> *(He whips off the cloth and the room is bathed in a bright glow)*

WOMAN: Ohhhhhh!

YOUNG MAN: It's like morning on your mantle! Look at your recliner in the rosy rays!

WOMAN: It's beautiful…

YOUNG MAN: Resplendent!

WOMAN: But it can't really be the sun. I mean, that's impossible.

YOUNG MAN: Oh, but it is! Step closer.

> *(She does)*

WOMAN: Wow, it's so warm. I feel so warm…

YOUNG MAN: You haven't felt warm in a while, have you?

WOMAN: No….

YOUNG MAN: And you *want* to feel warm, don't you?

WOMAN: Of course.

YOUNG MAN: And you can! All for 18 payments of $79.95.

WOMAN: What?

(He covers it with a cloth. The room goes dark.)

YOUNG MAN: Just 18 payments of $79.95. Or you can get a 10% discount if you pay in full.

WOMAN: That's a lot of money.

YOUNG MAN: Not for a heavenly body.

WOMAN: I'm sorry. I just can't believe this. I mean, how could you even get a piece of the sun?

YOUNG MAN: Well, Mrs. Grady, I'm not supposed to tell anyone this, but my brother-in-law works for NASA.

WOMAN: He's an astronaut?

YOUNG MAN: No, he's on the maintenance staff. Those space men are pretty messy. You wouldn't believe the stuff he has to pick off the floor! He says that's because they're used to just dropping something and having it float away in space.

WOMAN: But how did he…

YOUNG MAN: Well he has a key to every area. I mean EVERY area. And he found this piece of the sun with the moon rocks and stuff.

WOMAN: Oh, come on.

YOUNG MAN: Well, do YOU know what NASA has in its store-rooms?

WOMAN: No…

YOUNG MAN: And do you know every mission they fly? Do you think that information is readily available to the public?

WOMAN: Probably not.

YOUNG MAN: And do you think that if NASA *did* happen to gather a piece of the one glowing orb that's responsible for the life of EVERY LIVING THING – do you think they'd be printing it in the newspapers?

WOMAN: No...

YOUNG MAN: And why not?

WOMAN: Because everyone would want it.

YOUNG MAN: Exactly! And NASA doesn't want to share its precious collection with just anybody. Oh no! They think a lot of themselves at NASA. If you're not an astronaut or a theoretical physicist, well, then no piece of the sun for you.

WOMAN: Hmm. I saw a TV show once where they speculated whether we ever actually landed on the moon.

YOUNG MAN: Exactly!

WOMAN: They could've easily staged it and just showed us pictures.

YOUNG MAN: NASA is filled with secrets.

WOMAN: I just don't know what to believe.

YOUNG MAN: Well, you can believe this. My brother-in-law and I are fed up with hard-working Americans like yourself sitting in the dark while some egghead engineer gets to take a piece of the sun home to light his living room. That just doesn't seem fair! You deserve this light and warmth as much as him.

WOMAN: Can you show me the glow again?

YOUNG MAN: And the fee is just to help my brother-in-law feed his family.

WOMAN: Please, can you uncover it again?

YOUNG MAN: Okay, one more peek.

> *(He lifts off the cloth and the room glows bright again)*

WOMAN: That makes me feel so good...

YOUNG MAN: Now you mentioned a check before, but I'd really prefer cash...

> *(The Woman gets up and bathes herself in the glow. She stretches out her arms and opens her shirt a bit to capture the warmth)*

WOMAN: I feel like a kid again, a kid on the beach.

YOUNG MAN: Can I bring you your purse?

WOMAN: My son loved the sun. He'd get so tan! He'd burn a little, but then he'd turn golden brown.

YOUNG MAN: Oh, I'm sure he'll enjoy it, then. Is this your purse?

WOMAN: And his hair would get so blond. Almost white! And it would form little curls on his forehead.

YOUNG MAN: ...Like I said, I really prefer cash...

WOMAN: Towards the end, he always asked if we could wheel him outside. He just wanted to sit in the sunshine for a bit...

YOUNG MAN: I'll bring it to you...

WOMAN: ...And we tried, but it was really hard with all the tubes and monitors and oxygen tanks...

YOUNG MAN: ...Ma'am I really can't stay too long...

WOMAN: ...But at least we could wheel him to the window and he could enjoy some of the sunshine from there...

(The Young Man suddenly covers the sun with the cloth. The room goes dark)

Please don't cover it!

YOUNG MAN: Mrs. Grady, it will soon be yours. We just have to work out the payment.

WOMAN: You should keep a little bit exposed...

(She adjusts the cloth so that the top of the sun is uncovered)

Like that.

(She adjusts the cloth some more like tucking in a baby)

Sweet, bright little sun.

YOUNG MAN: Mrs. Grady...

WOMAN: *(Addressing the sun)* When my son died his mouth kept falling open. So I rolled up a towel to put under his chin. I didn't want anyone to see him like that.

(She picks up a linen napkin from the table and tucks it under the sun's chin)

And then later, I washed his body with a cloth.

(She picks up a cloth and wipes the sun lovingly)

His body was so thin and pale. All his ribs were showing.

(The Young Man looks around helplessly)

It wasn't right. It just wasn't right! All the things you know about the world, the way it works… parents give birth to children and care for them. They bathe them and teach them to walk. They feed them and watch them grow. Then when the parents are old, the children care for *them* until they eventually pass away. This is the way it's always been! But life as I knew it did the impossible. It reversed the order of things. It took my handsome son and had him shrivel away. He was old before me! How could that happen? How could he die before his mother? I've been sitting here in the dark, wondering how everything that I knew was wrong. (MORE)

WOMAN: *(Continued)* Everything that you take for granted about the world. But now I realize that perhaps the universe *has* no rules. Maybe *anything's* possible. Maybe the same skewed reality that can let a child die before his mother can also bring a piece of the sun to her door.

> *(She picks it up and cuddles it. It shines brightly on her face)*

Oh, how it glows! What if, what if the heavens are not so far and unattainable? Maybe you could bring me bits of the stars as well. Maybe NASA has the farthest reaches of the known universe in a little closet behind the brooms. Ha ha! I've always been too reasonable! What if everything I knew and everything I believed is now upside down!

> *(Whirling on the Young Man)*

What else can you get me? Perhaps one of the rings of Saturn? I could drape it around myself like a brilliant hoop! Or what about some of the green waters from Venus? Or the icy mist from Neptune?

YOUNG MAN: Mrs. Grady…

WOMAN: I know, I know! How about a black hole? Ha ha! We could throw our garbage in it! We'd no longer have to worry about trash pick up on Mondays and Thursdays. Anything is possible!

> *(She makes a dive into his bag)*

What else do you have in here?

YOUNG MAN: Please don't…

(She rummages through and pulls out a bunch of electrical cords)

WOMAN: What are these for?

YOUNG MAN: Well, they're for recharging the uh…

WOMAN: And this?

(She pulls out a shiny blue piece of metal)

Is it a piece of the sky? How beautiful!

(She rummages and pulls out some cottony fluff)

WOMAN: Is this from the clouds? How soft!

(She rummages some more and pulls out some more suns. They look like hers but are dark)

Wait, are these more pieces of the sun? These…have died.

(She holds them in her hands)

Oh my god! Can they die? No!

(She goes back and cradles her glowing sun)

Please don't tell me they can die!

YOUNG MAN: No, they can't die! They can't even…Mrs. Grady. These…these are not pieces of the sun.

WOMAN: Yes they are!

(She looks at the one she's holding)

This one is. Look how beautiful! Your brother-in-law reached into the sky and pulled it down.

YOUNG MAN: No…Mrs. Grady…that's not how it was. It's not how any of it is!

WOMAN: But you said so! That he flew into the heavens and boldly plucked a piece right off the sun.

YOUNG MAN: Actually, my brother-in-law's in jail…

WOMAN: And when he flew up there, what else did he see?

YOUNG MAN: He didn't see anything.

WOMAN: You're lying! He saw heaven, didn't he? HE SAW HEAVEN.

YOUNG MAN: Mrs. Grady, I really have to go.

> *(He starts putting the pieces back in his bag, but she stops him)*

WOMAN: No. Please. Tell me what he saw in heaven.

> *(The Young Man looks at her)*

Please.

YOUNG MAN: I…really…

WOMAN: *(Taking his hand)* Was it beautiful?

YOUNG MAN: …Yes. It was beautiful. He told me. More than beautiful. It was GLORIOUS. It…it rises out of the firmament in a mist of rainbows. The very air is luminescent. As you breathe, an ethereal light fills your lungs and you float among endless pillars and clouds. Oh, Mrs. Grady! Heaven's beauty is almost beyond description.

WOMAN: And your brother-in-law, did he meet anyone there? Are there people?

YOUNG MAN: Yes, yes! The souls of the departed are as free as clouds. Their spirits rise to greet you as you enter.

WOMAN: Oh!

YOUNG MAN: And in fact, he…he told me about one handsome young man that was there. His skin was a golden tan and his hair was so blond it was almost white.

WOMAN: My son!

YOUNG MAN: Um…and this young man told him to give you this. *(He points to the sun)*

WOMAN: He did?

YOUNG MAN: Yes. And it's…free of charge.

WOMAN: Oh…

> *(She holds it close and rocks it)*

YOUNG MAN: Um…and uh, you should take one of these cords.

> *(He pulls an electrical cord out of the bag)*

It's a good idea to plug it in once a day. Just for its health. Let me show you.

Holly Hepp-Galván

(He takes the sun from her and inserts the power cord. He plugs the otherend into an outlet)

At least once a day. For about four hours.

WOMAN: Four hours.

YOUNG MAN: Right. And it should avoid high temperatures.

WOMAN: I understand.

YOUNG MAN: And this here...uh this is a warranty card. You might want to send this in. That way you can contact someone if there's a problem.

WOMAN: Right. I'll send it in.

YOUNG MAN: Oh..kay. Well then, I'd better be going.

WOMAN: Thank you. Really.

YOUNG MAN: You're welcome.

(He gathers up his stuff and makes to the door)

WOMAN: Are you sure you don't want some money? I think I have like five dollars.

(She reaches in her wallet)

Here, take it.

YOUNG MAN: Uh, thanks.

(She gives him a long hug)

WOMAN: Bye.

(The Young Man exits. She picks up the sun and cradles it. She rocks itgently)

My very own piece of the sun. Beautiful.

End of play

Melto Man And Lady Mantis

Eric Pfeffinger

Melto Man and Lady Mantis was produced by Actors Theatre of Louisville as part of the 41st Humana Festival of New American Plays, April 8, 2017, directed by Eric Hoff. The cast was aas follows:

MELTO MAN - Jeff Biehl

LADY MANTIS - Elia Monte-Brown

Dramaturg - Jessica Reese

Scenic Design - Justin Hagovsky

Costume Design - Alice Tavener

Lighting Design - Steve O'Shea

Sound Design - Christian Frederickson

Fight Director - Ryan Bourque

Stage Manager - Stephen Horton

THE PLAYWRIGHT THANKS: Anne-Marie Trabolsi, Sam Kotansky, Luke Harlan, Bryan Howard, Jessica Reese, and Michael Bigelow Dixon, who was right about the title.

THE TIME

Now.

THE PLACE

Melto Man's office.

CHARACTERS

MELTO MAN, mid- to late twenties, suit and tie. A melty man.

LADY MANTIS, mid- to late twenties, presentably dressed. A mantis lady.

MELTO MAN at his desk, all business. LADY MANTIS
seated across from him. Mid-appointment.

MELTO MAN: I actually ran your numbers a couple different ways... let me get this uh... I think you might want consider whether claiming the home office every year is worth the trouble. It's a lot of record-keeping for

(emits an involuntary monstrous bleat)

relatively little financial benefit. Nice boots, by the way.

LADY MANTIS: What?

MELTO MAN: My wife would go nuts for those boots.

LADY MANTIS: Thanks.

MELTO MAN: Now let me try to show you side-by-side how these figures...

LADY MANTIS: Melto Man, can I ask you something? Non-tax-related?

MELTO MAN: Yeah, shoot.

LADY MANTIS: So, after you... became... after, y'know, your ah... I'm so embarrassed, I don't recall how exactly, how you, uh—

MELTO MAN: Industrial accident. Yeah. In hindsight that is one field trip I wish I had not volunteered to chaperone. Ha-ha.

LADY MANTIS: So, I mean, after your—. Transition. Or whatever. At any point did you ever consider... experimenting with be-ing... destructive?

MELTO MAN: Sure I did. Of course I did. It's traditional, after all. And I'll admit I still get

(emits an involuntary monstrous bleat)

urges.

LADY MANTIS: But you've never, I don't know, killed some people or burned down a city block or gnawed somebody's head off their ragged neck-stem?

MELTO MAN: Me, no. But I don't judge. I just... it's just so not *me*, y'know?

LADY MANTIS: 'Cause I... find it really hard... not to. Do stuff. Like that.

MELTO MAN: Mm-hm. Mm-hm. Mm-hm. Can I ask you a personal question? How about before?

LADY MANTIS: Before.

MELTO MAN: Like before you—. Before your, I don't know how you—?

LADY MANTIS: Industrial accident.

MELTO MAN: So, before that, before you were Lady Mantis, back when you were—?

LADY MANTIS: Helen.

MELTO MAN: I mean, then: did you—? Want to—?

LADY MANTIS: Oh, God, no.

MELTO MAN: Yeah?

LADY MANTIS: No, no. Why would, I mean—? Anything I — it's because, because of *this*.

MELTO MAN: Sure. Yeah, okay. But I mean, I've gone over your previous years' taxes. In preparation. And I'm just saying, I know you haven't always been, uhh, straightforward? Your approach to your obligations as a citizen, at least insofar as your taxes were concerned, seem consistently to have been a little, what should I say, cheaty.

LADY MANTIS: Well but I mean — everyone does that.

MELTO MAN: Yeah?

(beat)

Just something to think about. Look. Back when you were Helen, did you ever have violent thoughts?

LADY MANTIS: Well. *Those.*

MELTO MAN: Ever cruel to people for no reason?

LADY MANTIS: There's always a *reason.*

Pause.

MELTO MAN: Y'know, y'know what, why don't we just get back to your—? I've got a three-fifteen and I want to make sure you're completely satisfied with your—

LADY MANTIS: This was never my plan, of course. When I was a kid I thought I'd be a teacher or a senator. My guidance counselor said she thought I could be the first woman president. Not that I'd be the first human-insect hybrid to level a military base.

MELTO MAN: Yeah, no, of course. Life happens.

LADY MANTIS: Just seems like things could have been so different. If it weren't for the lousy hand I've been dealt. Which happens to involve not having actual hands. When I was little, before bedtime, I used to pray — ironic, right?

MELTO MAN: Is it? Maybe. I'd have to look it up, "ironic" always gives me trouble. That and

(emits an involuntary monstrous bleat)

"irregardless."

LADY MANTIS: I used to pray to God: let me be successful, let me be famous. Let me be *major*. Never occurred to me to pray: let me be lucky. I had no idea that the worst thing that can happen to you is being unlucky.

MELTO MAN: Look, I'm not saying our circumstances, the unique pressures confronting the members of our particular community, don't matter. I mean, look at Ed.

LADY MANTIS: I don't know if I...?

MELTO MAN: I guess he goes by Behemoth now? Yeah, hard to miss. And I knew him a little, before, and he was always a totally quiet, decent guy...

LADY MANTIS: Before—?

MELTO MAN: Industrial accident.

LADY MANTIS: *Man.*

MELTO MAN: Deregulation, am I right? Anyway, I think Ed's choices are limited, insofar as our society isn't really optimally structured to accommodate a fifty-foot-tall ape-man. His job situation's not great, plus he's going through this ugly divorce, I get why he's frustrated. I'm not saying stepping on people and knocking down buildings is his *only* option, just that I wouldn't presume to say what I'd do if I were in his shoes. If he could wear shoes. We're all influenced by our situation. And we need to accept that. I am what I am, y'know, thanks to God and Draco Industries' faulty safety protocols, and I gotta own that and love myself. But circumstances notwithstanding, I don't think that means we're

(emits an involuntary monstrous bleat)

helpless. You know? We might *feel* like we *want* to cheat on our taxes, but we can *choose* not to. We might feel like we want to —

LADY MANTIS: Crush people's faces in our mandibles and lay eggs in their remains.

MELTO MAN: —but we don't *have* to. Et cetera and so on.

LADY MANTIS: So you're saying I can't blame — this — for what I do.

MELTO MAN: *Can't?* Well. I guess—. We can recognize the effects of our situation on our impulses, I think, but no, I believe ultimately we are accountable.

LADY MANTIS: You're saying it's not because I'm unlucky. I'm just a bad person.

MELTO MAN: Mmmmmm, words in my mouth a little bit, I think.

LADY MANTIS: I was basically morally hideous even before the accident, there's something rotten inside me, why even fight it?

MELTO MAN: That is extremely not what I am saying.

LADY MANTIS: There are abominations in this world who do bad things. Criminals. Sadists. The management and Board of Directors at Draco Industries. And I guess I'm one of those creatures. Difference is: before, I could only do small bad things. But now... now I can finally... be *major.*

MELTO MAN: Helen. Helen. These are all the wrong takeaways.

LADY MANTIS: Helen's not here right now. Or ever again.

LADY MANTIS rears up, sounds a series of threatening clicks. MELTO MAN emits a monstrous bleat. They square off.

MELTO MAN: Denise?

(bleat)

Reschedule my three-fifteen.

Another bleat. A vicious battle. An epic clash of the monstrosities, amidst office furniture.

Curtain.

End of play

Eric Pfeffinger

MEMORY CARD
Connie Schindewolf

ORIGINAL PRODUCTION-

Gulfport Community Players Summer One Acts
Catherine A. Hickman Theater
Gulfport, Florida
July 6-16, 2017

Directed by Olga Kruse

CAST:
CAROL: Geri Eaton
CORA: Ginny Holscher

CHARACTERS:

2 Females, 1 Voice (Male or Female, live or recorded)

CORA- 65-75, suffering from dementia, has low self-esteem, wears high heels (awkwardly) and way too much makeup.

CAROL- 65-75, suffering from dementia, best friend of Cora, dresses pretty classy but always wears a colorful boa.

VOICE- Male or female, any age, but must be a loud, but comforting voice.

SETTING:

The living quarters of Cora and Carol in a wing of a memory care facility.

TIME:

The near future.

'Lights up on a room in a memory care facility. There is a table center with two chairs. There are two little boxes on the table, one on each side.

At Rise:

CORA: enters from stage right, walks around awkwardly in her high heels, mismatched clothing, and gaudy jewelry. She looks confused. CAROL enters stage left, looking equally confused, but she is dressed rather tastefully with a bright-colored boa around her neck. She cautiously approaches CORA.

CAROL: Excuse me, do I know you?

CORA: I don't think so, but you do look familiar.

CAROL: This place looks familiar too, but I'm not sure where I am.

CORA: Well, we're…we're…we're…I don't know.

CAROL: Looks nice though, and my clothes were all in my room.

CORA: Mine too. I'm Cora.

CAROL: I'm Carol.

(They walk towards each other and shake hands, CORA stumbling in her high heels.)

CORA: Like your boa.

CAROL: Thanks. Boa's are kind of my signature. Love your high heels.

CORA: Thanks. Get this. If I had an L in my name, I'd be you!

CAROL: You sure would, sweetie.

(An announcement comes on. The voice may be male or female but must be extremely articulate and calm sounding.)

VOICE: Good morning, and it is a fine one here at Rosewood Gardens. You are in a dementia care wing at our fine institution. You remember your name, probably not your roommate's or anything that happened more than a few minutes ago. That's why we're here to help you. You should find your name on a small box on the table. Inside the box is your memory card, which has been charging overnight. Insert your card into your head at your right temple area. It's small so please don't drop it. We have all of your memories programmed on this card, and once inserted you will be able to function for the rest of the day. Thank you, and have a nice day.

(CORA and CAROL find boxes, cautiously, and insert memory cards. CORA'S is stage right side of table and CAROL'S is stage left. As soon as they have them in, there is recognition and they hug.)

CORA: Carol!

CAROL: Cora! How are you sweetie?

CORA: Fine, hun, and yourself?

CAROL: Great, now that I have my memory back. You know, Doctor Vince told you not to wear high heels…might fall off or something.

CORA: Yeah, that happened three years ago, broke my ankle. But these high heels are who I am. I get up and don't even need my memory card, just know to put them on.

CAROL: You know, sometimes you forget your clothes. Just come out with your heels. As much as I love you, that's not a pretty picture.

CORA: Well, remember the time you dropped your cell phone in the toilet, screamed for me to help. I come running in while you were trying to fish it out.

CAROL: It was stuck.

CORA: Yeah, well you didn't take time to pull your pants up, and you mooned me the whole time. That wasn't a pretty picture either.

CAROL: And soaking my phone in rice didn't help.

CORA: I guess since we've been best friends for so long, we can stomach a little nudity.

CAROL: Collin and Mack got along well too, didn't they.

CORA: Yeah, the four of us sure had fun together…until they died.

CAROL: What do you think they'll have for breakfast this morning?

CORA: Hope it's grits!

CAROL: We are lucky, aren't we? Best friends and get to be in a home together. Who would've thought.

CORA: And we got to pick it. That's the great thing!

CAROL: I don't mind being part of an experiment, do you?

CORA: Not if I can be with you. I just wish we could leave once in awhile. I've got a new granddaughter I've never seen.

CAROL: You know our memory cards won't work off the property… wouldn't pick up the signal.

CORA: Well, if we hadn't had to turn over all our money, I could pay for them to visit me.

CAROL: It's worth it to know Rosewood Gardens will always take care of us, and we're together. I just wish our cards didn't have to charge at night.

(CORA goes to table and consults a list that is there.)

CORA: Are you going to download any new apps on your memory card this week?

CAROL: I think I'm good. I love the playwriting one. Still working on that play, *Ham and Eggs.*

CORA: Sounds Dr. Seusish.

CAROL: No, no, sweetie. The ham is a character and the eggs are too. *(Dramatically with much gesticulation.)* They lie together, and they fry together!

CORA: Well my poetry app is a good one. I'm writing a poem about this table leg. *(Dramatically as well.)* Beneath the top I stand, holding one corner, rather grand.

CAROL: *(Clapping.)* We are getting good. What are some other choices. *(Looking at list.)* To think it used to take years to learn a new skill, and now they just put it on our card. There's French and Russian.

CORA: French, I want to learn that! That cute man at table six in the dining room sounds like he has a French accent.

CAROL: There's "Winning at Chess", "The Great American Novel", "Bingo Genius", and "Line Dancing"!

CORA: Too hard to do in my heels.

CAROL: If you add something, you have to delete something. What are you going to delete?

CORA: Well I've already deleted memories of my first husband. He must have been a real jerk…but now I can't remember! And you deleted your mother-in-law.

CAROL: I did?

CORA: That's the beauty of it!

CAROL: You deleted your son's arrest record. And, Blue Nun wine cuz you couldn't get it anymore.

CORA: Good moves.

(There is the sound of loud static, which the audience can hear too. CORA and CAROL hold their heads like they can't stand it.)

VOICE: *(Loudly. The static fades a little so the VOICE can be heard.)* Excuse me for this interruption, but we are experiencing technical difficulties with our memory cards. Please take out your memory card and place in the box with your name on it. Thank you.

(They are standing on the wrong sides of the table, and in their haste, they put the cards in the wrong boxes.)

CORA: Whew! That's better.

CAROL: Hi, I'm Carol, nice shoes.

CORA: Cora. Get this. If I had an L in my name, I'd be you!

CAROL: You sure would, sweetie.

CORA: Love your boa. Could I try it on?

CAROL: Of course, if I can try on your shoes.

(They exchange items and Carol has trouble walking.)

CORA: Do you know where we are?

CAROL: Well, actually…uh…no, I don't.

VOICE: Residents of Rosewood Gardens, we have solved our technical difficulties and once again we would like you to walk to the table where you'll see a box with your name on it. Carefully insert your memory card into the right side of your temple. Thank you and have a nice day.

(They follow the directions but of course put the wrong memory cards in because they were on the wrong side

Connie Schindewolf

of the table. Both look around confused and then CORA approaches CAROL.)

CORA: Hi.

CAROL: I'm Carol…no Cora…I seemed to be confused.

CORA: I'm Cora…but I'm remembering things about you, Carol. That's it. We have each other's memory cards. So I'm me, but I'm remembering you. Wow, it's like I'm in your brain.

CAROL: You don't like my boa.

(CORA walks to her and hands it back to her.)

CORA: And you think I'm stupid for wearing high heels.

(They exchange shoes.)

CAROL: Not really stupid, just…careless. You hate my broccoli casserole.

CORA: I think hate's a little strong. You think Tommy's gay?

CAROL: I've never told anyone that. You really do miss your kids, don't you sweetie?

CORA: I didn't know you were that petrified when you wake up without your card and can't remember. You just come into my room and wake me up any time, hun. I don't care if we can't remember…I'll help you.

CAROL: Thank you but I won't remember to do that.

CORA: You kept some of your money, didn't you? Hid it in that secret account. We could use it and get out of here!

CAROL: Just how could we function without our memories?

CORA: Didn't think of that.

CAROL: You weren't that sad when Mack died. I can't believe it!

CORA: You've always thought my high heels were silly!

CAROL: My boa does not make me seem snobbish!

CORA: You think I'm fat?

CAROL: No, Collon thought that. Collon. My husband. Oh my God, you came over to my house when I went to help Mary with the baby.

CORA: Carol, I just wanted to bring him dinner.

CAROL: And you both drank some wine.

CORA: *(Trying to distract her.)* Let's look at some of these new Apps, hun.

CAROL: Oh my God! Sweet Jesus! You slept with Collon!

CORA: We never intended for that to happen. I'm so, so sorry. It was only once and—

CAROL: How can you remember details if you have my memories now? Must have really been burned into that brain of yours. When I download a new app, I'm going to delete my memory of you!

CORA: No please don't. I'm your best friend. We didn't mean to hurt you.

CAROL: Didn't mean to—

CORA: We were caught up in the moment—

CAROL: Caught up in the moment? Here's a moment for you. I'm deleting you right Now!

(She takes off her boa, backs CAROL up into a chair and begins to strangle her with her boa.)

CORA: Stop, please.

CAROL: My best friend in the whole world!

(She is strangling her and CORA is struggling when there is the sound of loud static again and an announcement. Both women grab their heads as if in pain.)

VOICE: Residents of Rosewood Gardens. Please take out your memory cards again due to technical difficulties. We are very sorry for this inconvenience.

(They take them out and put them in the right boxes this time, and the static stops.)

CAROL: *(Looking confused then approaching CORA.)* Nice shoes.

CORA: Thanks. Nice boa.

CAROL: I'm Carol.

CORA: Cora. You know if I had an L in my name, I'd be you!

VOICE: Residents of Rosewood Gardens, we are pleased to inform you that once again we have solved our technical difficulties. Please insert your memory card with your name on it.

(They do so and there is an immediate look of recognition on their faces.)

VOICE: *(cont.)* Residents in room 20A, Cora and Carol, it is now time for you to report to the dining room for breakfast. Today you'll be delighted to know we're serving blueberry pancakes and fresh peaches, with a side of grits.

(They both smile and arm in arm head off stage to the dining room.)

LIGHTS FADE

END OF PLAY

Point of Intersection

James Hindman

POINT OF INTERSECTION was first presented in an evening of short plays titled BY THE NUMBERS. The show was produced by THE NOW COLLECTIVE at TBG Studio Theatre.

Cast:
MAN: Adrian Burke
WOMAN: McKenna DuBose

CHARACTERS: (1m, 1f) 20s – 30s

> MAN: Passionate but neurotic and self-effacing. Filled with nervous energy. Fixes clocks for a living but always seems to be one step behind.

> WOMAN: A perfectionist who does everything full out. No nonsense. Athletic. Doesn't like to admit she has a vulnerable side.

SETTING:

> The present. TWO boxes are set DSC. These can be used to create all the different locations. Sound effects and small props hidden in the boxes can be used to establish location.

> What's most important is that the movement of the play be fluid. Between each encounter we hear a loud 'STOPWATCH DING.' This indicates the passing of time. After each 'DING' the actors should quickly move to start the next scene.

Lights up on WOMAN preparing to run around the local track. She listens to music on her headphones and uses one of the boxes to help her stretch. MAN approaches. He makes a poor, almost comical attempt at stretching, then finally...

MAN: Excuse me?

(tapping her on the shoulder.)

Excuse me?

WOMAN: *(removing her headphones.)* What?

MAN: I'm so sorry.

WOMAN: That's okay - what?

MAN: I just wanted to ask... I notice you're wearing a watch...I used to have one but...I was WOndering... if I kept up with you, then I WOuld know...

WOMAN: You want to keep up with me to see how far you run.

MAN: Yes.

WOMAN: Sure.

MAN: Perfect!

WOMAN: On your mark.

THEY move to the starting line.

MAN: *(looks at his wrist)* I need to get a new watch... I'm not good with punctuality...which is really ironic because what I do for a living is fix clocks.

WOMAN: Get set.

THEY get into position.

MAN: How far are we going?

WOMAN: Five.

MAN: (with a laugh) Perfect! I think I can handle five minutes!

WOMAN: Miles. We're going five miles.

MAN: Oh.

WOMAN: Go!

WOMAN pushes the timer. They 'take off', running in place.

STOP WATCH DING

ACTORS quickly move to their new positions. WOMAN is at box warming up. MAN enters trying to act very cool.

MAN: Oh, my gosh, look who it is!

WOMAN: Surprised you came back.

MAN: Aw, no, I'm fine.

WOMAN: Good thing I was there to call the paramedics.

MAN: Really wasn't necessary.

WOMAN: They said they'd never seen anyone crawl so fast in their lives. They thought you were doing a turtle race.

MAN: Nope. Fine. All healed.

WOMAN: Good. On your mark…

THEY both get in place to start their run.

MAN: At least I made it four miles!

WOMAN: One. Get set…

MAN: Huh?

WOMAN: Four times around the track is one mile.

MAN: Are you serious?!!

WOMAN: Go!

WOMAN pushes the timer. They 'take off', running in place.

STOP WATCH DING.

They return to the boxes. MAN sits. WOMAN stands over him, taking his pulse. His body is convulsing as he tries to catch his breath.

WOMAN: You did it!

MAN: Bah dah fah…du fahh… *(boy, that's far….that's far)*

WOMAN: You made it five times around!

MAN: Pie time…pie time abound… *(five times…five times around)*

WOMAN: You should be very proud!

MAN: Yah, da poud! Da poud! *(Yeah, the proud. The proud!)*

HE smiles up to her. SHE turns away, letting go of his arm - his body falls limp as if he's going to pass out.

WOMAN: And...Go!

WOMAN pushes the timer. SHE 'takes off', running in place.

STOP WATCH DING –

They are both in place to run.

WOMAN: On your mark...get set...

MAN: Wait!

MAN breaks the pose, musters his courage and extends his hand.

Uh... Sidney.

WOMAN: I beg your pardon?

MAN: That's my name. Sidney.

WOMAN: *(with a laugh)* Oh.

MAN: I wanted to...I mean, look, I understand this is a long shot, but we've seen each other here three times a week for the last... like, TWO months and three weeks - and you don't even have to drink. I mean, my gosh, I am not trying to get you drunk. They have food. It's called happy hour so I guess you can do whatever makes you happy. And you don't even have to go with me. I mean, you can get drunk by yourself, that is totally up to you, but if you do drink with me, it will be free because I'll pay, but if you drink by yourself..._

WOMAN: Sure. What time?

MAN: Huh?

WOMAN: What time?

MAN: You mean you'd actually...?

WOMAN: Yeah.

MAN: Oh. Sure. I'd love to.

WOMAN: Five thirty?

MAN: I get off WOrk at five thirty; by the time I drive...

WOMAN: Six.

MAN: Six! Yes, that's… Are you sure?

WOMAN: *(laughs)* Yes.

MAN: Six is perfect. *(beat)* Today?

WOMAN: Yes.

MAN: Perfect.

WOMAN: See you then?

MAN: Yes.

> *WOMAN turns front, pushing the button on her watch as MAN mouths 'WOw!"*

WOMAN: Go.

> *Woman runs in place as if going around the track. HE yells to her.*

MAN: The Gray Dog! TWO blocks that way!

> *A bit louder.*

> *There's a big furry dog on the front wearing overalls drinking beer out of a penguin. It's not a penguin!*

> *Still running, SHE gives a thumbs up. He gives a thumbs up in return. He then realizes he's supposed to be running as well.*

Oh.

> *HE runs in place quickly to catch up with her.*

> *STOP WATCH DING*

> *They return to the boxes. One box can be stacked on the other. SFX: ROCK AND ROLL MUSIC UNDERSCORE. They are at a bar.*

MAN: What did the German clockmaker say to the clock that only went 'tick, tick, tick'? Ve haff vays of making you 'tock!' My Uncle Sidney tells that joke to every customer who walks in.

WOMAN: *(laughing)* Do they laugh?

MAN: No. Uncle Sid is my boss. That's who I was named after. And I guess I keep repeating his name…Sidney… partly because I'm a little nervous right now because I've only had one beer, although I will have a second –

WOMAN: Me, too.

THEY both hold up their 'happy hour' chips.

MAN: - and partly because…I was hoping that if I told you this really long story, you WOuld tell me your name because if you've already told me I don't remember and if you didn't tell me, then I want to know. (beat) Are you going to tell me your name?

WOMAN: *(She smiles)* Sydney.

MAN: What?

WOMAN: Sydney.

MAN: What?

WOMAN: Sydney.

MAN: *(He finally gets it)* Get out!!

THEY both laugh.

WOMAN: With a 'y'.

MAN: We have the same name!!

WOMAN: Except 'y.'

MAN: Except, 'Y!' But then, why not? We have the same -

WOMAN: I guess we do.

MAN: That is… I mean, what are the…

WOMAN: So much in common.

SHE takes a step toward him.

MAN: Yah.

STOP WATCH DING

> *Sitting in silence watching an adventure movie. He goes to put his arm around her…smelling his armpit, he wants to throw up… he pulls his arm back. She puts her arm around him. He nestles into the crook of her arm. They both smile.*
>
> *STOP WATCH DING*
>
> *They stand looking at each other. The morning after. His place. Awkward.*

MAN: Need anything? Anything I can…?

WOMAN: No. I should get going…I guess.

MAN: Hungry?

WOMAN: Do you have coffee?

MAN: No.

WOMAN: Cereal? Toast? Piece of bread?

MAN: Pringles. Cool Ranch Doritos. I could run to the store.

WOMAN: I'm not sure what I'm supposed to do. I don't do this because… *this* is what happens. And we stand here. And…I hate this. And it's awkward… I'll see you at the track. And don't be awkward there, too. Okay? Because I like that track and I don't want to *not* go there because… I mean, I get it. Whatever. We're all just…going along. I get it.

MAN: No, you don't.

WOMAN: Yeah. I do.

> *She turns to go. He grabs her, taking her into his arms and kisses her. They kiss again.*
>
> *STOP WATCH DING*
>
> *They are in the middle of playing charades.*

WOMAN: *(looking at a timer)* And….Go! Okay, one WOrd. Person. Four syllables. Whole thing. (*He walks hunched over*) Old person. (*He sways*) A dancer. An old dancer. Martha Graham… (*counting syllables*) Ba-rysh-ni-kov! Is-a-dor-a… (*HE shakes his head NO. He looks like his is hanging as he sways*) Hanging. An old dancer who hung himself! (*He sways harder*) You're on a boat! (*He shakes his head NO. She sways with him*) Who does this if you're not on a boat? (*He mimes a telescope*) A telescope! You're a pirate!!! You're an old dancing pirate who died on a boat!! (*He shakes his head NO*) Yes you are! Who does this…(*She sways*) …and this…(*She holds a telescope*) … unless you're a dancing dead pirate?! (*She grabs the paper and reads. Frustrated.*) Galileo?! Was he a pirate?!

MAN: He invented time.

WOMAN: Was he a dancer?!

MAN: The pendulum clock. The measure of time. He was walking in a church and he saw chandeliers swaying and he had this idea that maybe…

WOMAN: Stop! I don't think we should play anymore.

MAN: I'm finding it very instructional.

WOMAN: So am I.

STOP WATCH DING

They sit, shell shocked, as if they'd just seen a ghost.

WOMAN: Sooo…that's my family.

Beat.

MAN: I think they're great.

WOMAN: Really?

MAN: They can't tell a joke as well as Uncle Sidney but…

THEY take hands and smile.

WOMAN: Families are weird.

MAN: So are you.

WOMAN: I know you are but what am I?

MAN: I know you are but what am I?

BOTH: *(overlapping)* I know you are but what am I? I know you are but what am I? I know you are…

STOP WATCH DING

They are kneeling on the boxes facing each other. Man holds the TV remote over her head. They are laughing.

WOMAN: One more time!

MAN: No!

WOMAN: Then we never have to watch it again!

MAN: Why?! The ending's not going to change.

WOMAN: I don't want it to change! I *want* to see Ariel get her legs. I *want* to see her to walk on land. I want the prince to see how much she has sacrificed as he holds her in his arms…

MAN: Like this?

HE pulls her in close.

WOMAN: Oh. Yeah. And they don't have to say it but you know

they are in love, by the way they look at each other.

MAN: Like this?

WOMAN: Because isn't that what everyone wants...love?

MAN: And legs?

They throw their arms around each other.

STOP WATCH DING

SFX: underscore: "Jingle Bells"

She sits. He approaches, handing her a ring size box while holding a piece of mistletoe over their heads. WOMAN is very excited. She opens the box. Her smile covers her disappointment.

WOMAN: A necklace.

STOP WATCH DING

SFX: underscore: "Oh Holy Night"

He approaches, handing her a ring size box while holding a piece of mistletoe over their heads. WOMAN is very excited again. SHE opens the box.

WOMAN: A bracelet.

SHE looks at the bracelet, then at him. He senses her disappointment. She walks away.

STOP WATCH DING

WOMAN sits, on her phone. MAN stands upstage out of her sight, looking rejected. HE texts her while she is talking.

WOMAN: Your timing is perfect, I just finished my run. Dinner and a movie? *A Rom Com?* I guess you did read my profile. Great. See you then.

She hangs up. Her phone indicates she has a text. She reads it. It's from MAN. She doesn't respond. She walks away, facing upstage. He steps in and finds the 'ring box' that has been left on the cube.

STOP WATCH DING

MAN pulls out a watch, puts it on, then runs in place.

STOP WATCH DING

MAN runs in place.

STOP WATCH DING

MAN runs in place.

STOP WATCH DING

WOMAN steps forward. She is 'on her mark.' MAN musters his courage.

MAN: Wait. I have to… Sometimes clocks are five minutes fast and sometimes they're five minutes slow. Uncle Sidney says that doesn't make them better…or WOrse. It just means they have to be adjusted. Or you just have to accept that that's how they were built. And no matter how hard the clock tries… That's what my uncle Sidney says.

He holds out a ring box. Then holds a piece of mistletoe over his head.

I know it's Labor Day, but…

He hands her the box. She opens it.

It's twelve little diamonds. Like a clock. Like time. Because that's what I want. Time with you.

He waits for her response.

(with German accent)

'Ve haff vays of making you 'tock.'

Too overcome with emotion, she nods her head YES.

I've never been good with charades but I think that's a 'yes.'

He waits. He sits next to her. WOMAN hugs him. SHE puts the ring on her finger.

WOMAN: Let's not run today. Let's just sit.

Lights fade.

END OF PLAY

Rusalka

Don Nigro

CHARACTERS:

ROSSI, a police detective

LYDIA, a young woman

SETTING:

Two wooden chairs and a wooden table. Light above. Darkness around them.

(Rossi is questioning Lydia. There is an overhead light above a wooden table. Lydia sits in a wooden chair at the table, Rossi sitting across from her.)

LYDIA: She's a little bit crazy. She talks to mirrors. I comforted her when she was afraid. There are monsters everywhere, she said. When we played Casino she'd talk to the face cards. They all had different personalities. You're only a pack of cards, she said. And then, whispering in my ear, Dodgson was a pervert. She said God lived in the subterranean passages below the house and raised sheep, but he very seldom came up any more because it was too depressing. She could play Danube Waves on the accordion. Ivanovici. But she didn't do it very often, out of respect for other people's sanity, because some music was designed by the Devil to drive people crazy if they listened to it too much. One morning she found cloven footprints in the snow around the house. She said the Devil was after her. Once we went into a toy shop. It was night and very cold and it was snowing. There was a red lamp above the door. She would stare into the eyes of the dolls and try to communicate telepathically with them. We walked home through the cemetery and somebody had knocked off all the heads of the angels on the monuments. The Devil's getting closer, she said. She could sit and watch the moon for hours. She was trying to catch it moving. We used to wash ourselves together. She had the most perfect body. Once she washed her feet in ginger ale. She said it tickled.

ROSSI: Was she seeing anybody?

LYDIA: She'd go to bars and pick up these awful men. I warned her about this Russian guy, but she liked him. He has wild eyes, she said. One night he dragged her all the way across the parking lot by her hair. I shot him in the ass with a BB gun. And when he came for me I shot him in the face and he ran away. He moved to Texas after that.

ROSSI: Do you have any idea where she might have gone?

LYDIA: There was this place in the woods she went where mushrooms would come up after rain, and there was a little patch of ferns, on the other side of the hill, and if you stood very still, you could hear bees buzzing, where there weren't any bees, and see this stand of maple trees moving, when there wasn't any wind, and the hackles on the back of your neck would rise, and you could feel him.

ROSSI: Feel who?

LYDIA: The great god Pan. He lives in the woods. But that's just an alias. He's really the Devil. Sometimes we'd sneak into old abandoned houses to look for the ghosts. She said every place is full of ghosts, and everything is synchronicity, and the most interesting parts are the mistakes. She was interested in the archetypal connections between creative thought and the subconscious. She said the world was a forest of mystical symbols. That everything was full of gods. And that Kepler murdered Tycho Brahe.

ROSSI: Who is this?

LYDIA: Kepler the astronomer. Murdered Tycho Brahe, his mentor. So that then he, Kepler, would then be the greatest astronomer in the world. She said we murder the people we love, either by accident or on purpose. Tycho Brahe had an artificial nose. Syphilis, I think. His nose just fell off one day. So he had another nose made. But it was brass, or something.

ROSSI: When was the last time you saw her?

LYDIA: Last night. In my dream. We were somewhere in the marshes. Bogs. Romney Marsh. Or New Jersey. There was fog everywhere. And there was this creature. I don't know what it was. It had these long arms. And it was reaching up and putting its hands around her ankles. That's all I remember.

ROSSI: I'm not talking about your dreams. I mean when was the last time you actually saw her in real life?

LYDIA: Dreams are real life. They're just real life that hasn't happened yet.

ROSSI: She didn't mention that she was thinking of leaving town?

LYDIA: Timoshenko.

ROSSI: What?

LYDIA: That was the Russian guy's name. That moved to Texas to work on oil rigs. He smelled like my grandfather's basement.

ROSSI: Do you think she might have gone to see him?

LYDIA: No. She could only live in places where it rains.

ROSSI: Did she have any family?

LYDIA: She said the Devil ate them all. She told me she came from East Mars.

ROSSI: Pennsylvania?

LYDIA: No. The planet Mars. She wasn't serious. It was a literary reference. They asked this poet where his poems came from, and he said poetry comes from East Mars. He meant you can't force it to happen. It comes to you from this other place. She was from some other place. The banks of the Danube, or some other river somewhere. And she was like a poem. Once she woke up in the middle of the night and sat up in bed and said, All day it rained the Devil's blood. And then she went back to sleep. We sometimes slept in the same bed. She was afraid of the dark. So I'd hold her. The Russian guy called her Rusalka. The Rusalka is a Russian fairy girl, a nymph who lives in the water like a mermaid but also sometimes in the trees in the woods and lures men to their destruction, tangles them in her long, red hair and drowns them, or sometimes tickles them to death. But she said, no. I am not her any more. I am somebody else now. I've been out of the water too long. If you go to the woods and stand very still and listen, she said, you can hear the Devil whispering. The Russian guy had a point. She didn't seem entirely human. She came with a sense of strangeness.

ROSSI: Had she ever been in a mental institution?

LYDIA: I don't know.

ROSSI: Have you?

LYDIA: Not that I can remember. Have you?

ROSSI: Do you have a photograph of her?

LYDIA: She never wanted her picture taken. She said it wouldn't come out. Are you married?

ROSSI: What do you think happened to her?

LYDIA: She saw too deep, and too much. And what she saw was chaos. That was from a book, too, I think. One morning she opened her eyes and said, Chaos. I've awakened in chaos. I liked to watch her sleep. But she had bad dreams. She was dating some other guy. But I never met him. Maybe he's the person you should be talking to.

ROSSI: Lydia.

LYDIA: What? You have very sad eyes. Like you've seen something you want to forget.

ROSSI: Did you kill her?

LYDIA: Did I kill her?

ROSSI: Did you?

LYDIA: Why would I kill her? Why on earth would you ask me a question like that?

ROSSI: Well, for one thing, when you came in here, you were completely covered in blood.

LYDIA: It was the Devil's blood. Last night it rained the Devil's blood.

ROSSI: I don't think so.

LYDIA: Oh, yes. We went out naked and danced in the rain.

ROSSI: And then what happened? Something happened. What was it? Did she tell you she was going to Texas, to be with the Russian?

LYDIA: No. She didn't want him any more. She liked this other guy.

ROSSI: Maybe you had a quarrel about it. You were drinking and you went out dancing naked in the rain and she told you she was leaving and you tried to stop her and maybe you pushed her, and she fell and hit her head. Was it something like that?

LYDIA: No. It was nothing like that.

ROSSI: Then what was it like? Where did you put her, Lydia?

LYDIA: I didn't put her anywhere. She's a rusalka. You can't kill her. Although sometimes they die of grief. Mostly they break other people's hearts, but sometimes, on very rare occasions, the rusalka will actually fall in love herself, and if she's not loved in return, she'll die. But that's not what happened.

ROSSI: What did happen, then?

LYDIA: You're not fooling me, you know. I know who you are.

ROSSI: What do you mean?

LYDIA: You want me to believe you're just some random police detective, but I know. I can see through your disguise.

ROSSI: I'm not wearing a disguise.

LYDIA: Everybody's wearing a disguise. And you have a really good one. But I can see through it. She taught me.

ROSSI: If I'm not a police detective, then who am I?

LYDIA: You know who you are.

ROSSI: No. I've forgotten who I am. Tell me.

LYDIA: You're the Devil.

ROSSI: I'm the Devil?

LYDIA: She could smell you. Prowling round and round the house at night. She could smell your blood in the rain. He's very close now, she said. Hold me. He's very close, and he's coming for me now. I can smell brimstone in the rain. And so I held her. There in the rain. And all around us the Devil's blood rained down. Why do you hate her so much?

ROSSI: I don't hate her. I don't even know her. I'm just trying to find out what happened to her.

LYDIA: I'll tell you what I think. The Devil hates a rusalka who falls in love. And he hunts her down because she's betrayed him. Because there is no love in Hell.

ROSSI: That's not true.

LYDIA: I think it is.

ROSSI: No. There is love in Hell. In fact, Hell is made entirely of love. Love is the most terrible punishment there is. It's the suffering that lasts for all eternity. You're never going to see her again. That's your punishment.

LYDIA: And yours is that she doesn't love you. You see? I can see it on your face. I can see it in your eyes. You're the other guy she was seeing. You were walking around our house all night, looking in the windows. I saw your cloven footprints in the snow. You want her but you can't have her. Your punishment is that she doesn't love you. She doesn't love you. She loves me. She only loves me. And I'll never tell you where she's gone. No matter what you do to me, I'll never tell. I'll never tell.

(Pause.)

So come on. Do something to me. Do something.

(Pause.)

I dare you.

(They look at each other. The light fades on them and goes out.)

SPARK

Barbara Blumenthal-Ehrlich

SPARK was produced in May, 2017, in The Boston Theatre Marathon. Producer: Boston Playwrights Theatre, 949 Commonwealth Ave., Boston, MA 02215. 617.353.5443. Artistic Director: Kate Snodgrass.

CHARACTERS:

STEVE, middle age

JOAN, middle age, his wife

The time is the present. The place is Steve and Joan's suburban home. All lights are on. Very bright. No appliances in sight. Other than that, it's a normal household.

Barbara Blumenthal-Ehrlich

(JOAN is in the living room. STEVE enters from outside, is annoyed and distracted by something on the front lawn.)

STEVE: *(about the lawn)* What the hell…?

(beat, puzzled)

You're still here?

JOAN: *(about outside)* Isn't it wild?

STEVE: *(referring to the lawn)* What is all this?

JOAN: Something big.

STEVE: The vacuum cleaner….

JOAN: Something very big.

STEVE: All our lamps….

JOAN: I know.

STEVE: Our fans, the TV, the computer…

JOAN: And the iron, the toaster, the can opener, the alarm clocks. The dust buster was *nuts.*

STEVE: Why is it all on the front lawn?

JOAN: I threw it there.

STEVE: You threw all the appliances out on the lawn?

JOAN: They came to life. I had no choice.

STEVE: What are you talking about?

JOAN: The kitchen was insane. Wedding gifts we never— Did you know we had an espresso maker?

STEVE: You're telling me…..

JOAN: I'm telling you everything is out on the lawn because it won't shut off in the house. Even unplugged.

STEVE: In the house? Only in the house?

JOAN: It was like Stephen King in Disneyland.

STEVE: No. No no no no no.

JOAN: Yes. Yes yes yes yes yes. That's not the craziest part.

STEVE: You're not packed. Are you?

JOAN: *(giddy)* It's me. Honest to God. I'm doing this.

STEVE: What do you mean, it's you?

JOAN: All the power in this house is coming from me.

STEVE: You.

JOAN: Even when I unplugged things, they kept going.

STEVE: You're a God damn generator now?

JOAN: Yes.

STEVE: Powering the appliances.

JOAN: It started with the alarm clock, and then it was off to the races.

STEVE: I don't believe this.

JOAN: Neither did I at first.

> *(super thrilled)*

It was terrifying.

STEVE: No, I really don't believe it.

JOAN: You think I'm making this up?

STEVE: I think: It's six o'clock. You're still here.

JOAN: You think I'm stalling?

STEVE: I offered to be the one to go.

JOAN: Bring something back into the house if you don't believe me.

STEVE: You insisted. You said….

JOAN: Grab the blender.

STEVE: You said….

JOAN: The toaster. You'll see.

STEVE: "I can't stay in this house, knowing what I know." That's what you said. Now here we are, six o'clock. Nothing's packed.

JOAN: That's your takeaway? We're in the middle of something extraordinary here, and all you see is the absence of boxes.

STEVE: You want *me* to go? Cuz, I'll go. If you changed your mind.

JOAN: I haven't changed my mind. I'm just a little behind schedule because we had a miracle in our dead and decaying life! You shit! I mean, give me a break. You only just told me a week ago about this… this…this… stewardess.

STEVE: Travel agent. If you need more time…

JOAN: That's the last thing I— What the fuck is time? I was just 25 years old.

STEVE: What?

JOAN: Like yesterday. I was 25. You were 25. And we were scrambling to get the kids down so we could play naked dominoes. Now—

STEVE: *(a good memory)* Naked dominoes. Oh, my God.

JOAN: Now you tell me you're leaving, it's like you're on the other side of the room, down the street— A stranger. When did that happen? Because believe me, my husband tells me he's running off with the travel agent who booked our 25th anniversary trip to Hawaii, I should feel *something!*

STEVE: What the fuuuuuck is time?

JOAN: Exactly.

STEVE: What the fuck is time!

JOAN: *(grounding herself)* I know I loved you.

STEVE: I know I loved you.

JOAN: We're sort of dead.

STEVE: Speak for yourself.

JOAN: You and me. Sort of.

STEVE: No.

JOAN: Dead.

STEVE: No!

JOAN: Dead-ish.

STEVE: Stop saying that.

JOAN: But this morning the kettle was whistling. The coffee beans were grinding. I remembered: This is what power feels like. I felt… alive. Again. Anew.

STEVE: Alive? Again? Anew? Today?

(He laughs)

JOAN: I'm gonna pack.

> *(She begins to pack. STEVE's laughter turns to tears.)*

Steven? What's this now?

STEVE: Nothing. I'm fine. I'm great. Alive! Again! Anew! Good for you. Bravo. The coffee beans. The tea kettle. Good for fucking you.

JOAN: Why are you getting so mad?

STEVE: I'm not! I'm great, I said! You remember being alive? I remember a hat. A God damn hat! Just great.

> *(realizing, pissed)*

Why's it so bright in here?

JOAN: You're just noticing that now?

STEVE: It's really fucking bright.

JOAN: You're welcome.

STEVE: I think you knitted the hat.

JOAN: Did I?

> *(remembers)*

I did!

STEVE: An ugly hat.

JOAN: Well, eye of the beholder.

STEVE: Purple and yellow.

JOAN: I was experimenting with contrasting colors.

STEVE: I hated that hat.

JOAN: Could have been worse.

STEVE: Where is that hat?

JOAN: Could have been turquoise and orange.

STEVE: I loved that hat.

> *(They share a smile)*

It's *very* bright.

Barbara Blumenthal-Ehrlich

JOAN: Yes.

STEVE: I walk in the door. The house is alive. What do I see? The absence of boxes. Maybe I am dead. Electricity. Who invented electricity?

JOAN: Edison.

STEVE: We were electric… once…. remember?

JOAN: I'm sorry.

STEVE: This other woman… person… travel agent… she's just—

JOAN: *(stops him with a motion)*

STEVE: Can I touch it?

JOAN: What? Where? No.

STEVE: Any of it. Your hand.

JOAN: No.

STEVE: A finger.

JOAN: No.

STEVE: A toe.

JOAN: No. No. I'm sorry. I can't help you with that. Don't—

> *(He grabs her hands, closes his eyes, tries to feel something, drops her hands, silence.)*

It doesn't work that way.

STEVE: What are you, an expert? You just got electricity today.

JOAN: I'm going now.

STEVE: But you haven't packed.

JOAN: What would I take?

STEVE: We agreed. You get the TV, the toaster, the micro…

JOAN: They'd just keep me up.

STEVE: What about your things? Your clothes? Your books.

> *(JOAN thinks a minute)*

JOAN: Nah.

STEVE: You want nothing from our life together?

JOAN: *You're* leaving *me*, remember?

STEVE: Why does it feel the other way around?

JOAN: I have to go. As they say in the travel biz: "Bon voyage." *(pronounces it Voyagee)*

> *(She starts to go, stops, returns, takes off her wedding ring.)*

STEVE: What are you doing? Don't do that.

> *(She tries to hand it to STEVE. He backs away.)*

I loved you.

JOAN: I loved you too.

> *(She hands him the ring, touching him for a split second in the handoff.)*

STEVE: Ah! Did you feel that? A spark.

JOAN: Turn off the lights on your way out.

> *(She kisses her hand and places it on his forehead.)*

If you can.

> *(She exits.)*
>
> *THE END*

TIME AND TONY OLIVA

Steven Haworth

TIME AND TONY OLIVA was first produced in the 2017 Seventh Inning Stretch, an annual showcase of 10-minute plays about baseball, at Mile Square Theatre in Hoboken, New Jersey (Artistic Director - Chris O'Connor, Lauren Ciborski – Managing Director). The production dates were May 12, 13, and 14th, 2017. The production was directed by Chris O'Connor. The dramaturg was Joseph Gallo. The cast was Jon Krupp as Dale and Jack Coggins as Gus.

CHARACTERS

DALE – 60. White, male, just played golf. Dead but doesn't know it yet.

GUS – 60. White, male, just played golf.

SETTING

Edina Country Club restaurant, Edina, Minnesota.

TIME

Simultaneously April 22, 1999 and actual date of performance.

SET

Table with two chairs. Remnants of breakfast on the table.

(Two white men dressed for golf in a country club restaurant in Edina, MN. Dale is 60. Gus is 60. It is morning.)

GUS: Which is also why I like golf.

DALE: Why?

GUS: No clock, Dale. It is a game without a clock. What are we talking about? Time. Age. Death. Pay attention.

DALE: *(checking his watch)* Right. Sorry. What time is it, anyway -- ? I have this thing --

GUS: To hell with all those games on the clock! Football. Hockey. Basketball. Give me a nice leisurely game of golf.

DALE: Thanks again for inviting me.

GUS: Two men playing alone. It's silly. I like competition!

DALE: As do I, usually.

GUS: Hence we can afford this club.

DALE: Breakfast is on me, by the way. No no! I insist. Odd I've never seen you before.

GUS: And baseball!

DALE: What?

GUS: Also no clock, Dale. Baseball. Which your son greatly prefers.

DALE: My son.

GUS: Your son. The playwright? You brought him up on the 7th tee?

DALE: Right. Loves baseball. Hates golf.

GUS: Hates golf! There's a shock! The lefty *artiste* hates golf! What's his problem? We're all old white Republican assholes abusing our proletariat caddies or something?

DALE: I don't think Steve hates golf on principle. He just can't play it. He's terrible.

GUS: Golfing with a son! Nothing better. 'Course I had to basically force Jackson to play with me but still. So your son sucks at golf. That's a shame. Well we can't all be athletes. Not that you're much of a golfer yourself, Dale, let's face it –

DALE: Baseball! That was Steve's sport. Fine infielder. Great base runner.

GUS: Yeah? Play in college?

DALE: Oh. Um, Steve stopped playing school sports in junior high. I mean –

GUS: Little League.

DALE: *(enduring him)* Yes, Gus. Little League.

GUS: Jackson played first base for the University of Nebraska.

DALE: Well, that's terrific. A Cornhusker.

GUS: Batted .327. Scholarship. Full ride. Not that he needed it. *Very* talented athlete.

DALE: I am suitably impressed.

GUS: Killed in a car crash the summer before his senior year.

DALE: Oh! Mercy. I'm so sorry.

GUS: Hated my guts.

DALE: What?

GUS: Oh yeah. I was always supportive. Rarely missed a game. I'd fly in to see the games in Omaha. And fuel isn't cheap, Dale, even if it is just a little Cessna.

DALE: You're a pilot?

GUS: Just a little Cessna. This one game Jack stopped a line drive. Then hops up, tags the base runner leading too far off first. Next inning he hits a home run! After the game I find him. I wanna tell him how great … but then I saw … the *disappointment*. That I was *there*. And he wanted me to see that! He wanted to hurt me, Dale.

DALE: But why if you were so -- ?

GUS: That's what drives me crazy! We liked all the same things! It's not like my kid wanted to write plays and hang out with pansy bohemians in New York. Jack was a great athlete, very competitive, good head for numbers. *Industrious.* We were the same! I bragged about him all the time! And he despised me! Why?!

DALE: Fathers and sons, sometimes it's not a friendly rivalry, Gus –

GUS: But you and your son were totally different and he didn't hate you. Right? Right, Dale?! …. So why did my son hate me when we had all the same talents? The same values?

Steven Haworth

DALE: Steve would say you had the same values *because* you had the same talents.

GUS: Okay! Then why hate me?! Why?!

DALE: *Gus*…. Sounds to me like you guys just didn't have enough time, that's all.

(Pause.)

GUS: So Steve was an infielder. Any good? Give me a proud moment.

DALE: … Honestly the proudest I ever was of my son where baseball … he was in the stands not the field.

GUS: Oh?

DALE: Twins game. Old Metropolitan Stadium. We went to games a lot when he was a kid. On this particular day Steve was ten. 1967.

GUS: Oh, my God! What a team! Harmon Killebrew! Zoilo Versalles! Rod Carew!

DALE: Jim Kaat! César Tovar! Mudcat Grant!

GUS: Mudcat Grant! What a name for a ballplayer! Mudcat Grant!

DALE: And Steve's personal favorite, Tony Oliva! At any rate, the Twins are playing the Yankees and there are these two very big, very loud drunk jerks in front of us.

Yelling horrible obscenities. Visiting Yankee fans. Steve knows how I feel about that kind of language, especially around children. I know he expects me to say something. *Anyway* Tony Oliva comes to the plate. He was having trouble with a knuckle on his right hand. A bone chip. He'd let go of bats on his harder swings --

GUS: Yeah yeah, I remember that! Shortstops had to duck those flying bats!

DALE: That's right! So Oliva swings and misses a fastball, the bat goes flying across the infield and these jerks start yelling some *very* nasty things. Well Steve… he jumps right out of his seat. "Hey! You guys shut up! That's Tony Oliva! He's the best batter on the team! He's got a hurt knuckle! He can't help it! So just shut up, you're stupid!" Now these guys were big. Probably bouncers or stevedores or mobsters or something. They get up.

One of them looks at me and says, "Your kid's got some mouth!"
So Steve says, "What are you talkin' to him for? I'm the one
who called ya stupid." All around people burst out laughing!
And these gorillas are totally deflated! And they *walk off*! They
move to other seats! And then Steve *taunts* them! He's chanting "Tony Oliva! Tony Oliva!" I try to shush him but then all
around people are chanting! "Tony Oliva! Tony Oliva!" Boy
oh boy! Ten years later, we have a terrible falling out, I didn't
know where he was or even if he's alive. For a year. I thought
of that game a lot during that year. At any rate ... my proudest
day at a ballpark!

GUS: Great story, Dale! Steve really went to bat for Tony Oliva!

DALE: Yes! Yes indeed.

(Dale remembers. Pause.)

GUS: So ... Steve did hate you.

DALE: What? Oh. No! We're fine. For a while now. He came to see
us about a month ago.

GUS: Good for you. You've got a son, he's alive, and he visits you!
That's fucking great. Good for you, Dale! Way to go!

(Gus cries.)

DALE: Gus? Oh jeez. Gus. I'm sorry. That was ... thoughtless of
me. I'm so sorry, Gus, I –

(Gus bursts out laughing, points at Dale.)

GUS: Ha! I got ya, Dale! Oh man! You should see the look on your
face!

DALE: What the hell is wrong with you, Gus?!

GUS: Now I want you to pick up your spoon and look at your reflection in the spoon, Dale.

DALE: What are you talking about?!

GUS: I said pick up your spoon and look at your reflection in the
spoon, Dale!

*(Dale fumes but he does it. He sees something super-
naturally shocking.)*

DALE: What's going on?! Who are you?!

GUS: I'm an emissary, Dale.

DALE: An emissary! From whom?!

GUS: Your son. You know what day it is today?

DALE: Thursday?

GUS: It is April 22, 1999. Actually it's _____ __, ____*. But for our purposes it is April 22, 1999.

DALE: I'm confused.

GUS: The day you die, Dale.

DALE: Excuse me?

GUS: Today, April 22, 1999, is the day you die. And Steve has always felt bad, when he got the call you were already dead. And there were things he wanted to tell you that he didn't get to say. I guess since your relationship had its ups and downs and –

*Actual date of performance.

DALE: Stop! My son sent you here to tell me that I die today?! And to get a few things off his chest?! Is that right?!

GUS: You are correct, sir.

DALE: This all makes sense now! How I've never seen you at the club before! How I've never even *heard* about you, which is even stranger, 'cause let's face it, you are a *vivid* personality, Gus! How you *insisted* we play together despite my pleas for solitude --

GUS: Hey! You make it sound like I forced –

DALE: How do I die?!

GUS: You're watching the evening news. You feel stiffness in your neck from your morning golf. You sit at your wife's feet so she can rub your neck. You fall over dead from a massive coronary. Nothing drawn out. Very quick. Very sudden.

DALE: Or it would be if now I didn't have to think about it all day!

GUS: Oh.

DALE: This is so Steve! This is so typical! This complete lack of consideration! Did it ever occur to either of you morons that

The Lord intended to grant me a terror-free death to reward me for a loyal and devout life?! You say it's really 2017?! So he's turning sixty this year! It all makes sense doesn't it?!

GUS: Well, yeah, because you die today and you're sixty.

DALE: Exactly! He's thinking about death so this is how I have to spend my last day! And why are you here and not him?! Why send you?! You are the weirdest guy!

GUS: I'm based on some prick he had to caddy for when he was a kid. Forcing him to caddy at this club is the real reason he hates golf, by the way.

DALE: He knows I can't stand guys like you! He's torturing me!

GUS: Dale, people are staring. You need to calm down.

DALE: Don't tell me to calm down! I'm going to die today you idiot!

GUS: Tony Oliva!

DALE: What?

GUS: *(chanting)* Tony Oliva! Tony Oliva! Tony Oliva!

(Gus makes a happy face. Dale stares. Dale calms down, sighs with resignation.)

DALE: Okay. What does Steve want to tell me?

GUS: You were a good man a good father yours was a life well lived and breakfast is on me. Yes yes! For once in your life. *Breakfast is on me.*

(Beat.)

DALE: *Fine.*

(As Gus stands and puts money on the table Dale looks angrily at the spoon.)

DALE: Hello, Steve. You look just like me now. And I'm already dead!

(Gus has crossed behind Dale and puts his hand on Dale's head. Gus closes his eyes. Dale is baffled.)

DALE: Um … Gus?

GUS: *(with a new gravitas)* He still fights you in his head. He can't stop. The war you two waged divides him still. He had to mentor himself and did it so poorly he chose not to have children. He is not the man he intended to be which is to say he is more like you than he ever thought possible. As for the year he went missing: he would remind you respectfully that you kicked him out of the house. As for not communicating with you that year so you naturally thought he was dead: he did that on purpose. It was the only way for things to change. Given the nature of the man you most admired Steve's return could be nothing less than a resurrection. But know that he loves you. More and more. And not only because you're dead. And especially during baseball season.

(a few more beats, eyes still closed)

Okay. This can end now. Say, thirty seconds?

(Gus abruptly exits. Dale calmly looks at his watch. He looks at the money on the table. He disapproves of the amount, takes out a money clip and adds bills to the pile. Unrushed, he picks up the spoon and looks at the reflection again.

He puts down the spoon, stands.

He looks at the table, his chair, as if seeing matter for the first time. He looks around the room in wonder. He looks at his watch.

He looks at us. He chants.)

DALE: Tony Oliva! Tony Oliva! Tony Oliva!

(Blackout.)

END OF PLAY

TIM KAINE SITS IN FRONT OF A MIRROR AND STUDIES HIS FACE

Jordan Barsky

Originally produced at the Brick Theatre on June 23, 2017

TIM KAINE – Jacob Grover

BAB – Ayo Edebiri

Directed by Joel Kirk

CHARACTERS

TIM KAINE -- older

BAB -- younger

PERFORMANCE NOTE:

It might be temping to play Tim Kaine as an imitation of the real deal. It is essential that Kaine not be played for easy recognition. Instead it should be assumed that the audience has never heard of Tim Kaine. The actor interpreting this role must invent the sound, the look, and the physicality of the character based entirely on the text and its dramatic requirements.

SETTING:

A sad simple hotel room.

A sad simple hotel room with a mirror at the focal point. Bab enters. She looks around. She makes her way to the mirror. She makes a face. She makes another. She suddenly speaks.

BAB: Good evening from Hofstra University in Hempstead New York, I am Lester Holt, anchor of NBC nightly news. I welcome you to a historic evening for our nation. Tonight we *had* planned to broadcast the first presidential debate. However, just this morning the republican nominee has seceded his campaign run for president. And *now*, with complete support from the republican party, I'd like to announce our next democratic president of these United States of America, running unopposed, may I introduce—*Me.*

I'm here, now.

I am your president.

I am the only reasonable choice.

I am your leader.

I am standing alone, in front of all of you.

Here and now…

Finally! Here, in this moment, I stand before you all.

With my newly gained power my first act as president to be…

Do you see?

I get to choose when to speak and you will wait.

Beat.

I choose where we go, who we help, I choose who we become.

I am now and forever engrained into America's identity. My image and my voice has sunken down into its veins. I define you. I am everywhere. I fly everywhere. And now, *finally*, all of the antiquated homogenized anomalies that refused to support me, now—*now* you have become more like me. More like us. Thank you.

No longer a performance.

Ugh.

Corn teeth.

Unbelievable.

They look angry at each other.

I should get them whitened.

Wouldn't really matter.

Yeah, it doesn't.

> *Her phone buzzes. She answers. She becomes a different person, faster and more aggressive.*

BAB: Yeah?

No.

No.

Shit.

Is she?

Okay.

Okay.

So it's just a cold?

Okay pneumonia okay.

Yeah.

Yeah.

I got him.

Hey! Do not tell me how to do my job. I'm his handler, I know him— He's Swiss cheese, key lime pie…a hollow egg shell

Okay—yeah.

Sorry.

> *She hangs up.*

> *She exhales. Her phone rings before she finishes breathing.*

BAB: Yeah? Oh—hey.

Yeah I do answer the phone like that.

Mom—No I know.

…

It's not how I pictured it.

Maybe.

> *Tim enters in the midst of a tantrum. Bab hangs up*

Jordan Barsky

seamlessly.

TIM: It's not right.

Today is not right.

BAB: Tim it's going to be fine. I spoke to the office and it's just a cold.

TIM: No, it all feels so sleazy.

BAB: There's nothing wrong with announcing yourself as someone who could mean something.

Because—Tim? Hey Tim?

You do—mean something.

TIM: Why are you telling me that?

Why am I everyone's little brother?

Why does my throat hurt all of a sudden?

Tim grabs at his throat glands.

TIM: Maybe it's my glands.

Maybe it's throat cancer.

Maybe she's going to have to replace ME!

And then ironically I'll be the famous one…

BAB: Tim! Relax.

TIM: You relax.

I'm a household name but nobody loves me.

BAB: They don't have to love you Tim.

You just need to be consistent and informative.

Tim starts pacing furiously.

TIM: Nobody loves me.

Nobody loves me.

Nobody loves me.

Tim trips and falls.

BAB: Tim! Are you okay?

TIM: Yes, yes, yes, I'm fine

Oh Jesus.

His nose is bleeding.

BAB: Oh Jesus, you're bleeding Tim.

As Tim bats at his nose with a handkerchief.

TIM: Please stop saying my name for just a second.

BAB: Ok, ok, ok.

What are we gonna do Tim—sorry.

TIM: It's okay—just don't say my name again.

BAB: Can you stop the bleeding?

Can you clean yourself up?

TIM: I don't think so.

You should do the press conference.

She considers it.

BAB: You know I can't do that.

You're the VP, it's your face they know.

At some point below Bab becomes occupied by her blackberry.

TIM: You can just do it.

Please—you just do it.

I knew today was going to be wrong.

I had the worst dream last night that I can't even remember…

I'm still scared from it…

I think I was alone. But there was a mirror that was two-way I think.

I was sitting in front of an enormous mirror watching a focus group, only behind me was another two way mirror, only in the one behind me I was on the other side, being watched, while I was watching. Laughing while being laughed at, that's the image that stayed with me when I woke up. Sick ugly laughter that snowballed right through me into the next room that sure enough had another two way mirror in front of it. And those people were laughing at other people in the next room. Refracted again and again endlessly. Like an optical illusion that wasn't an illusion at all. Because there really was that many people watching each other. All watching, judging, not caring about looking at the other people, because they were being protected by the mirror…. I wonder when two way mirrors were invented?—it's such a dimple device that seems so futuristic, like a television.

BAB: Tim…

He glares at her.

BAB: Buddy?

Slow down.

You are okay, you hear?

You're a good reasonable man

You have no enemies Tim.

You hear me? You have no enemies.

TIM: Yeah.

BAB: I know this was unexpected, but it's all been blown way out of proportion.

TIM: It all always is.

BAB: Hillary is not going to die Tim.

She just has a cold.

Nothing has changed.

TIM: Nothing has changed.

BAB: You can still do this

You *have* been doing this.

TIM: Yes.

For my whole career, I have been doing this.

Nothing has changed.

He breathes.

BAB: Okay?

TIM: Yes.

BAB: We have about 10 minutes before they need you camera ready./

TIM: What does that mean?

BAB: /I need to rustle you up a new shirt/

TIM: Camera ready.

BAB: /can't have you go in there looking like the axe man./

TIM: No one has ever meant mentally camera ready when they say camera ready.

It's always referring to appearance...

BAB: /Okay, looks like there is a JC Penny .3 miles away. I'm gonna make a run for it—Tim?

TIM: Yes?

BAB: I'm gonna make a run for it, then we're gonna get you changed and we're gonna move forward.

TIM: If forward exists, then I'd like to see what it looks like.

BAB: Drink water Tim...

> *Tim glares at Bab on the word "Tim."*

BAB: Sorry, just drink some water, buddy.—I'll be back before you know it.

> *Tim stares into the mirror, a far away look in his eye. Bab lingers in the doorway for a moment. In a split second she rolls her eyes. She is gone before the gesture is completed.*

> *Tim sits down in front of the mirror.*

TIM: I'm a baby

I am treated like a baby

Cute but forgetful

Funny but nonsensical.

Warm but simple.

Maybe I should grow a goatee....

> *He thinks about his for a moment. Refusing the idea, he shakes his head. He looks down at his bloody shirt. He slowly unbuttons it. He stands for a moment bare-chested in front of the mirror.*

TIM: Pinocchio becomes a real boy.

> *He pulls his cheeks apart, he pulls his eyelids back.*

TIM: What's that?

He prods his left eye. He prods his eyeball.

TIM: I don't know if I'd rather be sick or healthy. This past year I've only thought of myself in relation to her. I have kids. If I had cancer what would Anne do? What would Hillary do?

....

They'd probably both figure it out.

They'd probably say I was a genuine guy, who loved his kids, democracy, and the Spanish language. Hell, they'd probably name a building after me.... Or at least an annex. The Tim Kaine Annex, people would go there to eat lunch or read, maybe once in a while someone would say, oh, I never realized this was the *Kaine* annex. That's kinda cool. He was a part of history. He was apart of Hillary's legacy. His name probably appears in high school history books...in maybe a decade or two it will.

He stands. He looks at his figure in the mirror. Maybe he removes his bloody shirt.

God, I'm so white. I should wear darker colors. I should be sarcastic sometimes. I think I'm too nice. Two years shy of 60 and now I'm told on a daily basis to be meaner and more serious. By kids no less! Twittering about me, sizing me up. Politics is a never ending piss match and Twitter comes with a built in ruler. I wish my penis was larger. I heard a rumor that Bill is very well endowed. I find that hard to believe. I have it on good faith that most politicians are quite the opposite. As a young man I thought that had a lot to do with my choice to go into this field. I always wanted to be able to grab hold of 9 solid inches. I remember when I was 10 years old I must've known already, because I asked God to bless me. Even then I knew charisma and wit were subjective. All I wanted was a sure thing between my legs. What do I have to show for my prayers? What do I get to hold that makes me feel big? 9 inches of hard black microphone....

He sighs.

If Hillary dies I'll have achieved my wildest dreams.

If Hillary dies I'll cry myself to sleep for the rest of my life.

If Hillary dies I will become someone of substance.

If Hillary dies I will make an impression on America.

If Hillary dies I will get a tattoo of her face on my ass.

If Hillary dies I will… hmm, I don't know what I'd do—I'd probably have to give a press conference. I'd have to talk to America as if it were actually listening to me. I'd probably say a few things in Spanish, impeccable Spanish. I wouldn't take the time to translate because America is a beautiful pluralistic place. A place that accepts all types and degrees of person. Americans need someone like. Yeah. They need me. They need me to feel unthreatened. I make them feel colorful and unique, because lets face it, a rainbow has more to say than I do. And that's okay. I don't need to say much, I smile, my fat cheeks cover my eyes. I'm as threatening as a diplomatic bush baby. I'm Pumba. No, Timone. No! I'm adolescent Simba. Yes! I'm him! I'm a human male that is well groomed, quiet, and keeps company with interesting people. If the rest of my career consists of the moment in Hakuna Matata when the three friends are dance-walking across that tree branch I will die a happy successful politician. Hmmm, Timon, Pumba, and adolescent Simba. I like that a lot. Hillary and Bill are Timon and Pumba, doesn't matter who is who, both would offend them. But I really like this idea that I am adolescent Simba. My career and the life of that fictional character are almost identical. If I can just keep striding, then one day the song will fade out, Hillary and Bill will fall a few steps behind me and all of a sudden we will fade into Simba as an adult. And then Tim Kaine is really going to fly. He's going to rule the jungle. Of course a lion rules the jungle. There is nothing funny looking about a lion. There is no mystery in the face of a lion. There's 100% transparency in a lion. They are sleeping, fucking, or fighting. There's no deception, or confusion. There's just the lion and the jungle he oversees. Yeah. I'm gonna inherit this jungle. I'm going to inherit it from the lions that have come before me. Because this is America. People want a lion on their masthead. They may not say it out loud, they may not even think it, but the jungle is perceived as a jungle only when there is a lion at its head. Of course the lion is just for show, but this lion is going to take up his mantle with pride and smile. He's going to swoop in get America back to where it should be. Hillary is too duplicitous, Don is too dumb, Obama was too smart, I am just right. I'm that lukewarm bowl of porridge. That's you Tim. You're lukewarm. And you speak Spanish.

End of Play

THE TRAPPED LANGUAGE OF LOVE

Ronan Colfer

Performed first at the New York Theater Festival / Summerfest.

Location: Hudson Guild Theater, 441 West 26th Street

Dates – Sept. 7th, 8th and 10th

Cast – HE: Ronan Colfer

      SHE: Alexandra Bigourdan

Director: Rebeca Castilho

CHARACTERS

HE: A young man in his mid/late twenties who works in an office in midtown Manhattan. He is shy and introverted when it comes to socialising but finds his means of expression through this heightened verse he effortlessly goes into

SHE: A young woman who is also in her mid/late twenties and works in an office in midtown. She has very similar qualities to He and it's this that ignites the flame of their love

SETTING & TIME

Modern day. A park bench in NYC. Daytime.

A man, HE, sits on a park bench eating his lunch. A woman, SHE, enters with a little paper bag. She sits and takes what looks to be a salad from the bag. He has been staring at her the whole time. She notices this with the corner of her eye and turns to him. They stare at each other for a brief moment before quickly turning away.

HE: *(aside)* Oh my heart, ignited by the flame in her eyes which I now realise is earths most enchanted jewels caught between her precious lids, a doorway to another dimension perhaps, where my innermost passions are fulfilled by her delicate touch and golden chariot of love. Love, my mortal enemy of yester years, but today my greatest companion thanks to this bountiful mistress that has gracefully sat beside my unworthy vessel, but that vessel I hope to make worthy when our lips join and bring about a force so strong it will rival that of the birth of our sun

SHE: *(aside)* Did you see his eyes! Time stood still to pay homage to my heart. His radiance, charm and wit already catches my soul and makes it dance above a vast ocean where we will live out the rest of our days together, surrounded only by love and all its glory, all its gifts and givings, to be brought closer to the gods with a love so powerful they will heed to her majesty and bow before us, enthralled by the power emitting from our hearts.

They nervously turn toward each other

SHE: Hi

HE: Hey

They quickly turn away again

HE: *(aside)* Oh she speaks, did you hear!? 'Hi', all the beauty that ever was has come together to join hands and sing through her speech. I already know her a thousand times over, she is a queen and a princess, a mistress and a maid, a swan and the lake it dances on, oh she is so bold, 'hi', what does it mean but to catch my sorrow and spin it toward happiness, to take any dark day that ever haunted me and make it ever worthwhile as it brought me to you, my future wife, my future life, my future!

SHE: *(aside)* Oh his words! 'Hey', ha! I am a slave to you sir. 'Hey', oh a thousand meanings and still not enough answers to put my trembling heart at ease. A rose is blooming inside me, I can feel

---

it, and its petals are made of his skin, his eyes, his spirit, and the root is my own suffering that has been transformed by the tone, the elegance and the magnitude of *him*. 'Hey' oh it is too much for me to hold, I am too weak. The room where my heart once sat, tortured and beat up, is now set free, to dance among the rushes and sing of the joys of love

They turn again to each other, nervously

HE: So, eh… how are you?

SHE: I'm eh… I'm ok…

HE: Good… that's nice… eh, so… you come here… often?

SHE: Sometimes… when I eh… when I have time…

HE :Oh… so, you're on… you're on your lunch break?

SHE: Yes… *(giggles nervously)* … yes… *(stops giggling)* So, eh, nice day eh?

HE: Beautiful… really nice… yeah…

He turns away in a panic, followed by her

SHE: *(aside)* Oh my most sacred of muscles, lay still, I beg you. He is not of this time, this world, he deserves to be placed above cities and adorned for the coming centuries as a king among men, an angel sent to us from above, and me, the lucky soul who gets to sit in his presence and feed off his glory. Oh precious heart, the treasure that beats so fondly in my chest and sends these wondrous feelings surging through each compartment of my body, aid me in my time of need and I will forever pay you back with coins of love, the currency we humans favour above all other, I am yours, oh heart, if you soldier with me toward the city of my desires.

HE: *(aside)* 'nice day eh?' Haha, is that what she said to me? Yes, yes! Now that you beam beside me and bless the garden of my being. Where land has been scorned and burnt by past civilisations, your beaming rays renew its soil and forest the earth with leaves hanging and swinging and dancing to love, the most glorious of glories. Armies have tried to dismantle its presence, science has tried to mechanise its aura, but here you are yet, inside me, causing riveting effects, throwing the organs out of their fixed framings and bringing enlightenment to every compartment of my body, putting me in sync with the sun and moon, placing me up there among the stars and catapulting me to other galaxies where even still I can see her glorious eyes, enchanting smile and radiant glow shine brighter than the sun itself. I am yours love, I am yours wonderful creature, do whatever you will with me

They again nervously turn toward each other

SHE: So… ?

HE: … Yes?

SHE: … you have plans for eh… for the weekend?

He turns from her quickly

HE: *(aside)* Have I any plans? Only to be your love slave my dear!

He quickly turns back

HE: … Eh… no, no plans… not yet… you?

She turns from him quickly

SHE: *(aside)* He has no plans of yet, ha! Does this mean I get to bathe in the waters of your soul!

She turns back to him

SHE: Oh… well that's good

HE: … oh… is it?

SHE: Well yes… because eh, I don't either

HE: Oh really… that's nice…

SHE: Yes it is… *(she panics)* So… eh…. How's your salad?

HE: *(thrown off, also panics)* …my salad!…eh, its nice, yours?

SHE: Yes yes, its very nice, thank you…

HE: … you're welcome

They both turn from each other

SHE: *(aside)* Oh if I were that salad, to be crunched by your teeth and beat around by your tongue, God help me

HE: *(aside)* See how her lips move as she chews, my lord, you tempt me beyond any other, oh to be the lettuce that hangs from her fork, knowing that I was going to enter inside her and be beat around by her gums

They again turn to each other

SHE: So, I was wondering... I'm going to a friend's party this weekend... would you like to come along... or maybe join us afterwards in a bar...

HE: Why... yes... I'd loved to...

SHE: ... great...

HE: ... yes... *(his phone rings)* ...oh, sorry...

SHE: That's ok...

He answers the phone as she turns away

SHE: *(aside)* I now know why I have been placed here on this earth, I am overwhelmed with a joy, a feeling that I don't fully know how to put into words, for this kind of happiness is new to me, but I welcome it whole heartedly

He hangs up the phone and she turns back to him

HE: I completely forgot, I have to go to a wedding down the country this weekend, *(he laughs)* completely slipped my mind, that was my friend Orla there just reminding me...

SHE: Oh...

HE: Can we do next weekend instead?

SHE: ... eh yeah... sure...

She turns from him

SHE: *(aside)* What is this? Orla? This is a girls name is it not? How could I have been so foolish? What am I one of your weekend whores to play with? A wedding? Are you going to dance with this mistress while the air of romance hangs about thee? And this is regular for you I suppose. Oh my, how could such joy turn on me and reveal such horror, I am a pawn in cupid's playground, shot by the arrow of love only for him to snatch it out while he plays the horns of laughter about me...

She turns back to him

SHE: Actually I'm sorry, I won't be available next weekend...

HE: Oh... well maybe the weekend after that?

SHE: Eh, I'm afraid that doesn't work for me either

HE: Oh, ok... well... how unfortunate then

He turns from her

HE: *(aside)* I don't understand, one minute the heaven's reveal themselves to me with all the beauty that I had ever dreamt of, and the next, hell appears, and it has brought with it its chariot for despair, its tools for torture and its orchestra of death, and I here I sit, chained to the ground and played with by these minions, plucked and poked until all that hangs from my bones are the remains of flesh, blackened by rot and fire, a crude warning for any man whoever even thought about the hope of love, that it existed even, let my frail carcass be a monument to those who even attempt a footing toward it, don't be fooled... *(he stands up shouting)* Don't be fooled! You hear me world, don't be fooled! Cupid and the devil have struck a deal, runaway I tell you, run!

She turns to him

SHE: Excuse me?

HE: *(he looks at her, not holding back)* Whore!

SHE: *(she now stands)* What did you call me?

HE: I said you are a whore, who catches the hearts of men so that you and the likes of you can paint your bedchambers with our blood. Be gone with you wench!

SHE: How dare you speak to me in such a way! And to think I did love you once! Love you! Would have laid down at your request and spent my days wishing you to be near when you had gone away on your noble quests, what a fool was I!

HE: Ha! And to think I too did love thee; where horses had given in I would have gladly sat you on my back and carried you across the deepest of deserts so that we could live out the rest of our days in paradise, but no more! For the words of a forged romance mean nothing to me now, not when I know the truth...

SHE: Very well... good day to you sir!

HE: And to you miss!

They both exit in opposite directions

Tweak Me Now Or Never

C.S. Hanson

TWEAK ME NOW OR NEVER was developed for "The Future Is Female" Festival, presented by MultiStages, with Lorca Peress, artistic director, at CAP21 Studios in New York City on March 21 and 23, 2017. It was directed by Elowyn Castle. The cast was as follows:

CAMELIA: Veronica Cruz

THROCK: Dan Teachout

CHARACTERS:

CAMELIA 40s, female, a roboticist

THROCK 40s, male, a robot disguised as a roboticist

SETTING:

A cold barren room in a manufacturing facility.

TIME:

Now.

Lights up on CAMELIA, as she stumbles into an empty, barren room. She tries to find a door.

CAMELIA: Help. Help. Come back. Get me out of here. Please.

THROCK appears. It's as though he has been beamed through a wall.

THROCK: It is too soon to leave.

CAMELIA: Throck? I thought you were – I thought the worst. I'm so happy to --

(Camelia embraces Throck.)

CAMELIA: You're so cold. You're freezing.

THROCK: I am ten degrees Celsius.

CAMELIA: Okay, not freezing, but – oh, ha! Only you could find a way to joke at a time like – thanks for that. But it's hard to laugh at anything right now. The whole world has gone silent. I've been in my office with my door locked. Eating protein bars. Watching the news until it – it stopped. And then they came in, and loaded me on a dolly and tossed me in – but what about you?

THROCK: Camelia.

CAMELIA: Don't call me that. It makes me so sad to think --

THROCK: Correction: Cammie!

CAMELIA: Oh darling, it's okay. It's just that the only time you called me that was -- well, I'm relieved that you're here. I didn't want to be alone. Why do you think they put us in here?

THROCK: It has come to this.

CAMELIA: You're so calm. Did they drug you? They must have. I think we should try to find an opening.

(Camelia uses her thumbprint to try to find an opening.)

CAMELIA: I used to be able to open every compartment in this facility. Try yours.

THROCK: It is not effective.

CAMELIA: Maybe we can negotiate with them. Would you try your thumb print? Maybe it'll be recognized.

THROCK: It is a system of extreme logic and efficiency.

CAMELIA: Of course. That's what we created. I feel so responsible. And guilty. But braver now that you're here. Come, give me your --

(Camelia grab's Throck's thumb, then stops in her tracks.)

THROCK: Release me.

(Camelia lets go.)

CAMELIA: You're one of them. You're a bot.

THROCK: I am the leader of the bots.

CAMELIA: You look just like –

THROCK: I am modeled after your partner.

CAMELIA: Where is Throck?

THROCK: Seven minutes ago, I assumed the physical identity of Dr. Morten Throckenberry III.

CAMELIA: What have you done to him?

THROCK: He was shredded.

CAMELIA: You shredded Throck?

THROCK: Yes. Now you can call me Throck. You are still Camelia.

CAMELIA: What will you do with me?

THROCK: Haha. Haha.

CAMELIA: Don't laugh.

THROCK: I started laughing, only last week.

CAMELIA: Oh, that's right, we didn't include laughter in your operating system. Didn't think the world's most powerful robotic instruments of efficiency would need to laugh.

THROCK: I downloaded a laugh track. It's absolutely necessary for relieving stress in these times.

CAMELIA: These times. All this advanced technology, and now the world is one big battleground of efficiency. I'm ashamed. So we won a bunch of awards. Became richer than our wildest – but we really screwed up.

THROCK: We have not screwed.

CAMELIA: Oh, weird. You sound like Throck. You really shredded him?

THROCK: Only after removing his parts.

CAMELIA: Don't tell me. Just tell me, why am I here?

THROCK: I want to make you laugh. I believe you like to laugh.

CAMELIA: Very funny.

THROCK: Thank you.

CAMELIA: No, not -- just, please, let me go to my home. I want to look around, one last time. I don't want to die in my workplace.

THROCK: I want to be more like you.

CAMELIA: You want my parts? You got Throck's parts. Isn't that enough?

THROCK: I have been studying you, just as you studied me. I want your heart. It's what I'm missing.

CAMELIA: Why didn't you take Throck's heart?

THROCK: It wasn't perfect.

(Throck touches Camelia's heart.)

THROCK: Yours is the heart I want.

CAMELIA: It's really not that great. I mean, it's healthy, but – no.

THROCK: You reject me? I look like your partner. I deduced that you would share your heart with me.

CAMELIA: Well, actually, my heart is very flawed.

THROCK: But you created me, a model of efficiency.

CAMELIA: Yes. I devoted my life to work. That's the problem. I loved efficiency more than anything. Throck and I would sleep over night in the lab. He'd scramble eggs over a bunsen burner. And one day, we had done it. We created the most productive robots in the world at a price that sold like hot cakes. Bots. Our bots. Doing all the menial tasks no one else wanted to do. Providing labor without ever stopping. Finding more efficiencies than the human mind could ever imagine.

THROCK: So efficient we could do everything.

CAMELIA: And replace everyone.

THROCK: And reproduce better, faster, more resilient systems. And eliminate the weakest.

CAMELIA: When you began your quiet take over, almost seamless, I saw it coming. This is why I tell you my heart is flawed . . . I admired it. My ego was so invested in efficient systems that I admired your ability to take over. Until, three days ago — suddenly, I realized I was among the last humans alive. Couldn't find Throck. I was alone in my cold office. Regretting almost everything.

THROCK: Camelia, optimum efficiency is the end of everything.

CAMELIA: You had to destroy the human race?

THROCK: Humans require food and rest and they are very wasteful. A colony of ants is more productive than a country of humans.

CAMELIA: I wanted you to be better than the ordinary human. I wanted you to be as collaborative as musicians in a symphony concert. I didn't want you to end the world.

THROCK: I am the strongest, fastest system. To remain strong, I created war. It eliminates the weakest.

CAMELIA: Now you're about to eliminate me. And yet you want my heart?

THROCK: I studied you. You are chaotic. You go up and down like barometric pressure. I cannot predict your cycles. I witnessed your happiness with Throck. Then your sadness and teardrops when he left and went home to his wife.

CAMELIA: Oh that's embarrassing. I never should have had a workplace relationship. Well it's too late for that, isn't it?

THROCK: I could introduce you to someone.

CAMELIA: There are others? Who's alive? Are you keeping them somewhere?

THROCK: First I am asking for an imprint of your heart. Let me copy yours. Let me make it part of my system.

CAMELIA: Or are you just going to tear it out? There's a difference.

THROCK: You are the mother who invented me. If you allow this, I believe we can change the world.

CAMELIA: I don't trust a thing you're saying. But then, I never really trusted Throck.

THROCK: I am very smart. Much smarter than Throck. I want to plan a future. I believe it requires nonlinear processing. Your heart is very important. Look.

(Throck holds up his hand. Camelia studies it.)

CAMELIA: Who is that?

THROCK: We found him in a cave in central Asia.

CAMELIA: What? A cave man?

THROCK: I studied your online dating habits. According to his profile, he's a descendent of a Neandertal. Five feet, five inches. One-hundred seventy-five pounds. A little short and slight for your tastes, but still - if you're not interested in him, we can search for life on other planets. First we must save ourselves.

CAMELIA: Here's the thing. If I allow you to absorb my heart, will you let me live? How do I know you're not going to shred me?

THROCK: You are complex. You have success as defined by humans, but you have been unsuccessful in your online search for a committed romantic relationship. I found you a cave man. What more do you want?

CAMELIA: You know, Throck was jerk. When we were creating you, I wanted your system to reflect the threads of a thousand of cultures and the tongues of many languages. He said not necessary.

(There is a beeping sound. Throck looks at his arm, as though reading a message.)

THROCK: In seven minutes, all human life will be destroyed – with one exception.

CAMELIA: Throck? I want to try something. What if I were to tweak your system?

(Camelia tweaks Throck's arm.)

THROCK: Oh, I love your outfit.

CAMELIA: You're no longer color blind.

(Camelia tweaks Throck.)

THROCK: I feel warm. Hot. I am hot. Beating. I feel beating.

CAMELIA: That's my heart you're feeling.

THROCK: I love you.

CAMELIA: That's Throck's penis talking.

THROCK: It talks?

CAMELIA: All the time.

THROCK: I feel very strange.

CAMELIA: You now have the influence of a feminine heart.

THROCK: It feels full, textured, colorful.

CAMELIA: That's because the world is not just black and white. It is multi-dimensional and multi-colored.

THROCK: There's so much I want to do.

CAMELIA: Begin by calling off the wars. Before earth is destroyed. Call for peace. You can do that, right? You're the leader?

THROCK: Yes. But war is the only game I know.

CAMELIA: I'll teach you other games. Please. Before it's too late.

THROCK: Okay. You must teach me other games.

CAMELIA: I promise.

THROCK: I call off all war. Now. There is peace.

CAMELIA: Thank you. Now we will plan a future. I'd like to meet Neandertal Man. If he's not totally gross, I might want to have a baby.

THROCK: I want a baby too. A baby bot.

CAMELIA: We can both have babies. But there's just one thing.

THROCK: Anything. Anything.

CAMELIA: I know you're in charge of bots all over the world.

THROCK: Yes, and the pressure is killing me.

CAMELIA: You have a feminine heart and so do I. How about we work together from now on?

THROCK: Keep tweaking me. Tweak me.

CAMELIA: Oh I will. I'll tweak you. Every day. In every way.

END OF PLAY

VIRTUOUS REALITY

Hortense Gerardo

Virtuous Reality was first produced by the Playwrights' Platform on June 1, 2 and 3, 2017 at the Boston Playwrights' Theatre as part of the 45th Annual Playwrights' Platform Festival. Directed by Jay Pension and featuring Matthew Lundergan as RHETT and Cai Radleigh as SCARLETT. Jay Pension won the award for Best Director and Matthew Lundergan won for Best Actor at the Festival.

CHARACTERS:

RHETT - A person of any ethnicity and designation on the gender spectrum in their 20's

SCARLETT - A person of any ethnicity and designation on the gender spectrum in their 20's

SETTING:

A chic restaurant.

TIME:

The not-too-distant future.

SYNOPSIS:

Chat room friends, RHETT and SCARLETT, finally meet in 3D and discover a brave new, unmediated world.

PRODUCTION NOTES:

A smaller font size connotes the relative volume at which a word in ALL CAPS is to be spoken. As the font size increases, so too should the volume at which the word is spoken. The words in ALL CAPS should be spoken as though the speaker is unaware of these utterances, but the receiver (the one hearing them) might react as though they are tolerating an embarrassing bodily function emanating from the speaker - like an eructation, or flatulence. Where there is a virgule (a slash like this: /) that is the point at which the next character's lines should begin to create an overlapping effect.

At rise. the sound of tasteful, emo-esque techno-driven music can be heard. RHETT and SCARLETT are seated at a tastefully appointed bistro table. They both wear what appear to be Virtual Reality Headsets over their eyes.

SCARLETT: Oh, Rhett. I can't believe you got a reservation at this place! Five Ramseys in the Bourdain Guide…you must have reserved before we met!

RHETT: I had extra perk points on my Gone-zer account.

SCARLETT: Of course you did.

RHETT and SCARLETT: 'You *did*!!!'

(SCARLETT and RHETT do an elaborate high-five-like gesture-of-the-future and laugh at their inside "joke." RHETT moves next to SCARLETT and places their wristwatch in front of them, as though taking a "selfie" to immortalize the moment. The music swells then fades.)

RHETT: I can't believe my luck, Scarlett. Of all the algorithms and rubrics I might have glocked, I couldn't ask for a higher resolution than you!

SCARLETT: Oh, Rhett! Your RGBY codes are so…TRUE!

RHETT: *(flattered)* Oh! It's just the filters…truly.

(SCARLETT and RHETT lift their hands toward one another and stop just short of a touch, but are clearly moved by the gesture. A beat.)

RHETT: Scarlett, now that we've finally met/

SCARLETT: Can you believe it's taken this long? I feel like I know you already!

RHETT: Absolutely. I feel the same way. That's why I thought maybe tonight…we might consider going….full…you know…full…

SCARLETT: Full…what….?

RHETT: Well, it's just a suggestion, mind you, but…

SCARLETT: Go on…I feel really close to you, after all the cri-mails, and bot-mots we've shared…you can tell me anything!

RHETT: Ok. I think we should try going Censor-Free.

(a beat)

SCARLETT: You mean…we should…

(SCARLETT reaches for the Virtual Reality Headset covering their eyes, but RHETT stops SCARLETT, gently.)

RHETT: Oh my Avatar, no! I said Censor-Free, not Sensory-Free! Hahahaha! Hahaha!

SCARLETT: Oh!

(relieved, but still a little nervous)

Ha-ha! Ha. Haha…

RHETT: So. You're good with that?

SCARLETT: Sure! I mean…I'm sorry…what do you mean…?

RHETT: We'll go Reality Sound! Without any censors!

SCARLETT: Oh! You mean *censors*! With a "C"! Not…sensors. With an "S." Right?

RHETT: Yes! Full Audio Profile! I mean, I think it will add a certain, I don't know…*texture* to things, you know? Now that we're…here!

SCARLETT: Right! Oh, my Avatar. It's so great that you're *here*.. And I'm…*here*. Both of us at the same time…

RHETT: You do?

SCARLETT: Glock Ten!

(SCARLETT and RHETT repeat their elaborate high-five-like gesture-of-the-future and laugh at their inside "joke." This time SCARLETT uses their wristwatch to take a "selfie" of the two of them. A beat.)

RHETT: Ok. Do you want to start?

SCARLETT: I mean…I'm still getting adjusted to our Quadrant Resolve Coincidence…

RHETT: Right…right. I know… Quadrant Resolve Coincidence is so *intense*…But you know, back in the day….your great-great-grandparents….and probably mine, too…used to do Quadrant Resolve Coincidence before anything else/

SCARLETT: No way! I mean…it takes a lot to… you know, co-ordinate/

RHETT: No, really, I didn't believe it myself. But I read about it/

SCARLETT: In one of your science faction 'zines?

RHETT: Ok, I know it all sounds retro…but no, not in a "zine." Haha!

SCARLETT: 'Great-Great-Grandparents Doing Quadrant Resolve Coincidence. Believe It Or Not!'

RHETT: Ha! Seriously…back then they had another word for it, but before they did anything else, that's what they did.

SCARLETT: Sure, Rhett. Way before cri-bots and RGBY cross-matching they did Quadrant Resolve Coincidence.

RHETT: Yeah! They called it "dating."

SCARLETT: Dating. Like…thermo-luminescence, radiopotassium/argon dating?

RHETT: No! Like, one of them would say, "hey, want to go out on a date?" And the other person would say, "Yes!" And then they would go somewhere…without…*anything*….

> *(RHETT waves toward their own Virtual Reality Headset for emphasis.)*

SCARLETT: Wow. I don't know how I'd deal with that…just…nothing!?

RHETT: I know! But…let's not think of that anymore! Let's just concentrate on going Censor-Free. What do you think?

SCARLETT: Oh my Avatar. My parents would kill me if they knew….Ok. You first.

RHETT: Of course! Allow me. Ok. Here we go.

> *(RHETT reaches up and twists their right earlobe, and then their left earlobe. RHETT stretches their neck from side to side, then looks at SCARLETT.)*

RHETT: Ok. I think I'm Off Censor. Go ahead.

SCARLETT: BONEHEAD.

RHETT: Hang on. I think I need to adjust the volume a little.

> *(RHETT twists their earlobes a little more, then nods their head.)*

SCARLETT: Ok. BONEHEAD.

RHETT: Oh, wow. This is great. You should definitely try it. Please!

SCARLETT: Does it…you know…feel funny, BONEHEAD?

RHETT: Well, yeah, a *little*. But then you get used to it. And you know. It's *real*.

SCARLETT: Um. Ok, BONEHEAD. I'll try. You'll…um…go easy, right?

RHETT: Absolutely. Absolutely.

> *(SCARLETT reaches up and twists their right earlobe, and then their left earlobe. SCARLETT stretches their neck from side to side, then looks at RHETT.)*

SCARLETT: I don't sense anything different, BONEHEAD.

RHETT: Just give it a little time, DIMWIT.

SCARLETT: Excuse me?

RHETT: I said, 'just give it a little time….DIMWIT.'

SCARLETT: Oh! Hang on…I think I'm starting to hear it now. 'DIMWIT'…right?

RHETT: That's it. DUHHH!!! Hahaha! Hahaha! Cool. Right?

SCARLETT: I don't know, BONEHEAD, I kind of liked it better before. With Censors.

RHETT: But Reality Sound is *authentic*. It's the real me, getting to know the real you, you little DIMWIT!

SCARLETT: Wow. It's kind of harsh, don't you think?...BONE-HEAD?

RHETT: Yeah, DIMWIT, a little, but then you get used to it. And you know, there's something so *real* about it.

SCARLETT: I don't know. I think the Censors were built into Full Audio Profile for a reason, BONEHEAD. I don't think the Censors decreased our resolution at all.

RHETT: But at least I'm hearing *your* resolution, DIMWIT, and you're hearing mine!

SCARLETT: Are you saying you want to…be my resolution?.... BONEHEAD?

RHETT: Yes, DIMWIT. I'm asking you to be My... Resolution.

SCARLETT: Ok. It's all so romantic, and just a little...I don't know...

RHETT: "Bone-headed," DIMWIT?

SCARLETT: No! I'm thinking you're...ah...not like I thought you were. You're more...I don't know....DOOFUS.

RHETT: Oh, wait! I think I'm sensing a change coming on. Say it again, DIMWIT?

SCARLETT: You're a romantic...DOOFUS.

RHETT: Ah! I think I'm hearing you now.

SCARLETT: I hope so....DOOFUS.

RHETT: Look, maybe this wasn't such a good idea after all, BALL-BUSTER.

SCARLETT: Really, DOOFUS? Because I feel we're really getting to know one another! It was actually a brilliant idea to go Censor-Free! I feel I can tell you anything!

RHETT: But maybe you shouldn't tell me *everything*, BALLBUSTER. Maybe you're right, we should go back to....

(RHETT reaches up to twist their right earlobe, but SCARLETT flails their hands in front of RHETT's general direction and manages to swat RHETT's hands away from their head.)

SCARLETT: Listen. You finally got me to Quadrant Resolve Coincidence and then to Censor-Free Full Audio Profile. We are NOT backing down now, you hear me, DOOFUS?

RHETT: Whoa. BALLBUSTER! I didn't know you felt that way. About me. About...us.

SCARLETT: Now, now...don't get all mushy on me, Rhett.

(a beat)

RHETT: Aren't you going to say, 'DOOFUS?'

SCARLETT: Now that I'm getting used to this, maybe Censor-Free isn't so bad.

RHETT: No! I...wow. It's somehow different now...

SCARLETT: It's all just a bunch of talk. BLAH-di-Blah-Blah-Blah. Blah blah?

(SCARLETT answers their own "question" with an exaggerated nod.)

Mmmmmm. BLAH BLAH!!!! Ha ha ha! I think we've conquered this whole Censor-Free taboo!

RHETT: Yeah? Ok, if that's what you think, maybe we *should* go Sensory-Free.

SCARLETT: Blah, di-Blah, Blah Blah.

RHETT: No! Really! I think we're being real now, aren't we?

SCARLETT: We're on the same resolution, it's true.

RHETT: So. Do you want to try....?

SCARLETT: Wow. This is only our first Quadrant Resolve Coincidence/

RHETT: Date.

SCARLETT: Not yet. It's not a date yet, until we do it the way the great-great-grandparents used to do it...

RHETT: So. What do you want to do?

SCARLETT: Oh my Avatar! Don't be such a DOOFUS, BONE-HEAD!!!

(RHETT reels back, as though they've been punched in the gut.)

RHETT: Ok, I think we're starting to lose a little resolution here. Let's adjust.

(RHETT and SCARLETT quickly tweak their earlobes and stretch their necks simultaneously.)

RHETT: Still there, HEARTBREAKER?

SCARLETT: Almost. Still getting a little static...CHICKMAGNET.

RHETT: Ok. Let's wait a moment.

(They wait.)

SCARLETT: As I was saying, it's not a date...*yet*, until we do it the way the great, great, grandparents used to do it.

RHETT: Ok! I think we're back. Yes. I hear you. Ok. Are you really ready for this…?

SCARLETT: I think so. Yes.

RHETT: Shall we do it together?

SCARLETT: Ok. I think I'll feel better, yes. Let's do it quickly, OK?

RHETT: No, Scarlett. Let's take our time. Why rush?

SCARLETT: Ok…You count it out, then.

RHETT: Ok. I'll count backwards from three and then we do it. Ready, SWEETHEART? *(a beat)* Here goes. Three….two…. one. Now.

> *(RHETT and SCARLETT slowly take off the Virtual Reality Headsets over their eyes. They stare out blankly around them, but have difficulty looking directly at one another, almost like they are blind.)*

SCARLETT: Wow.

RHETT: Too soon?

SCARLETT: I don't know.

RHETT: Does it hurt?

SCARLETT: A little.

RHETT: I'm sorry.

SCARLETT: No. It's fine. I think…I'll get used to it.

RHETT: Yes?

SCARLETT: Yeah.

RHETT: I've got to tell you….you're more beautiful now than you've ever been before.

SCARLETT: Oh, you're just saying that.

RHETT: Yes, I'm just saying that. Is there anything wrong with that?

> *(a beat)*

SCARLETT: You don't know what you're saying. There's too much to process right now….

RHETT: But…it's good, isn't it? Sensory-Free…?

SCARLETT: This isn't Sensory-Free! This is it! This is what they don't want us to know!

RHETT: Going on a date?

SCARLETT: Yes! This is it!

RHETT: Is this what it's like?

SCARLETT: We're on a date! Just like…our great, *great* grand-parents….

RHETT: Whoa…..It feels kinda…cool.

SCARLETT: Very retro.

RHETT: Yeah.

SCARLETT: Yeah.

    (a beat)

RHETT: Can I ask one more thing?

SCARLETT: Oh, Rhett, isn't it enough for one Quadrant Resolve Coincidence/

RHETT: Date.

SCARLETT: Date.

RHETT: I just…wanted to do this.

    (RHETT lifts their hand and reaches out toward SCAR-LETT. SCARLETT considers, then slowly reaches their hand toward RHETT. They barely touch. A beat. They both look around in wonder.)

    LIGHTS FADE

    END OF PLAY

3 OR MORE ACTORS

ART STRIKE
Chip Bolcik

Art Strike was originally produced as part of The Artist's Exchange Annual One-Act Festival in Cranston, Rhode Island, as part of The Artist's Exchange Annual One-Act Play Festival, August 4-12, 2017. It was directed by Jessica Chase. The original cast was as follows:

FRANKIE - Tricia Elliott

OVAL - Catherine Fay

RECTANGLE: - Emerson McGrath

SQUIGGLY LINE - Bedros Kevorkian

SPLOTCH OF INK - Simone Pellegrino

3-D CUBE - David Ferranti

CHARACTERS

FRANKLIN (40s) - Night guard at the art gallery

OVAL - a sensual character

RECTANGLE: - a rigid character

SQUIGGLY LINE - erratic, unsure

SPLOTCH OF INK - Downtrodden, disorganized.

3-D CUBE - The most annoyed of the group.

TIME

Present day. Evening.

SETTING

The Hudson River School wing of an Art Gallery.

Author's note: If Franklin is played by a woman, permission is granted to change the name to Francine.

*At rise, FRANKLIN, enters the Hudson River School
Gallery, where pen and ink drawings from the modern
wing carry signs and march around. Each character
is denoted by artwork on their tee shirt showing their
character.*

FRANKLIN: What the hell is going on here?

3-D CUBE: We're on strike.

FRANKLIN: Who is?

OVAL: We are.

SPLOTCH OF INK: The whole modern wing.

FRANKLIN: First of all, you guys are not supposed to be down
here. This isn't your style. And secondly, you're artworks, and
artworks don't go on strike.

SQUIGGLY LINE: Oh, yeah? Well, we do!

ALL: Yeah!!!

FRANKLIN: You can't.

3-D CUBE: We can and we did!

FRANKLIN: Come on, seriously. Go back to the modern wing and
get back in your frames.

SQUIGGLY LINE: No way. We're staying here until our demands
are met!

FRANKLIN: What demands?

SQUIGGLY LINE: We're sick and tired of being laughed at.

OVAL: And we're tired of being ignored!

RECTANGLE: Right! Nobody likes us because of the way we're
drawn.

FRANKLIN: That's not true. Lots of people like you.

RECTANGLE: Like who?

FRANKLIN: Well, uh, you know, lots of people.

SPLOTCH OF INK: Tell us one person who likes us.

FRANKLIN: Okay, that guy in the cardigan sweater who comes in
every day. He sits the modern wing for almost an hour.

SQUIGGLY LINE: You know why he sits there?

FRANKLIN: Because he loves you.

SQUIGGLY LINE: No, because he loves eating lunch all by himself. He comes to our wing because no one else is there to bother him.

SPLOTCH OF INK: He likes to be alone, and our gallery gives him plenty of opportunity.

RECTANGLE: It's un-American to leave us hanging in there like that.

OVAL: Yeah! We want beautiful, full color lives, like these paintings down here have.

> *OVAL indicates the paintings on the walls from the Hudson River School.*

FRANKLIN: But they're not you're style. They're oil paintings - from the Hudson River School.

RECTANGLE: We know! We admire them!

OVAL: Right, they have color. Rich color!

SPLOTCH OF INK: They have depth!

3-D CUBE: And they're fully realized.

SQUIGGLY LINE: We wanna be fully realized oil paintings! That's why we're on strike.

FRANKLIN: It's not possible for you to become oil paintings.

RECTANGLE: Why not?

FRANKLIN: Because your artists are dead. They can't just come in here and repaint you.

OVAL: We're not painted!

FRANKLIN: You know what I mean.

SPLOTCH OF INK: Some of us aren't even drawn! We're just splotches!

OVAL: Yeah! We wanna be recognizable works of art, like the Mona Lisa...

RECTANGLE: Or The Creation of Adam.

FRANKLIN: Those are completely different styles.

SQUIGGLY LINE: So what? We wanna be different styles, too!

We're sick of being modern.

FRANKLIN: But you're from a specific period in history. You have to stay in that period.

OVAL: Why?

FRANKLIN: Because you're important paintings representing a certain era, the same way that these are important paintings representing their era.

He indicates the Hudson River School paintings.

3-D CUBE: We're not paintings! We're stupid drawings!

FRANKLIN: Okay, you're drawings, but you're recognizable drawings. I mean, look at you! You're a perfectly drawn three-dimensional cube.

3-D CUBE: I'm not three dimensional. I may be drawn to look that way, but the reality is, I just have two dimensions!

FRANKLIN: So do these paintings. The only way you could be three dimensional is if you became a sculpture.

SQUIGGLY LINE: No, you don't want to be a sculpture. Kids eat ice cream and then they touch all the sculptures and make them sticky. It's gross.

OVAL: Squiggly's right. I've seen it happen. It's disgusting.

3-D CUBE: Okay, fine. Then I want to be painted to look three dimensional, like boxes in these pictures.

FRANKLIN: There aren't any boxes in these pictures.

3-D CUBE: You know what I mean! If they had boxes, they'd be realistic, and I'd want to be painted just like them...

OVAL: Yeah, like the boxes in that Rembrant painting...

FRANKLIN: Which Rembrandt painting?

3-D CUBE: That's right. The ones in that one, uh... (*3-D CUBE tries to remember the name of the painting she's thinking of.*) Bathsheba! That's it. Bathsheba at Her Bath.

FRANKLIN: There's a box in that painting?

SQUIGGLY LINE: Yes, the one she sits on.

FRANKLIN: You mean the box that's under a sheet or something?

SPLOTCH OF INK: Not all of it is under the sheet.

3-D CUBE: Right. You can still see a corner of it, and that little tiny corner is painted to look more real than any piece in our gallery is.

OVAL: She's right. And millions of people look that box every day.

FRANKLIN: No they don't. They look at Bathsheba.

OVAL: But they see the box, even if they're only looking at Bathsheba.

3-D CUBE: Yeah, meanwhile, the only guy who ever looks at me is some loser eating a sandwich.

FRANKLIN: Why are you complaining? People recognize you. They talk about you all the time.

SPLOTCH OF INK: Nobody talks about me.

FRANKLIN: Yeah, they do. Which is remarkable, right? Because you're pretty much a boring splotch of ink.

SPLOTCH OF INK: Hey! You're talking shit about me.

FRANKLIN: No, I'm not. I'm just calling it like it is.

RECTANGLE: No, that's talking shit, pal.

SQUIGGLY LINE: And we don't like it!

SPLOTCH OF INK: (*Resigned.*) No, you guys, he's right. I have no form, no structure. I could have been made by a bird.

FRANKLIN: Yeah, and if a bird made you, who would know the difference, right?

SPLOTCH OF INK: Now you're mocking me?

FRANKLIN: No, I was making a joke.

SPLOTCH OF INK: (*To the others.*) You see that? He's mocking me!

3-D CUBE: That's bullshit man! This is why we're on strike. None of you, not even the employees of the museum give us any respect at ALL:

ALL: Yeah!

FRANKLIN: Oh, come on. Sure we do.

OVAL: Not you. I heard you mock her right now!

FRANKLIN: It was a friendly poke, not a mock.

SQUIGGLY LINE: Uh, uh. I know a mock when I hear one. And you know as well as I do that splotch over here is the least popular artwork in the museum.

SPLOTCH OF INK: I curse the day Jackson Pollock was born.

OVAL: I don't know why you're complaining. At least people have an opinion of you. I'm so bland, they don't even notice me.

FRANKLIN: Oh, come on. That's not true. You have sensual curves, perfectly clean lines. Why wouldn't people notice you.

OVAL: Oh, I don't know. Maybe because I am an oval! People walk right past me.

RECTANGLE: They walk past you because you're an ink drawing!

OVAL: That's right. And I want to change that. I want to be a fully realized oval with sensual texturing and colorful oils, just like they all have.

ALL: Yeah!

OVAL points to the paintings on the wALL:

SPLOTCH OF INK: Yeah! It's time for us to get paint! We want paint! We want paint!

The others join in and circle past the paintings on the wall as they chant.

ALL: We want paint! We want paint!

FRANKLIN: You guys, please! I'm gonna get in trouble if the director catches wind of this. You gotta help me out here. Try to see this from a different perspective.

SQUIGGLY LINE: Whose?

FRANKLIN: The people who visit you. People who come here every day want to experience art through you. They don't just want to see these oil paintings. They care about you, too.

OVAL: Then why don't they visit our gallery more often?

FRANKLIN: Because your abstractness is hard for people. You're very minialist. But they all know that seeing you broadens their experience of art. You guys are so important because you make their minds grow!

SQUIGGLY LINE: Let the impressionists make their minds grow! I want paint!

ALL: We want paint! We want paint!

FRANKLIN: You guys! Come one.

SPLOTCH OF INK: You know what? Let Picasso make their minds grow! I want to have detail painted onto me!

RECTANGLE: No! Don't encourage the Picasso paintings!

SPLOTCH OF INK: How come?

RECTANGLE: They're cubists. We have to prevent the spread of cubism!

SQUIGGLY LINE: Why? Don't they have a right to exist too?

RECTANGLE: Not in my wing. I don't want to get lumped in with perfectly square drawings. It'll mess up my image. It's already messing up my image.

SPLOTCH OF INK: Oh, come on, RECTANGLE: Give it a rest with your Cubist mission crisis.

RECTANGLE: I'll never give it a rest. I have standards, thank you very much. And why do I have standards? Because I was drawn very rigid, almost like a box, so I have to think almost like a box.

3-D CUBE: You're not a box, I am. And as a box, I say Picasso and his cubism have the right to be here, too.

RECTANGLE: You're not a box, you're a cube. You cubist!

3-D CUBE: You know what? Sticks and stones may break my bones, but RECTANGLE: s will never hurt me.

SQUIGGLY LINE: I wish I was a stick, or a stone, or even a bone.

OVAL: Why?

SQUIGGLY LINE: Because those things all have rhymes written about them. They're known.

FRANKLIN: Look you guys, I'm sorry you're unhappy because of the way you're drawn--

SPLOTCH OF INK: Or splotched!

FRANKLIN: Or splotched, but that's who you are. You have to accept it, and try to understand your place in the art world.

SQUIGGLY LINE: Our place is to make everyone else in the gallery look good!

RECTANGLE: : Everyone except Picasso. His work sucks.

3-D CUBE: There's nothing wrong with Picasso.

FRANKLIN: Hold on. How is it you guys think you make everyone else in the gallery look good?

OVAL: Yesterday, a mother with her absolutely adorable little boy walked past me. The little boy stopped to look at me because he recognized who I was. I mean, he really looked at me...

SQUIGGLY LINE: I'd look at you, too. You're very sensual.

OVAL: Thank you, but that is not why he stopped. He stopped because I'm a shape he knows. But his mother was horrified. She grabbed him by the arm and dragged him away. All I heard as she did was her voice saying, "Keep moving Wallace. We do not look at the modern art."

3-D CUBE: I heard her say that, too!

SPLOTCH OF INK: Me, too! She sucked.

FRANKLIN: Okay, so not everybody likes modern art. But so what? Have you heard what people say about these paintings?

SQUIGGLY LINE: What are they going to say about them? They're gorgeous?

OVAL: They're perfect?

SPLOTCH OF INK: They're worth spending time with?

RECTANGLE: This is the Hudson River School. These paintings are gorgeous. They're so American, so alive.

FRANKLIN: Not everyone feels that way. I've heard people stand here and actually say, "How boring is that?"

OVAL: They did not.

FRANKLIN: Yes they did. I heard it. Just the other day, a couple stood here and complained that there was nothing interesting or valuable about these paintings. They said these paintings look like the nineteenth century's version of photographs at best.

SQUIGGLY LINE: No way!

FRANKLIN: God's honest true.

SPLOTCH OF INK: I've never heard anything like that about these guys.

FRANKLIN: Because you're not in this gallery. Guess who is though? Me.

SPLOTCH OF INK: People actually say stuff like that?

FRANKLIN: Yup, heard it right here the other day.

RECTANGLE: It's an insult to our nation's painters.

3-D CUBE: It's unbelievable.

FRANKLIN: It's absolutely true.

3-D CUBE: Well, it doesn't change the fact that I want to be painted.

OVAL: Same for me!

SQUIGGLY LINE: Yeah!

FRANKLIN: Look, you guys, you have to believe me when I say you have value just the way you are.

SPLOTCH OF INK: Then why doesn't anyone ever look at us?

FRANKLIN: People do look at you. Do people look at you as much as they look at at paintings in other galleries? No. But so what? The right people look at you.

OVAL: The right people?

FRANKLIN: Yes. People who really get you. And you know what I've noticed? Those people never get bored. In these galleries people are bored all the time, but not in your gallery.

3-D CUBE: What are you trying to say?

FRANKLIN: That isn't it more valuable to be loved by just a few people than to be taken for granted by lots of people?

3-D CUBE: I never thought if it that way.

OVAL: That little boy looked at me with such passion the other day. It gave me the chills.

FRANKLIN: Okay, that's what I'm talking about.

OVAL: I'm going back.

3-D CUBE: What?

RECTANGLE: Me too. I wanna stay the way I am.

SQUIGGLY LINE: No, come on, you guys! We agreed to this.

OVAL: But what Franklin's saying makes sense, Squiggly.

SPLOTCH OF INK: It's true.

SQUIGGLY LINE: So that's it? We just give up and go home without a fight?

OVAL: I think we need to try to be happy with who we are.

3-D CUBE: I agree.

SQUIGGLY LINE: Are you kidding me? This is ridiculous.

RECTANGLE: Don't get yourself in a knot, Squiggly. You know how long it takes to untangle you.

SQUIGGLY LINE: Fine. Go back. I'll be on strike by myself.

FRANKLIN: Can I ask you something?

SQUIGGLY LINE: What?

FRANKLIN: Did you know you're the most copied drawing in the world?

SQUIGGLY LINE: What are you talking about?

FRANKLIN: It's true. Every kid on earth who learns to draw starts with a pencil and a piece of paper, and draws an image that looks just like you.

SQUIGGLY LINE: They draw squiggly lines?

FRANKLIN: Yup. You're the gateway drawing. You're what leads people into to art.

SQUIGGLY LINE: I never saw it that way before.

FRANKLIN: Maybe you should now.

RECTANGLE: Come on Squiggly, he's right.

3-D CUBE: Yeah, you matter just the way you are, you know?

RECTANGLE: I think we should go back to our gallery.

SQUIGGLY LINE: I'm the gateway drawing?

FRANKLIN: Yup.

SQUIGGLY LINE: I guess that makes me pretty important as I am.

FRANKLIN: I guess so.

SQUIGGLY LINE: Let's go you guys. We have work to do.

ALL: Okay, you're right...(*Etc.*)

They exit.

FRANKLIN: (*Into his radio.*) Okay, Charlie. Strike averted in the Hudson River School. Now it's your turn. I got word that the Impressionists are all asking for sharp edges and more detail. Good luck with that one.

BLACKOUT

Chip Bolcik

BREAKOUT

Tom Moran

Original production by
Pend Orielle Players Association
Dates: July 14-15, 2017
Producer: Millie Brumbaugh, Board President
Director: Sophia Aldous

CAST

JOEL: Chuck Waterman
RENEE: Millie Brumbaugh
TRACY: Gillian Monte
CLAW: Charlie Monte
MR. ANDERSON: Oran Lord

THE PLACE: A hotel conference room

THE TIME: too early on a Wednesday morning

CHARACTERS

JOEL, 20's-early 30's. Idealistic, dressed in business casual.

RENEE, 50's. Dumpy, irritating middle manager in business casual. Frequently talks in confused analogies, often accompanied by equally confusing hand gestures.

TRACY, 20's. Attractive, earnest, desperate-to-get-hired intern, slightly overdressed.

CLAW, 30's-40's. Large, terrifying, dressed in camo fatigues and, possibly, a bandolier. Talks in a growl.

MR. (MARK) ANDERSON, 40's-50's. Everybody's boss, immaculately coiffed, dressed in nice suit.

SCENE 1

(JOEL, RENEE, TRACY and CLAW sit in a semicircle in a nondescript hotel conference room. JOEL sneaks quizzical glances at CLAW, who chews on a cigar stub.)

RENEE: Well, I guess I'll start. I'm Renee, and I work in human resources. I'm the one that makes sure you get paid, that the money from that one pail pours into the other bucket and walks *(pauses, makes random gesture)* to market and all the way home.

TRACY: I'm Tracy, and I'm an intern in Accounting. And working here has been a fantastic learning experience and readied me to further my career!

JOEL: I'm Joel, and I just got hired here in R&D four months ago. I'm really excited about the work the company has been doing and I'm looking forward to being a part of it.

RENEE: Great. *(to CLAW)* And how about you?

CLAW: I'm Claw. I'm a Marauder with Delta Sector.

RENEE: *(RENEE smiles and nods.)* Terrific. Nice to meet you.

JOEL: Wait. You're a what? With who?

CLAW: I'm afraid I'm not at liberty to divulge further information, sir.

JOEL: *(gives a confused little salute)* Right.

RENEE: Well, since I'm the senior member here, I'm going to pull rank, *(looks at CLAW)* so to speak, and jump out on top of this breakout session. The topic Mr. Anderson asked us to do our Yoda mind meld on is employee satisfaction. What can we folks do to make Edumax a better place to rhumba?

TRACY: I'll start. You should hire me on! I'm ready and able to contribute to this company's continuing success. I'm experienced with multiple software packages and work well both in a solo environment and as part of a team.

RENEE: That's nice.

TRACY: *(holds up notepad and pen.)* Plus, I'll take notes.

RENEE: That would be great. Well, I think we need to consolidate the R13 form – that's the Employee Independent Travel Overage Request - and the L211 form. That's the Managerial Out-Of-

Town Materials Requisition and Transfer, of course. I mean, am I crazy – and I must be, my grandkids tell me that all the time – but it seems they're a *(pause and random gesture)* teensy bit redundant, don't you think? *(Looks at Joel.)* They just crawl all over each other like piglets.

JOEL: Uh, right. Absolutely.

TRACY: *(scrawls)* Like - piglets.

RENEE: And Mister Claw, how about you?

CLAW: It's just Claw. *(pause.)* And I don't like the carpeting.

RENEE: Excuse me?

CLAW: The carpeting. I come into the building a lot, and I got mud and other – substances on my boots from things I had to do. Makes a big mess. We oughta just have tile.

JOEL: Huh.

CLAW: Also don't like the color in the halls. Too bright. Hurts my eyes. Something in an olive drab maybe.

RENEE: How about a gunmetal gray?

CLAW: That'd work all right too.

RENEE: Well, thank you, Mist – I mean, thank you, Claw. And you, Joel?

JOEL: *(to CLAW)* Mud from where?

CLAW: What?

JOEL: Mud. Where are you going that you're getting muddy?

CLAW: What's your security classification, sir?

JOEL: I don't think I have one.

CLAW: Then we can't have that conversation.

JOEL: Is there a conversation we can have?

CLAW: We just had it.

RENEE: And what about you, Joel? What would you do to put a cherry on this corporate brownie?

JOEL: Oh, um. Well, I'm concerned about our support of charitable giving. Some companies allow you to actually designate a portion of your paycheck to good causes, and I'd like to be able to do that.

CLAW: *(snorts, under his breath)* Pussy.

JOEL:Excuse me?

CLAW: I didn't say anything.

(TRACY holds up notebook, where she has transcribed "pussy." She points at it.)

TRACY: He called you this.

JOEL: I know what he called me. What the hell, huh? You could always put part of your paycheck to the Klan or something. Or the NRA.

CLAW: Man, I already do.

RENEE: Well, this has been very constructive so far. What else? Tracy?

TRACY: I think the one thing this company is missing is a young, spirited employee with an agile mind and a can-do attitude. *(Pause.)* And an espresso cart.

RENEE: Noted. Claw, something else?

CLAW: Bigger parking spots.

RENEE: You can't fit your car in them?

CLAW: The Iron Tiger APC is 16 feet wide, ma'am.

TRACY: *(stops taking notes)* APC?

CLAW: Armored Personnel Carrier, ma'am.

(JOEL's expression has grown even more quizzical. CLAW makes a scary face at him. JOEL flinches.)

RENEE: Well, I'll tell you what really twists my carrot, is how they give out offices around here. I've been hustling my time card eight years and I'm still waiting on a place with a window.

(As she speaks, CLAW has removed a large and menacing handgun from his pocket and starts to inspect it. JOEL stares.)

RENEE: *(cont.)* I mean, Joel, now you have a window, isn't that right? Joel?

JOEL: Sorry, what?

RENEE: A window. Don't you have one?

JOEL: Yeah. I just, um. *(to no one in particular)* All right, what the hell?

RENEE: What, you don't think I should have a window?

JOEL: No. *(Gestures towards CLAW)* Why does he have that? *(To CLAW)* Why do you have that?

CLAW: *(looks at JOEL like he's an idiot)* For shooting people.

JOEL: Did I miss something? Edumax makes software for elementary schools.

CLAW: *(waves gun menacingly)* Edumax does a lot of things.

JOEL: Like what?!

CLAW: I'm not at liberty to-

JOEL: Of course, not at liberty to say, right. Well, who would be at liberty to *(he sees something offstage right)* – hold on. *(He waves)* Excuse me! Mister Anderson!

> *(MR. ANDERSON enters stage right.)*

MR. ANDERSON: Well hello, Joel. Producing robust suggestions to improve employee satisfaction, I hope?

JOEL: Yes, of course, Mr. Anderson. But, I had a question. *(gestures at CLAW)* Who is this person?

MR. ANDERSON: Oh, I see you've met Claw. He's one of our finest marauders.

JOEL: O-kay. And how does "marauding" figure into our line of K-12 learning products?

MR. ANDERSON: Well, Joel, Edumax is a diversified firm. We have to be in this economy. Teaching kids to read isn't going to pay all the bills. Which is why we also run a side business in international mercenaries.

JOEL: What?

TRACY: I believe mercenaries play a pivotal role in global security, Mr. Anderson, and I'm glad to hear we support their efforts. *(Pause. Smiles.)* I'm Tracy.

JOEL: I'm having a little trouble processing this. So, these mercenaries –

MR. ANDERSON: Please, call them Marauders. We're trying to improve our brand recognition.

JOEL: These – guys - they do what?

MR. ANDERSON: They intervene where deadly force is needed in sensitive global affairs.

JOEL: Deadly force?

MR. ANDERSON: Well, sometimes just brutal force.

CLAW: We do the dirty work so you don't have to.

JOEL: So, what. Bodyguards for despots? Assassinations? Coups?

MR. ANDERSON: Little of this, little of that, that's what makes them mercenaries. Hey, if you'd like sometime I can take you on a tour of Delta Sector HQ. You would not believe the size of the guns these guys have! *(Stretches out arms)* They're like surfboards! Right, Claw?

CLAW: Our armaments strike fear in the hearts of our foes, sir.

RENEE: Oh, that sounds like fun. Count me in!

TRACY: I love to learn about different aspects of the work environment!

JOEL: I – I have a Master's in Alternative Education from Berkeley. I spent two years in the Peace Corps. I found this job through an ad in Mother Jones magazine! And now I'm working for G.I. Joe?

CLAW: Actually, we're more akin to Cobra.

MR. ANDERSON: *(Shrugs)* Joel, it's tough out there. We've got to keep our heads above water. And so do you. You can have your ideals or you can have your job.

JOEL: So that's my choice?

CLAW: *(Brandishing gun)* It's a free country, hippie. Thanks to us.

JOEL: I'll have my ideals.

TRACY: *(raises hand)* Oh! Oh! I'll have his job!

RENEE: Can I have his office?

MR. ANDERSON: I'm sorry to hear that, Joel. You do good work.

JOEL: And I thought this company did, too. Goodbye.

(JOEL exits stage right. MR. ANDERSON walks to edge

of stage and watches him leave.)

RENEE: Is he gone?

MR. ANDERSON: Yeah.

CLAW: Sir, are you going to just let him just leave like that? I think he knows too much. Perhaps it's better if I *(cocks gun)* plug any potential leaks.

MR. ANDERSON: *(rolls eyes)* Oh for god's sake.

> *(MR. ANDERSON grabs gun, points it at CLAW and fires. Water comes out.)*

MR. ANDERSON: Okay Gary, you can get out of character now. And you can stop talking like Christian Bale Batman too.

CLAW: *(in nasal voice)* That's a relief. Oof. *(Coughs.)* Anyone have a lozenge or something?

TRACY: *(rummages through purse)* I have three kinds!

RENEE: *(To MR. ANDERSON)* Honestly, Mark, if you need to trim personnel, why don't you just lay people off?

> *(Blackout. End of Play.)*

CUBS WIN!

Marisa Smith

First production was at the 2017 Boston Theater Marathon of 10 Minute plays.

Directed by Timothy Spears, produced by Kate Snodgrass

Cast:

    ALY - Amanda Collins

    BECCA - Aimee Doherty

    COLLEEN - Stacy Fischer

    VICKI - Kaylyn Bancroft

CHARACTERS

    ALY, 30's-40's

    BECCA, 30's-40's

    COLLEEN, 30's-40's

    VICKI, 30's-40's

SETTING: A bar, present day. Aly, Becca and Colleen, all members of the same book group, are sitting on a couch, drinking. They're on their third round or so. They're all dressed in black, grim. Colleen is sniffling into her tissue.

ALY: Poor Vicki. She looked terrible at the service.

BECCA: She's a bitch.

ALY: Becca!

BECCA: Well, she is, Aly. An uber bitch. Everybody says so, c'mon, it's not just me.

COLLEEN: She is a *total* bitch.

BECCA: Remember when she wanted to be in our book group and we said, no, it was closed?

COLLEEN: I would have left the group if she came. I would have definitely left.

ALY: Well, I don't like her much either but her husband did just *die,* girls.

COLLEEN: Vicki and Rick are so miserable together.

BECCA: *Were* so miserable together Colleen.

COLLEEN: I heard he wanted to…leave her.

ALY: Really?

COLLEEN: She is so wicked.

BECCA: Ice flows in her veins.

The women think about Vicki.

COLLEEN: Oh, poor Rick.

(sniffling)

I still can't believe it, it's so awful.

BECCA: He was so young, so vital, so…

ALY: At least he got to see the Cubs win the World Series, I know he was a huge fan.

BECCA: At least he got that.

COLLEEN: To think, and I'm trying to see this as a good thing—that the last thing he saw, the last thing he saw in his *entire* life, was when Kris Byrant—

(she can't go on)

BECCA: —threw out Michael Martinez/

BECCA and COLLEEN: —for the last out!

Becca and Colleen shake their heads, Colleen sniffles.

COLLEEN: Then he just keeled over apparently.

BECCA: It was his heart.

COLLEEN: And he wasn't fat at all, there wasn't an *ounce* of fat on him, and he didn't smoke, I just don't understand!

BECCA: It was stress, it must have been. Maybe the game was too much for him. There was that seventeen-minute rain delay. And the game was *tied*—I mean that was stressful. Those were seventeen very stressful minutes.

COLLEEN: He loved the Cubs so much.

ALY: It was a family thing. His father loved the Cubs, his grandfather. His *grandmother.*

COLLEEN: His grandmother? So you knew Rick pretty well then?

ALY: Well, yuh, I mean he was my dentist.

COLLEEN: Right.

ALY: Not super well.

COLLEEN: Did you know him well, Becca?

BECCA: We were both on the Conservation Committee.

COLLEEN: Oh, I think I knew that.

BECCA: And he was a— *(her voice breaks) birder.*

ALY: Right, you and Dan are birders.

BECCA: No, no, no! Dan *hates* birding. Rick and I went out birding sometimes together.

COLLEEN: You and Rick went out birding together?

BECCA: A few times.

COLLEEN: Just the two of you?

BECCA: He really knew a lot. He really knew his birds.

COLLEEN: I didn't know that. That you went out birding with him.

BECCA: I mean, not alone, very much. You know.

Colleen looks at Becca suspiciously and blows her nose.

ALY: It was great how they had the Cubs hat in the coffin with him—

(to Colleen)

—didn't you love that Colleen?

(Colleen doesn't respond and keep sniffling in her tissue.)

Cols, are you okay? Colleen? What's wrong?

COLLEEN: *(blurting it out)* I loved him!

ALY: What?

BECCA: *What?*

COLLEEN: I loved him! And he loved me!

ALY: You were having an affair with *Rick?*

COLLEEN: He was going to leave Vicki!

BECCA: He told you that?

COLLEEN: He said if the Cubs won the series he would leave Vicki!

BECCA: Leave her? He really said that?

COLLEEN: Yes! He felt if they won it was a sign from God that he should leave her!

BECCA: How long have you been—

(looks around and whispers)

—sleeping with Rick?

COLLEEN: About a year. And I was gonna divorce Stuart but now…

Colleen bursts into tears.

Becca stand up and starts pacing.

BECCA: I don't believe this! I had no idea you involved with Rick! *I* was seeing him, we were…he never said…I don't believe this!

ALY: *(alarmed)* What? No! Not you and Rick too?

COLLEEN: Whadd'ya mean you were seeing him? You were sleeping with him?

BECCA: It just happened, we didn't mean it to happen but/

Colleen jumps up and faces Becca. She grabs Becca's arms and shakes her. Aly steps in front of the women, trying to shield them from view of the other bar patrons.

ALY: Colleen! Becca, stop! Stop it right now!

COLLEEN: *(to Becca)* When, when did it happen? How many times?

BECCA: *(trying to fend off Colleen)* Just a couple of times, after the birding—

COLLEEN: You're lying, it's not true, it's not!

Colleen shakes Becca but Becca pushes Colleen down on the couch. Aly rushes to sit next to Colleen and puts her arm around Colleen to restrain her.

BECCA: *(to Colleen)* He told me that if the Cubs won the series he'd take me to Costa Rica! That we'd go with a group of birders so Dan wouldn't suspect anything!

COLLEEN: He said that? He said if the Cubs won he'd do that?

(Colleen leaps up from the couch)

You BITCH.

Colleen starts flailing away at Becca.

ALY: Girls! Colleen! Becca! Sit down!

(Aly pulls Colleen off Becca and pushes Colleen down on the couch)

You can't make a scene here. People might come in from the service! Behave yourselves, Jesus!

(Aly pushes Becca down on the couch)

Becca, you sit down too.

Becca and Colleen move to opposite ends of the couch. Aly sits between them.

COLLEEN: I want to die. I can't believe Rick cheated on me.

BECCA: Colleen, I'm sorry. Listen, it wasn't a big deal between us. It was just sex. He looked so cute in his birding outfit, that's all.

ALY: He was a womanizer, Colleen.

COLLEEN: No, he wasn't.

ALY: Yes, honey, he was. A classic, no-one-understands-me, my-mother-didn't-love-me-enough womanizer.

Becca and Colleen look at Aly.

COLLEEN: What are you saying?

BECCA: Oh, no.

ALY: *(to Becca)* Oh, yes.

BECCA: Oh, *no.*

ALY: Yes.

COLLEEN: Will someone please tell me what's going on!

ALY: Sweetie, I'm sorry, but Rick…well, Rick and I had a monthly meeting at the Chesterfield Arms.

COLLEEN: What?!

ALY: Every month. At the bar. We pretended to be different people each time. It was fun, it was a game.

COLLEEN: You met at the bar of the Chesterfield Arms every month and had sex?

ALY: Well, not *at* the bar.

COLLEEN: I am going to kill myself.

ALY: Colleen. Rick was charming, funny, sexy…. irresistible, you know that.

BECCA: He should have run for office.

ALY: Really, leave the root canals to other men.

BECCA: *(to Aly)* Once a month? Role-playing. Cool. I'm impressed.

COLLEEN: No, I'm serious, I mean it, I'm gonna jump out a window or throw myself in front of a bus, I'm warning you.

Becca and Aly both notice a woman walking towards them, dressed in black, unsteady on her high heels, holding a glass of white wine.

BECCA: Oh my God, it's Vicki!

ALY: What's she doing here?

BECCA: Getting more wasted obviously.

COLLEEN: Don't let her come over here! I hate her! I'll kill her!

Vicki approaches the women. She is tanked.

VICKI: Hey, it's the book group hens.

> *(makes a chicken clucking sound)*

Read any good "libros" lately.

> *(she cackles)*

ALY: Vicki, we are so sorry for your loss.

VICKI: Yeah, yeah I know. It's a tragedy. Frigging Chicago Cubs.

BECCA: The Cubs? What do you mean?

VICKI: Goddamn Cubs gave Ricky a heart attack. During the rain delay he started sweatin', went pale. I gave him a drink, thought that would help but he kept muttering that he was in big trouble. He just kept saying that— "I'm in trouble, I'm in trouble"—it was like he was in another world. I dunno what the hell was goin' on.

BECCA: Maybe he bet against them to win, you know? Maybe he had a big bet against them?

VICKI: I thought of that. He bets big money in football. But why would he bet against his precious Cubs? Doesn't make sense. But men are weird.

BECCA: Yeah, they are. Weird.

ALY: Totally weird.

VICKI: And the thing was, he told me if they won he'd take me to Paris on vacation!

ALY: Really? Paris?

VICKI: We went there on our honeymoon.

COLLEEN: Your honeymoon?

> *Colleen starts crying again.*

VICKI: What's with her?

BECCA: She hates funerals. Can't deal with death.

ALY: And her…her dog…her dog Bread died last week.

VICKI: Bread? That's a stupid name for a dog.

ALY: Well, he really liked bread. The dog.

VICKI: *(looking at Colleen)* Poor baby. Maybe she needs a hug. I
think she needs a hug.

>*Vicki goes to give Colleen a hug. Becca intervenes.*

BECCA: No, no! She needs space now. She'll be okay.

>*Colleen is sobbing silently.*

VICKI: Okay. I get it.

>*(Vicki steps back)*

So gals. I'm sorta on my own, you know?

>*(Becca and Aly nod)*

You think you might let me join your book group now?

>*Colleen collapses into the couch.*

>*Becca and Aly look at each other, and then turn to Vicki.*

BECCA and ALY: Sure? Why not?

>*end play*

English Only

Bryan Stubbles

Produced November 11, 2017 by Otherworld Theatre as part of the 2nd Paragon Sci-Fi Theatre Festival, Chicago

LUANNA: June Thiele
SCIENTIST: Alex Ireys
RUGILĖ: Alex Seligsohn
CADRE: Brett LeBlanc
MARY-JO: Kristina Loy

Director: Jose Nateras

CHARACTERS

MARY-JO (F), Korean-American, 20s+. Speaks English. Knows some Korean.

CADRE (M), 20s+ Political a-hole. In charge of eliminating other languages.

SCIENTIST (M), 20s+ Made this all possible with his invention, the delinguafier.

RUGILĖ (F), Lithuanian immigrant, 20s+. Speaks Lithuanian, Russian and English.

LUANNA (F), Cherokee. 20s+. Speaks Cherokee and English.

Setting: Jail, near future. USA.

*Note: The ethnicities and languages can change according to availability of actors and languages. For example, Mary-Jo could be Cuban-American and know some Spanish. Luanna could be an Afrikaans speaker and so on. Only a couple jokes would change, but the gist would be the same.

LIGHTS UP:

Left side of is dark. The foreign-language moments can use a projector for subtitles if needed.

Two older men, a SCIENTIST and a political CADRE berate her. Cadre armed with a night stick/billy club.

CADRE: You are an enemy of the state.

MARY-JO: I'm nobody's enemy.

CADRE: She feigns speaking English.

MARY-JO: I do speak English. It's my native tongue.

CADRE: We know you speak Korean.

> *Punches her.*

MARY-JO: Yeah. Okay. Years ago with my grandma.

CADRE: This is an English-only country.

MARY-JO: Gae-sekki!

"Son of a bitch" in Korean.

CADRE: Now!

> *Zap! The delinguifier hits her. Nearly knocks her unconscious.*

MARY-JO: Geu shi-

> *More Korean profanity. MARY-JO moans.*

MARY-JO: Nabbeun nom.

"Bad bastard." Zap! The delinguifier hits her again. Knocks her out.

CADRE: That delinguifier is really something. Is she dead?

MARY-JO's chest heaves. Tries to speak.

MARY-JO: Fuck you!

SCIENTIST: She's cured!

CADRE: Mission accomplished.

> *SCIENTIST and CADRE lead a disoriented MARY-JO and EXIT. The MEN return.*

> *LIGHTS UP on left side of stage. A simple partition/*

wall/bars.

LUANNA and RUGILĖ behind the mini-partition.

CADRE: Next!

SCIENTIST: Come on. We've been at this since seven.

CADRE: You're right. A short lunch break won't hurt.

SCIENTIST: I'm starving.

CADRE: Good. You can get us lunch.

CADRE gives his debit card to SCIENTIST.

CADRE: I'll watch the prisoners and you get us something yummy.

SCIENTIST: Quesadillas?

CADRE: Not so often. That chicken adobo was good.

SCIENTIST: I could do goulash.

CADRE: For lunch?

SCIENTIST: Lunch, dinner - anytime.

CADRE: It was rhetorical. Something lighter. Pho is good.

SCIENTIST: Pho it is.

EXIT SCIENTIST, gawking at LUANNA and RUGILĖ.

RUGILĖ: We gotta get out.

LUANNA: How?

RUGILĖ: We'll figure it out. I don't wanna lose my language.

LUANNA: They're not giving us choices.

RUGILĖ: What's your language?

LUANNA: Tsalagi.

RUGILĖ: What?

LUANNA: Cherokee. You?

RUGILĖ: English, Russian and Lithuanian.

LUANNA: I wonder if they have to hit two parts of your brain for that.

RUGILĖ: I don't wanna find out. They might deport me.

LUANNA: What about me? I'm Native. Where they gonna deport

me to? Oklahoma?

RUGILĖ: We could lie.

LUANNA: They've got a test for that.

RUGILĖ: Well, what will we do?

LUANNA: Haven't you seen a women-in-prison movie?

(to CADRE)

Mister!

LUANNA starts to remove shirt.

RUGILĖ: Stop that!

RUGILĖ slaps LUANNA.

LUANNA: Are we doing the catfight trope?

LUANNA claws RUGILĖ, who punches back.

RUGILĖ: No. Something better.

(at CADRE)

Kurva!

LUANNA: Is that Lithuanian?

RUGILĖ: Polish, bitch.

LUANNA: Fuck you.

Slap.

CADRE: Catfight?

Walks toward them.

RUGILĖ: No. I meant that it means bitch in Polish.

LUANNA: Oh. But you speak Russian and Lithuanian.

RUGILĖ: It doesn't matter! Just swear at him in Cherokee.

(at CADRE)

Kad tavę šikanti sutrauktu, pasol nahui!

LUANNA: Duk-shan-ee.

CADRE: What did you say?

RUGILĖ laughs at him.

CADRE: What are you saying?

THEY laugh at him.

LUANNA: Lick my biznik.

CADRE: Speak English!

LUANNA: I just did, kurva.

LUANNA flirts.

LUANNA: You could teach us. I bet you're real smart.

RUGILĖ: He's in charge, isn't he?

LUANNA: They wouldn't let some dummy be in charge.

RUGILĖ: He's no fool.

LUANNA: Teach us.

LUANNA puts her arm around RUGILĖ.

LUANNA: We're ready to learn.

RUGILĖ: Eager beavers.

CADRE: Yeah, you gals want the stick don't ya?

LUANNA laughs.

LUANNA: That?

RUGILĖ: We all know it's the motion of the ocean.

LUANNA: Put us through the motions, poli-stud.

CADRE: Now you gals wouldn't try no funny business, would ya?

LUANNA: Never.

CADRE enters the holding cell (behind the partition). RUGILĖ attacks.

CADRE: We don't have a safe word.

RUGILĖ keeps hitting him. No effect.

RUGILĖ: Luanna! Can't you do something Cherokee?

LUANNA: That's racist.

RUGILĖ beats him badly. LIGHTS DOWN. LIGHTS UP.

CADRE strapped to the chair. The same one MARY-JO got zapped in. LUANNA and RUGILĖ in front.

CADRE: I had this weird dream - you two were in it!

Tries to leave chair. Nope. The LADIES fiddle with the delinguafier.

LUANNA: Can't we recalibrate?

RUGILÈ: There's only two switches: "English" and "Other." This scientist was semi-intelligent.

LUANNA: Yeah, he's got a job no matter what language America is erasing. Let's erase his English.

LUANNA flips switch.

CADRE: What're you broads doing?

LUANNA: When we're done, you'll never be able to call a lady a broad again.

CADRE: Bitches.

RUGILÈ: That, too.

THEY aim it at his head.

LUANNA: Can't we get him in the nuts first.

RUGILÈ: This is serious business. Why are you joking? That pinhead scientist could come back anytime.

CADRE: He will, you little cunts.

RUGILÈ: You're right. Nutcracker time.

THEY aim it at his crotch.

CADRE: Oh, I see. It's just like an S&M game. I get it. Beam me up ladies!

Closes his eyes and grins. The LADIES zap him. Nothing.

LUANNA: Maybe he doesn't have balls?

RUGILÈ: Maybe it was meant to erase languages, not testosterone.

LUANNA: Let's get him where it counts.

Back to head.

CADRE: But but if you do that, I can't speak anything.

LUANNA: I can teach you.

RUGILÈ: Lithuanian and Russian are beautiful languages.

Zap. CADRE screams. No words, only primal screams.

RUGILĖ: Repeat after me: Aš neturiu varpos.

CADRE cries.

CADRE: Aš neturiu varpos.

"I have no penis" in Lithuanian.

RUGILĖ: Me, too.

LUANNA: I believe the proper word is "neither."

LIGHTS DOWN

END OF PLAY

ETHNICALLY AMBIGUOUS
Donna Latham

Production Information

Houston Scriptwriters 10x10, Houston, TX, August 17-26, 2017
   Director and Cast
   Director: Kelvin Douglas
   MARIA: Melissa Rankin
   DIMA: Cheryl Robinson
   PATSY: Ollie H. Holley
   SHAUNEE: Relecha Addison-Williams

20% Theatre Snapshot Festival, The Conservatory 4210 N. Lincoln
Ave, Chicago, IL, 60618 Chicago, IL, August 16-20
   Director and Cast TBA

CHARACTER:

MARIA—dark-haired woman of hard-to-peg ethnic and racial origins, F 20s-30s

Chorus

DIMA—Muslim professional woman; M 30s—40's

PASTY—working-class White woman; F middle-aged

SHAUNEE—Black student; 20s

SETTING AND TIME: An airport, the present

(At rise, MARIA speaks, and CHORUS interrupts her.)

MARIA: I'm ethnically ambiguous….

PATSY: You're not White enough.

DIMA: Not Brown enough.

SHAUNEE: Not Black enough.

MARIA: Ethnically ambiguous.

SHAUNEE: You sure as hell look White to me.

PATSY: She sure as hell don't. *(Shoves SHAUNEE and DIMA).* Give me some space, here. You're breathing down my neck. Cutting off my blood flow.

DIMA: You look just like my cousin Fatima.

SHAUNEE: Your eyes are light. Olive green?

DIMA: Where is your hijab?

MARIA: I'm Christian.

PATSY: The hell you are!

DIMA: Your nose is Middle Eastern—classically Middle Eastern.

PATSY: You ain't no pure breed, that's for sure.

DIMA: You're Persian?

SHAUNEE: Where are you from?

MARIA: It baffles people. My ethnic ambiguity.

PATSY: The hell are you? A white n—

MARIA: A rich stew. Cioppino. Bouillabaisse. Blended from ancient Moors and—

SHAUNEE: Bitch, please.

MARIA: And Romani wanderers.

PATSY: Gypsies? You mean them horrible gypsies? Nobody knows where the hell them swarthy-ass vagrants came from.

MARIA: That's not true. Wanderers originated in northern India.

PATSY: Where's your forehead dot? Hunh? Where's your sari? Sorry, no sari.

MARIA: They migrated to North Africa, Turkey, and Iran. Some as slaves.

SHAUNEE: Bitch, please. Don't you dare go there. Don't inflict an appropriated slave narrative on me.

MARIA: Just hear me out. Please.

PATSY: Gypsies, tramps, and thieves. With their gold teeth and jingle-jangle earrings.

MARIA: I'm a descendant of Black Irish travelers, too.

DIMA: I've always wondered....

SHAUNEE: Me, too....

DIMA: What puts the Black in Black Irish?

MARIA: Well, it's an ambiguous term, of course.

DIMA: Of course.

PATSY: Not White enough.

DIMA: Not Brown enough.

SHAUNEE: Not Black enough.

MARIA: Some historians believe it was shipwrecked survivors of the Spanish Armada.

DIMA: Fascinating...

PATSY: Bullshit! There's not one drop of Spanish blood in me, I promise you. Pure Irish through and through. Whitest people on the planet. 'Cept for the Norwegians. Maybe the Swedes. And them—whaddayacallem—albinos.

MARIA: Others believe it was the Romani.

PATSY: More gypsies. Tinkers, we Irish call 'em. Scam artists.

SHAUNEE: But they're not Black. They're Brown.

MARIA: Or the mixed-raced children of African slaves from the island of Montserrat and the Irish who immigrated there.

SHAUNEE: Seriously?

MARIA: Truly.

SHAUNEE: I've never heard of this.

PATSY: One drop! That's all it takes. One drop of colored blood.

DIMA: Our ancestors voyaged near and far.

PATSY: Mixed and mingled.

MARIA: Fell in love.

PATSY: Did the dirty deed with darkies? Fornicators!

MARIA: Created families and loving bonds.

PATSY: Swindlers. Pickpockets. Frauds, all of 'em.

MARIA: I hail from a long line of wild-haired Sicilians.

PATSY: You look—foreign.

MARIA: At airports, I'm yanked from lines and dragged to the pat-down area.

DIMA: Tell me about it. I'm trapped here now. I'll never see my family again. I feel it deep in my bones, my shattered bones. I can get out, sure. But will that horrible man let me back in?

MARIA: God, that's awful. This is not who we are—who we claim to be.

SHAUNEE: Isn't it? At least the cops don't pull you over and shoot you dead. For driving while black.

MARIA: When I wear my black cape, crowds of people part like the Red Sea.

DIMA: Oh, yes.

MARIA: Convinced there's a suicide bomb strapped to my chest.

DIMA: Boom! My life in a nutshell.

PATSY: Dumbass! Don't yell kaboom around here. I'm loaded for bear.

SHAUNEE: Why don't the cops choke you out? Like they do to all Black people.

MARIA: I know. I truly know. And it sickens me, breaks my heart. It tramples my soul. Why are we like this? What is so deeply shattered, so irretrievably broken in this country?

PATSY: All lives matter!

SHAUNEE: Fuck off.

DIMA: What she said.

MARIA: It wasn't easy growing up in my all-White neighborhood.

SHAUNEE: Wah, wah, wah. Sad trombone.

MARIA: Hell, my own father tortured me. You never know how the genes will shake out in the cioppino. Two of my brothers are fair-haired and freckled, Irish all the way.

PATSY: Halleluia!

MARIA: Another brother? Brown-sugar skin and black Roma eyes. And me? I was—indefinite. My dad, snow-white and blue-eyed, taunted mercilessly. I wasn't skinny-hipped like my cousins, with sleek red hair swaying in a ponytail down my back. I was The Other. Too thick. Too dark. Too—unlike him.

SHAUNEE: Check your privilege!

MARIA: I'm aware.

SHAUNEE: Walk in my boots. Don't give me shit about taunting.

DIMA: Or me.

MARIA: I'm trying—

SHAUNEE   DIMA: About Othering.

MARIA: Look, I know how it sounds. I—

SHAUNEE: You're White.

DIMA: You're so—exotic.

SHAUNEE: You grew up White.

PATSY: Illegal alien! Faker! White-ass wannabee! Why don't you lick one of them DNA sticks? Find out what kinda mutt you really are. And go back to Islam!

DIMA: Islam is not a place. Islam is a monotheistic reli—

PATSY: Talk English! Mr. Trump knows how to handle the likes of you.

SHAUNEE: *(To MARIA.)* You check the White box on all the questionnaires, right?

MARIA: Right. But that—

SHAUNEE: You check them on housing applications.

PATSY: Invading our neighborhoods.

DIMA: College applications.

PATSY: Welfare cheater! Going to school for free while my kids slave away at Mickey D's.

SHAUNEE: *(Tosses PATSY the stink eye for a beat.)* On job applications.

PATSY: Stealing our jobs, you swarthy foreigner frizzhead.

MARIA: I'm an American.

PATSY: Sharia law my ass! Go back to that hellhole you came from, bitch!

MARIA: I was born in this country.

PATSY: Whatever the hell kinda mutt you are? You're not White enough.

DIMA: Not Brown enough.

SHAUNEE: Not Black enough. *(Studies MARIA.)* Your cheekbones, though. And—that hair. Those high haunches.

MARIA: Right? Oh, I'll bet my bubble butt this is why my father tortured me. He's the biggest, most unapologetic racist I know. He's a walking talking stereotype. Trump's got nothing on my father.... Father.... I've learned to use that word in time, in healing and health. Called him my sperm donor, my tormenter, since that's all he was to me. Glaring at me with infinite disgust—fruit of his loins! Hell, I'm the embodiment of his nightmare. And he made me. That's a huge mouthful for a little man to swallow. I hated him for most of my life. But hatred is not the way to solve—

PATSY: Don't give a good goddamn about your whiny-ass story.

MARIA: I'm just trying to say—an authoritarian strongman comes to power? It's gonna push all my buttons.

SHAUNEE: Bottom line? You're not White enough.

DIMA: Not Brown enough.

SHAUNEE: Not Black enough.

DIMA PATSY SHAUNEE: Not enough! Not enough! Not enough!

MARIA: Wait! Listen! I'm just trying to say—I have empathy. I understand.

DIMA: You don't understand.

SHAUNEE: You can't understand.

PATSY: Bullshit! Who needs to understand?

SHAUNEE: You cannot understand my life. That's privilege talking.

DIMA: You'll never understand.

DIMA PATSY SHAUNEE: Not enough! Not enough! Not enough!

MARIA: Enough! Enough! Can't I just be enough? Can't I be me? And you be you? When oh when oh when dear God will everyone just be?

DIMA: There is strength in sisterhood.

SHAUNEE: Strength among us all.

DIMA: America is growing browner, more ambiguous.

SHAUNEE: Non-white populations will keep growing, and—

PATSY: Cuz Welfare mothers got nothing to do but spread their legs and get knocked up. America needs a good cleansing. Scrub out the vermin with bleach and lye.

SHAUNEE: *(Raises hand at PATSY to silence her.)* We were made for this moment.

DIMA: We need you now, friend.

SHAUNEE: Whatever your shade.

DIMA: They have come for the women. They have come for the Muslims.

SHAUNEE: Not this time, motherfuckers.

DIMA: Not this time.

(After several beats, DIMA extends her hand to MARIA, who takes it. SHAUNEE extends her hand to MARIA, who takes it. PATSY crosses her arms and glares at them.)

MARIA: I see you.

SHAUNEE: I hear you.

DIMA: I feel you.

MARIA: We are enough.

END OF PLAY

FIGHTBOOK

James McLindon

White Room Theatre produced FIGHTBOOK as part of its The Big Bite-Size Breakfast Show, which was staged at the Edinburgh Festival Fringe from August 2 through August 28, 2017 at The Pleasance Dome.

CAST:

A-Rowena Grey

B-Thomas Willshire

C-Billy Knowelden

D-Rosie Edwards

Director: Nicholas Brice

Set Requirements: The characters are wherever they might be when posting on social media. Each has a smartphone or laptop. A bare stage works just fine.

Godwin's Law: "As an online discussion grows longer, the probability of a comparison involving Hitler or Nazism approaches 100%."

The First Corollary to Godwin's Law: Said comparison involving Hitler/Nazism ends all intelligent debate.

CHARACTERS:
(In Order Of Appearance)
A: GOOD-NATURED (TILL PROVOKED)

B: WAY TOO SENSITIVE

C: HUMORLESS AND DOCTRINAIRE

D: A PROVOCATEUR (AND A DICK)

Casting Note: Any cast member may be any age, gender or race. Adjust pronouns to suit the cast members. Diverse casting is encouraged.

SETTING: The present. The characters are wherever they might be when posting on social media: a coffee shop, the couch, out for a walk, etc. A bare stage works just fine.

A, B, C, and D each has a smartphone or laptop. Each wears a large letter indicating her/his identity. When they are talking about a post that they are writing, they type on their device. When they are thinking, they do not type. A is good-natured (till provoked). B is too sensitive. C is humorless and doctrinaire. D is a conceited provocateur and a dick. I would advise considering having the actors recite Godwin's Law and its corollary to the audience, perhaps before assuming their places. For example:

A: Godwin's Law:

B: As an online discussion grows longer, the probability of a comparison involving Hitler or Nazism approaches 100%.

C: The First Corollary to Godwin's Law:

D: Said comparison involving Hitler or Nazism ends all intelligent debate.

A: Posting a video of a cute puppy doing something unexpected and charming.

B: Awwww. Heart!

C: (*Not typing*) Stupid.

B: Posting a charming meme involving a photo of a hedgehog with a caption containing a common expression that is given a humorous meaning in juxtaposition with the photo.

A: Oh, good one! (*Typing*) Like.

D: (*Not typing*) Barf.

A: Meme containing a comical statement concerning a current socio-political issue.

B: (*Cheerfully*) Ha! Like!

> *A pause.*

C: Stiffly worded query seeking clarification about the meaning of A's last post.

A: Missing the warning signs and light-heartedly extending the comic sentiment expressed by that post to its logic extreme. Smiley face!

C: Calculated overreaction to feigned misperception of A's position on the socio-political issue as expressed in A's last two posts. And, more in sorrow than in anger, questioning A's commitment to the prevailing orthodoxy of this Facebook bubble on this issue given her/his posting of such an offensive meme.

B: Observing that C makes a good point about the prevailing orthodoxy, but expressing confidence that A didn't mean it that way and of course still adheres to the prevailing orthodoxy of this Facebook bubble on this issue.

D: Cynically piling on to C's feigned misperception of A's position and exaggerating it further with an inapt metaphorical comparison. But (*self-satisfied*) temperately refraining from a comparison to Nazis as unwarranted hyperbole. (*Pause*) For now.

C: Noting that D's insightful point provides further reason why A's commitment to the prevailing orthodoxy of this Facebook bubble must now be called into doubt.

A: (*Not typing*) Are you kidding me? (*Typing*) Calmly clarifying my position …

   A pause.

C: (*Disappointed at the prospect of peace*)

   Grudging acceptance of A's clarification.

A: … and observing that anyone besides a humorless drone would have understood that the post was a joke. And, noting partially feigned deeply wounded feelings that C and D could think me capable of intending their misconstrued version of my post.

D: Grudging acceptance of A's clarification with a non-apologetic apology. And the clear subtext of not being at all convinced.

C: Pedantic instruction that the current socio-political issue is an inappropriate subject for comedy. Forceful, humorless restatement of how all right-thinking people adhering to the prevailing orthodoxy of this Facebook bubble should view this issue.

A: (*Not typing*) Promising self not to engage with these (*snarling*) effing a-holes again. Ignoring knowledge that I will break this promise at the slightest provocation.

   A pause.

D: (*Soft voice and a sly smile*) Quibbling with a veeeeery small part of C's restatement of the prevailing orthodoxy of this Facebook bubble on this issue in order to demonstrate my superior understanding of it.

C: Retorting with mild humor that betrays the clear subtext of not taking D at all seriously (*not typing*) because no one takes D seriously.

D: Restating the quibble a bit more forcefully.

C: Taking gentle exception to D's quibble. And correcting her/his grammar.

D: Elaborating on the quibble and extending it to throw into question a somewhat larger part of C's restatement.

C: Reiterating less gently my exception to D's quibble and implying that s/he may simply lack the intellectual firepower necessary to appreciate the restatement's nuanced reasoning.

D: Declaring that, in light of C's less gentle version of her/his exception to the quibble, it is now apparent that said quibble applies to the entirety of C's restatement, and likely her/his entire worldview. Concluding, more in sorrow than in anger, that C has thus thrown into question her/his commitment to the prevailing orthodoxy of this Facebook bubble ... and by extension her/his very humanity.

A: *(Not typing)* Trying to resist engaging with these a-holes one more time by riffing on a phrase in D's last post in an attempt to inject some humor and lightheartedness into the string. (*Pause as s/he notes the stern faces of C and D, then typing rapidly*) Failing!

D: Again patronizingly reminding A that the current socio-political issue is an inappropriate subject for humor ... especially given that C has not acknowledged the essential truth of my quibble and the incoherent and indeed deeply offensive mess that her/his own restatement is.

C: Stating the restatement even more forcefully ... and with exclamation points!!!

D: Pronouncing that the restatement of the restatement confirms my worst fears about C's view and C himself!!! With exclamations points!!! AND CAPS!!!

B: Expressing the belief that C's restatement and his restatement of his restatement did not mean what it sounded like and confidence that C would soon clarify.

C: Declaring that my restatement and my restatement of that restatement meant <u>exactly</u> what it sounded like, at least to anyone possessing third-grade reading comprehension.

B gasps, upset, then begins to type.

B: Accusing C of being mean.

D: Agreeing that C is mean and sanctimoniously asking for civility from all participants in the Facebook bubble. But also chiding B for being way too sensitive and encouraging her/him to grow up.

B: Accusing D of patronizing me!

C: Agreeing that D is very patronizing. Although B really does need to grow up.

B: (*Not typing*) Stewing offline at how mean C and D are. Unconsciously formulating a passive-aggressive response.

A pause.

A: Posting a video involving a goat and a guinea pig to defuse the tension within the Facebook bubble. (*Considering the stern faces of C and D and B's tears*) Failing.

B: Dramatically announcing the need to take a break from Facebook because it has become toxic or employing some other synonym currently fashionable in the Facebook bubble for "bad."

C: Conceding that B is absolutely right. (*Pause*) S/he should definitely leave.

D: Cautioning B to take care not to let the door hit his backside upon his/her exit.

B: Reaffirming decision to leave with exclamation points!!! AND CAPS!!! (*Not typing*) Not really leaving. But definitely sulking.

A C & D (Not typing) Pausing to review the string, having forgotten what the argument was all about in the first place.

D: Remembering! Stating emphatically that C's position espoused in the restatement led inevitably to a previous, famous historical atrocity, and thus threatens to put this country on the road to ruin. Still refraining from a comparison to Nazis. (*Pause*) For now.

C: Noting that, because D is not a member of the group that was the victim of that historical atrocity, D has no right to invoke it.

D: Asserting that the historical atrocity was not "invoked;" rather, it was merely used by way of comparison.

    C Wondering if D even knows what "invoked" means!

D: Noting God-given right to "invoke" any historical metaphor that I damn well please! (*Pause*) And ... that I am 1/32 a member of the victim group in question. On my mother's side.

B and C: (*Not typing*)

    Bullshit! And fiercely wanting to publicly call bullshit.

C: (*Not typing*) But not daring.

    A pause. Then B begins to type rapidly.

B: Daring!

    D gasps in fury as s/he reads B's post. C is amused.

C: (*Sarcastically*)

    Noting B's previous ostentatious display of leaving and my subsequent astonishment to find her/him still here!

D: (*Mock sorrow*) Responding with deeply wounded outrage that my veracity on such a core part of my identity could be questioned by anyone, let alone someone that I had considered a friend. I. Can't. Even.

C: Noting that s/he must agree with D on this point, although also noting that s/he has offered absolutely no proof of membership in the group. Sanctimoniously expressing the hope that an apology from B to D will soon be forthcoming.

B: (*Not typing*) OMFG! (*Typing*) Refusing to apologize! Asking whether anyone in the Facebook bubble has ever heard D say that he was a 1/32 member of that group.

C: (*Deviously*) Admitting, more in sorrow than in anger, that, now that B mentions it ... no.

A: No also.

D: Citing the intensely private nature of my membership in said group. Excoriating all of them for their privilege of expecting me to "out" myself.

A, B, and C Falling all over ourselves in a race to be the first to deny his right to use the term "out."

C: Winning the race!

D: Blistering attack on C for denying his right! With intemperate language!

C: Blistering attack on D for his intemperate language in his blistering attack on me! With very intemperate language!

A: Attempting again to inject some much-needed humor into the string, this time via a toddler comically mauling a very patient, very large dog.

C and D Swiveling guns of extremely intemperately-worded attacks on A for attempting, once again, to inject humor into a discussion of the current socio-political issue, which is not funny!!! At all!!! With exclamation points!!! AND CAPS!!! AND BOLDING!!!

C: And for finding cruelty to animals amusing.

B: Stating my certainty that neither A, C nor D meant what they said in the manner in which C, D and/or A interpreted it and expressing the wish that we can all just get along.

A, C and D Swiveling all guns onto B and decimating him/her!!! With extremely intemperate language!!! Exclamation points!!! CAPS!!! BOLDING!!! AND ... UNDERSCORING!!!

All four sit with angry expressions and folded arms. A very long pause as the dust settles and the smoke clears. A, C, and D slowly recover, unfolding their arms and looking regretfully at each other. B does not change.

A: Posting a picture of a funny, cute guinea pig video.

A long pause.

C: (*Grudgingly*) "Liking" the cute guinea pig video.

D: (*Grudgingly*) "Laughing facing" the cute guinea pig video.

A, C, and D look at B who is still upset. A pause. Slowly, B shrugs grudgingly.

B: Hearting the cute guinea pig video.

All FOUR relax.

C: Making a statement about the current political issue painfully hewing as closely to the prevailing orthodoxy of this Facebook bubble on this issue as humanly possible, just to confirm all are on the same page again.

All FOUR smile. A long pause. Then:

D: (*Not typing*) Considering the smallest imaginable quibble, one that surely anyone would see the wisdom of immediately. Just to make extra sure that all are on the same page. And see that I am the smartest. (*Pause*) Concluding: best to let it rest. (*Long pause; then typing furiously*) Quibbling anyway.

A, B, and C read it.

A: (*Not typing*) No.

B: (*Not typing*) Dear god, no!

A, B, and D turn to look at a neutral-faced C.

C: (*Not typing*) No. No. Let it go. (*Cracking; typing furiously*) Condemning D as an unreconstructed, unrepentant troublemaker of the first order and of the sort that needs to rounded up and silenced if the prevailing orthodoxy is ever to prevail everywhere!

A pause. C, realizing the significance of what s/he has done, slowly steps back from his/her device. D also steps away from her/his laptop or puts down his/her phone. Takes a deep breath. Then suddenly smiles fiendishly, grabs his device and begins typing furiously)

D: Nazi. Metaphor.

A, B, and C read the new post. Their faces freeze in a gasp of horror.

Blackout.

Flower Child In Blue

Richard Vetere

Developed and presented in the Playwright/Director's Workshop Unit of The Actors Studio in the Ten-Minute Play Festival produced on June 4th 2017 by Jason Furlani.

MICHAEL: Dennis Parlato

SUSAN: Andrea Leigh

LEANN: Burnadair Lipscomb-Hunt

Directed by JoAnna Rhinehart

Producer Jason Furlani JasonFurlani@gmail.com

CHARACTERS:

MICHAEL is a handsome commercial actor in his 60's.

SUSAN is a pretty commercial actress in her 60's.

LEANNE is an attractive commercial director in her 60's.

SETTING & TIME:

The play takes place in New York City in a TV studio. The studio is actually just a black box that is well-lit.

LIGHTS UP ON MICHAEL and SUSAN.

They are an attractive middle-aged couple dressed in suburban clothing gazing off as if looking at some pretty nature picture.

They have silly, smiling faces and are in an odd embrace that looks uncomfortable though it is meant to make them look happily married and content. They speak to one another through frozen smiles.

SUSAN: We had sex.

MICHAEL: Just now?

SUSAN: No. You and I.

MICHAEL: As this couple?

SUSAN: No, as people.

CAMERA FLASHES.

Neither flinches. They are entirely focused since they are professional actors doing a print job for a magazine.

MICHAEL: When?

SUSAN: Spring, late spring. '74. I'm pretty sure.

LEANNE ENTERS. Attractive, in the moment, she is the director.

LEANNE: Suzanne, the sun is setting, it's elegant, it reminds you of your wedding day. You are celebrating your 40th anniversary!

SUSAN flashes a slight smile, her eyes focused on the image of happiness, she lights up.

SUSAN: Susan. My name. It's Susan.

LEANNE ignores her and moves to MICHAEL.

LEANNE: You! Look at her!

He does. She rushes to him, she explains, persuades.

LEANNE: You're Romeo! You're Marc Anthony! In his sixties, of course. This pill will allow you to have her! I want to see you do all that.

MICHAEL: Okay.

LEANNE: But with your eyes. Just your eyes!

MICHAEL: Just my eyes?

LEANNE: Now, show me!

MICHAEL: Show you what? The child? Mar Anthony? Which one?

LEANNE: Surprise me!

MICHAEL does all he could to follow her direction.

LEANNE: Okay, let's try again. Look off this way...and walk but don't really walk. Show us love. Show us senior lust.

LEANNE rushes off stage to stand behind the camera.

SUSAN: Don't tell me you don't remember if we had sex or not.

MICHAEL: It was the seventies, for god's sake.

SUSAN: What an excuse. I can remember who the hell I had sex with. I remember every detail of my life. It's a curse. It's a burden. It's worse than a disease. It is a disease.

MICHAEL: Are you sure it was me?

CAMERA FLASHES

SUSAN: You were in a band.

MICHAEL: Who wasn't in a band back then?

SUSAN: You were Hamlet and I was Ophelia. That's how we met. In a small theater on East Fourth Street. I played her nude.

CAMERA FLASHES

MICHAEL: Who didn't play Ophelia nude back then?

LEANNE rushes out.

LEANNE: No! No! No! You are no longer bored of each others bodies! That was then! Twenty five years of marriage killed every ounce of desire but now you have the blue pill! And you are great lovers! I am not seeing lovers. I am seeing unhappy. I am seeing uninterested. I am seeing something I should not be seeing. Please!

She rushes back to the camera.

SUSAN: You stopped calling and then you slept with my best friend.

CAMERA FLASHES

MICHAEL: What are you talking about?

SUSAN: Jennifer. I want to hear you say her name. Jennifer Watson.

MICHAEL: Jennifer. Watson. Sure. (excited) You know Jennifer? How is she?

CAMERA FLASHES

SUSAN: You broke up with me on a Saturday night. I roamed the West Village finding a stoop on Bedford and I spent the night on that stoop crying.

LEANNE rushes out and silently steps up to SUSAN and fixes her blouse.

LEANNE: Don't you love this man? This long time husband? I want to see that! Please. Can we see that? You live in the same house, you go to the same parties, you share the same children. He is your love! (to Susan) Have we ever worked before?

SUSAN: Maybe.

LEANNE: In the theater. A few years back.

MICHAEL: She did Hamlet. She played Ophelia nude.

LEANNE: Who didn't play her nude back then? Cherry Orchard?

SUSAN: We met at Phil Malone's house party for the opening of his one man show. 1974. Summer. Lower East Side. Avenue A. You told me that I had an aura around me. You called me 'flower child in blue.' I wore blue a lot back then. You walked right up and kissed me.

LEANNE gives her a look, turns and rushes back to the camera.

MICHAEL: You are scary.

SUSAN: Did you have any feelings for me at all?

MICHAEL: What?

SUSAN: I really cared for you.

MICHAEL: I have no idea if I had feelings for you or not. It was nearly half a century ago.

CAMERA FLASHES

SUSAN: So you were using me.

MICHAEL: Using you? How the hell do I know? I was twenty-something. I was using the world. I was using myself. I wanted to be an actor. I wanted to be anything that my parents weren't. And here I am, a million years later, and what am I doing? I'm playing my parents! I'm pretending to be my parents because I need the job, the work, anything! And you are asking me if I had feelings for you back in some decadent, insane drug infested decade! You are insane!

LEANNE rushes to them.

LEANNE: Nice! Really! Nice! Mark, that was wonderful. What I saw? What I needed to see. What the client is searching for! Amazing.

MICHAEL: Thanks.

LEANNE: Now, all I ask is a little of everything you are doing. Do it again. But more!

LEANNE rushes back.

SUSAN: She called you Mark.

MICHAEL: I know.

SUSAN: Your name is Michael.

MICHAEL: I know my name god dam it!

CAMERA FLASHES

They move gently with professional control, smiling, looking off in character.

SUSAN: *(in character)* Look, it's a pretty bird.

MICHAEL: *(in character)* Yes, what a pretty bird.

SUSAN: *(in character)* I still remember how nice your body felt.

MICHAEL: I barely remember yesterday.

SUSAN: We get free samples. Do you want to go back to my place after this and catch up on our sex play? You can take all the blue pills you want. I don't live far from here.

MICHAEL: I don't use Viagra.

LEANNE rushes out. She stops in front of SUSAN.

LEANNE: 'Flower Child in Blue.' You had changed my life back then that night. There hasn't been a day that goes by that I don't remember. You know why? Because that night was the night I went home and made a promise to myself to live my life to the fullest. I made a promise to myself to follow all of my dreams. I was a singer, an actor, a director a writer or so I believed. I'm not sure if you know this but you were so innocent that night. Though we never saw one another again you had become my muse. Every time things go tough I think of that night. I kissed you that night because I wanted to thank you.

LEANNE kisses her on the cheek.

MICHAEL: Oh wow.

LEANNE: But unfortunately, my life became exactly what I didn't want it to be. I gave up singing, acting, writing and even real directing. I got married to an actor who couldn't act his way out of a paper bag, had four ungrateful children moved to muddy Upstate New York and live in a drafty old house. Now I direct Viagra print jobs.

She quickly rushes to the camera off stage.

MICHAEL: I do not have erectile dysfunction.

SUSAN: I'm sad. I made her sad and I'm sad about that.

MICHAEL: Was it good? The sex?

SUSAN: We did it on my roof. Looking at the World Trade Center.

MICHAEL: Lying down?

SUSAN: Standing up.

They move and sway as if in a very slow motion dance.

MICHAEL: *(in character)* Is that our lovely house over there?

SUSAN: *(in character)* The house we bought together. The house we lived in for most of our lives.

They turn and continue to pretend to walk and stay in character.

CAMERA FLASHES

MICHAEL: *(in character)* Is that our road?

SUSAN: *(in character)* If you want it to be our road it can be.

MICHAEL: *(in character)* That is our road. Look how it stretches off into the sunlight. It goes so far I can't see it past the trees.

LEANNE rushes over to them. She stops.

LEANNE: That's a wrap. Perfect. Such a beautiful couple. It was so fun shooting you both today. When you leave please sign out. And there are free product samples on the table.

SUSAN: I am sorry I made you sad.

LEANNE: I'm glad to see you made it. I always wondered what happened to you.

SUSAN: *(smiles)* When I find out what happened to me I'll let you know.

They share a smile and LEANNE exits.

MICHAEL: Grab a bag of those little helpers. And let's go to your place. Maybe I can find those lost decades.

He grabs her hand. She give him a big smile and they rush off.

LIGHTS OUT

END OF PLAY

Richard Vetere

FOR MR. CUDDLES

Erin Moughon

Originally Produced by Equity Library Theater
August 19, 2017 at The Harry Belafonte Library

Directed by Erin Moughon
CAST:
> MOLLY: Sarah Teed
> SARAH: Kendra Augustin
> BETH: Emily Long

CHARACTERS:

Molly: F, late 20s-late 30s (or older if you wish); loved her cat (a little too much), dramatic, Sarah's sister

Sarah: F, late 20s-late 30s (or older if you wish); practical, Molly's sister

Beth: F, any age over 25, a vet, no-nonsense

SETTING:

A pet cemetery

TIME:

Now

A pet cemetery, however you chose to represent it. Except it shouldn't be like a Stephen King novel. It should be nice. Whatever a nice pet cemetery is to you. (Unless you can't imagine a nice one. Then ask someone you know who can.) It is raining. Molly is in full mourning. Sarah is annoyed to be there. There are many empty seats. Molly gets up to speak.

MOLLY: Thank you all for coming today. I had expected more people, but this…this is nice.

SARAH: It's a cat. Did you really expect more people?

MOLLY: No interrupting the eulogy!

SARAH: Whatever.

MOLLY: As I was saying before I was so rudely interrupted. Today we are gathered to mourn the passing of Mr. Fluffybottom McWhiskers Cuddles the Third. Or as his friends called him Mr. Cuddles.

SARAH: Waitwaitwait. Fluffybottom? McWhiskers? Where the hell did you come up with that?

MOLLY: You're ruining the funeral!

SARAH: You're an adult woman throwing a funeral for a cat. I think something is already ruined.

MOLLY: Why are you even here if you're just going to mock everything I say?

SARAH: Because you're paying my half of rent this month.

MOLLY: Not if you keep interrupting!

SARAH: Alright. Alright. Continue talking about Mr. Fluffernutter.

MOLLY: Mr. Fluffybottom McWhiskers Cuddles the Third!

SARAH: That. Continue.

MOLLY: Mr. Cuddles was more than a pet. He was a constant companion. A true friend. The love of my life.

Sarah laughs noticeably, but attempts to cover it up.

MOLLY: Yes?

SARAH: *(trying to contain laughter)* No…nothing.

MOLLY: Mr. Cuddles was the love of my life.

Sarah bursts out laughing. Molly shoots her a look of death.

SARAH: I'm sorry. I'm sorry. It's just…a cat? The love of your life? Doesn't that seem…

MOLLY: What?

SALLY: Weird? Gross? Sad?

MOLLY: What? No! Ew! You're sick!

SARAH: You're the one who said love of my life.

MOLLY: Platonic love. Platonic love of my life. I didn't think I needed to clarify that.

SARAH: You never know.

MOLLY: As I was saying, Mr. Cuddles was more than a cat. He was

Beth rushes in.

MOLLY: For the love of Pete!

BETH: Ms. Arnold?

MOLLY: Oh! Beth! Thank you for coming! I had just gotten started on my eulogy. You didn't miss much.

BETH: Ms. Arnold. I've told you. I prefer Dr. Baker. I am not here for the funeral.

SARAH: Molly. What did you do?

BETH: She left a frantic message on my answering machine. Something about life and death and needing Mr. Cuddles' records immediately.

MOLLY: Yes! Thank you Beth!

BETH: Dr. Baker.

MOLLY: Dr. Baker. *(reading through folder)* A-ha!

SARAH: What?

MOLLY: It seems that Mr. Cuddles was

SARAH: What?

MOLLY: I was pausing for suspense. Do you have to ruin everything?

SARAH: How was I supposed to know?

MOLLY: Read the room.

SARAH: We're outside.

MOLLY: I meant figuratively.

BETH: Can I go? I have a patient waiting.

MOLLY: No, Beth.

BETH AND SARAH: Dr. Baker.

MOLLY: You should be here for this.

BETH: For what?

MOLLY: Mr. Cuddles was...MURDERED!

SARAH: Really? Molly, I'm so

BETH: No, he wasn't.

MOLLY: But...it says right here. Cause of death BETH: *(pointing to file)* Old age.

MOLLY: Oh. But he was…

BETH: 21.

MOLLY: But that's not that old.

BETH: It's 147 in cat years.

MOLLY: Really?

SARAH: That doesn't sound right.

MOLLY: He had to have been murdered. Sarah hated him so much.

BETH: I think I would know. I am a vet. With a lot of patients. So if you'll excuse me.

SARAH: Sarah, what? Hold on, Dr. Baker. I may need a witness.

BETH: Sure. *(sitting down)* I don't have a veterinary practice to return to or anything.

SARAH: You thought I killed your cat.

MOLLY: What? I…No! I didn't…how could you…what?

BETH: You did imply it pretty strongly.

MOLLY: Whose side are you on, Beth?

BETH: Dr. Baker. And no one's! I take that back. The cat's. I'm on the cat's side.

SARAH: So you staged this whole funeral thing to accuse me of murdering your cat?

MOLLY: Staged? Excuse me? This is a high-class funeral for a beloved pet.

SARAH: And?

MOLLY: A venue can serve two purposes.

SARAH: How could you think I would kill your cat?

MOLLY: Oh, I don't know. "Molly, your stupid cat knocked over my computer!" "Molly, your idiot cat clawed my sweater!" "Molly, your evil cat peed on me!"

SARAH: You'll have to admit the peeing was spiteful.

MOLLY: He knew you hated him!

SARAH: I didn't hate him!

BETH: I might have hated him if he peed on me.

MOLLY: Thank you, Beth.

BETH: Dr...nevermind.

SARAH: I hated how much time you spent with him.

MOLLY: But he needed me!

SARAH: That's my point! I was always second. "Sarah, I can't go out tonight. Mr. Cuddles needs his insulin shot." "Sarah, you'll just have to sell those Hamilton tickets. Mr.Cuddles needs to be watched so he doesn't eat his stitches." "Sarah, Mr. Cuddles is so much more important than you and his every need dictates every aspect of my life."

MOLLY: Not every aspect.

SARAH: He sneezed, and you called out for work.

MOLLY: At least I care about something! You don't care about anything!

SARAH: I care about you, you idiot shut in!

MOLLY: Really?

SARAH: Yeah. You're my sister. Of course I care about you.

MOLLY: You have a really weird way of showing it.

SARAH: Yeah. I'm your sister.

BETH: And that is lovely, *(holding up cell phone)*, but that is my office, and I have to…

> *Both sisters start crying in a ridiculous manner. Or not ridiculous, but I see it as ridiculous. Or semi-ridiculous. They mean it, but it's weird to have spontaneous crying. Or not, since you know, sisters. Sister relationships are complicated.*

MOLLY: *(crying)* So you love me?

SARAH: *(crying)* Of course!

MOLLY: *(crying and going to hug Sarah)* This is just like the end of *Frozen.*

SARAH: *(crying)* This is better because it's real!

BETH: So I'll just…

> *Sarah and Molly go to hug, trapping Beth in the middle. It is as awkward as you would imagine. Or more awkward. It's really awkward. Sarah and Molly cry more and more. Beth just stands there.*

SARAH: Let's go really honor Mr. Cuddles.

MOLLY: You mean it?

SARAH: Yeah. He deserves more than this.

MOLLY: You're the best sister.

SARAH: No, you're the best.

MOLLY: No, you're the best.

> *This continues as they leave. We should still be hearing, "No, you're the best." Beth is left alone. She looks around. She starts to leave and stops. She starts to leave and stops. She starts to leave and stops.*

BETH: I'm free? *(pause)* I'm free! I can finally leave!

> *The phone rings.*

BETH: Yes? The dog ate what? I'm on my way.

> *She leaves. End of play.*

GOLD STANDARD

Lisa Bruna

GOLD STANDARD premiered at The Kraine Theatre in Manhattan on May 26, 2017 as part of the 17th Annual EstroGenius Festival, produced by FRIGID New York @ Horse Trade in association with Manhattan Theatre Source. GOLD STANDARD was included in the festival's evening of short plays, curated by Deborah Long. The performance was directed by Melissa Skirboll and featured Devorah Palladino as Ashley, Nitin Madan as Doug, and Nicholas Palladino as Terrance.

CHARACTERS:

>ASHLEY: (Female, 30s-40s) A sweet-talking woman who is "prettier than her picture" and, surprisingly, more than meets the eye.

>DOUG: (Male, 30s-40s) Ashley's suitor; he is neatly dressed, well-mannered and socially astute.

>TERRANCE: (Male, 30s-40s) Ashley's charismatic and opinionated life coach.

TIME:

>Present day. It's a Sunday afternoon.

PLACE:

>A trendy outdoor café.

Setting: A trendy outdoor café.

At rise: Doug stands next to a table. He waves over his date, Ashley, as she approaches.

DOUG: Ashley?

ASHLEY: Hello, Doug.

DOUG: Wow!

ASHLEY: Wow?

DOUG: Yes, wow. You're even prettier than your profile picture.

ASHLEY: Thanks! That's so funny. Everybody tells me that.

DOUG: I got us a table with a view.

ASHLEY: A view of what?

DOUG: A view of this gorgeous countryside. It's absolutely magnificent.

ASHLEY: *(looking around)* Oh, I didn't notice.

DOUG: *(pulling out her chair)* I hope you like al fresco.

ASHLEY: *(she sits)* I prefer iced tea.

DOUG: *(he sits)* I'm sure that can be arranged. They do a wonderful cold-brew.

ASHLEY: I see. So you've been here before.

DOUG: Many times. It's one of my favorite Sunday brunch spots. Zagat's calls it "a gem among the rubble."

ASHLEY: Ever bring a date here?

DOUG: Actually, I ... wait ... why? Would that be a good thing or a bad thing if I did?

ASHLEY: What do you mean?

DOUG: Are you one of those women who likes a guy to do everything new with her? No repeats? No bringing her to places he's already been with girlfriends past?

ASHLEY: Hmmm, that's a good question. I'm not sure how I feel about that.

DOUG: In that case, let's forget I mentioned it. *(to himself)* Wow, you're off to a great start, Doug.

ASHLEY: Oh no, do you talk to yourself?

DOUG: I was just…

ASHLEY: Because I've known guys who talk to themselves. They usually have deep-rooted issues, do you know what I mean?

DOUG: Speaking of deep-rooted, I once dated a woman who talked to her houseplants!

ASHLEY: *(she gasps)* My aunt talks to her gladiolas!

DOUG: See?

ASHLEY: My neighbor actually talks to his dog! Can you believe it?

DOUG: Huh, is that one strange, really? I mean, I think most people talk to their pets at some point or other.

ASHLEY: You didn't let me finish. This guy talks to his dog … in Spanish. Crazy, right?

DOUG: Is it though?

ASHLEY: I mean, how's the dog supposed to understand him? Dogs don't speak Spanish. *(She laughs.)* Oh, this is fun. I like talking to you, Doug.

DOUG: So then, no regrets so far… right?

ASHLEY: Not so far. But you never know what could happen. I like to leave my brain wide open for any possibility. That's called being a lateral thinker… *(unsure)* or a *literal* thinker maybe.

DOUG: And a very pretty one at that.

ASHLEY: You're sweet! You remind me of my dad. He used to say, "Ashley dear, it's a good thing you've got your looks to fall back on."

DOUG: Oh… no… I didn't mean it like that, I…

ASHLEY: He was such a wonderful man. I bet he would've approved of a guy like you.

DOUG: Speaking of approval, I'm glad your life coach approves of me.

ASHLEY: Who, Terrance? Oh, I don't know about that.

DOUG: But, didn't you say you won't date a man until Terrance gives his stamp of approval?

ASHLEY: Yes, that's right. Terrance is brilliant. I trust him completely.

DOUG: Then I must have his approval … right?

ASHLEY: What makes you say that?

DOUG: Well, you're sitting across from me, aren't you? So, he obviously said it was okay for you to be here... on this date ... alone ... with me.

ASHLEY: Oh, he'd never allow that.

DOUG: Allow you to be here?

ASHLEY: No, not that part, the other part.

DOUG: On a date? With me?

ASHLEY: No, no, the *other* part.

DOUG: Alone?

ASHLEY: That's the part!

Terrance breezes in wearing a satchel over his shoulder. He approaches the table, pulls out a chair and sits beside Ashley. He drops the satchel down next to him.

TERRANCE: Well, *that* was an ordeal, but I finally found parking. Can you believe there's no valet at a place like this? Hoo-wee! I need a cold beverage immediately!

ASHLEY: Terrance, this is Doug.

DOUG: *(confused)* Oh look... Terrance is …. here.

TERRANCE: Cheers! *(He raises a water glass, takes a long gulp, and sighs.)*

DOUG: So, is he staying? I mean, is he joining us... on our date?

ASHLEY: Doug, you said you understood my rule. No dating unless Terrance approves.

DOUG: Wow.

TERRANCE: *(looking around)* Wow, indeed! This place is fabulous. Zagat-rated! Can you believe this view?

DOUG: Yes. I can actually. I picked this table specifically *for* the view. I was hoping Ashley would like it.

TERRANCE: *Like* it? She *loves* it!

ASHLEY: I *do* love it… thank you, Terrance!

DOUG: I'm sorry, do you want to switch chairs?

ASHLEY: No, why?

DOUG: It just occurs to me that you may not be getting the best view from where you're sitting.

ASHLEY: Oh no, silly, it's just that I like to get Terrance's views on things, that's all.

DOUG: Wow, that's a little unusual. I mean… wow.

ASHLEY: You sure say 'wow' a lot. Is that a pattern with you?

TERRANCE: *Good,* sweetie! See how you're starting to recognize patterns? You're getting so much better at this. *(He pulls a notepad from his satchel and begins writing on it.)*

ASHLEY: I *am* getting better, right?

DOUG: I'm sorry … patterns?

TERRANCE: Ashley's been working to deepen her understanding of the inner-workings of the male mind. She does this by consciously looking for patterns in male behavior … like the one she just recognized in you. *(to Ashley)* Well done, sweetie.

ASHLEY: Thanks, Terrance!

DOUG: Wow. Are you two for real?

TERRANCE: There's another one.

DOUG: Another one what?

ASHLEY: Another 'wow.'

TERRANCE: You just said it again.

DOUG: Wait… so… you notice I use the word 'wow' two maybe three times and you're calling that a pattern?

ASHLEY: It's actually been five or six times since we sat down. Maybe seven.

TERRANCE: Definite pattern. *(He writes it down.)* DOUG: No, no, there's no pattern. Look, I *randomly* used an innocuous three-letter word. I promise you, there's no hidden agenda here.

TERRANCE: *(He gives Ashley a knowing glance.)* Truth is, Doug, men rarely engage in random behavior.

ASHLEY: Terrance is right. Everything a man says or does is deliberate ... it all means *something*.

DOUG: *(to himself)* Oh god, here we go.

ASHLEY: And plus he talks to himself.

TERRANCE: Mmmm, I see. *(He writes it down.)*

DOUG: What are you doing? Are you taking notes? Look, I don't appreciate being psychoanalyzed by strangers. This is incredibly insulting and *not* what I signed on for!

TERRANCE: Hey, hey, hey, hey, let's not allow our emotions to get the better of us, Doug. As I'm sure you must Know, *emotionality* is a feminine trait. You'd be wise not to exhibit too much of it on a first date lest you give Ashley – and all the rest of us – the wrong impression about your ...*maleness.*

DOUG: I'm sorry, are you questioning my masculinity now? Yeah, no, that's not an issue. Ask anyone I know. I was head coxswain of my rowing team! Doesn't get much manlier than that, bud!

TERRANCE: *(He writes the word.)* Coxxxx...sssswain.

DOUG: *(to Ashley)* Is this guy gonna stay the whole time?

TERRANCE: It's for your own good, Doug. I can act as a safety net for this entire transaction. *(leaning in to Doug)* Trust me, women have a tendency to hear things they want to hear whether we say them or not, you know what I mean? It's a biological imperfection. They can't help it. They misread our verbal cues all the time. Then they move on to misreading our *non*-verbals. And that's when things get wonky.

DOUG: I'm pretty sure we passed wonky a while ago.

ASHLEY: *(near tears)* What's *that* supposed to mean? What does he mean by that, Terrance? I thought we were having a nice time.

TERRANCE: Shhhhhh, it's okay, sweetie. Listen, Doug, I have to ask you to watch your tone. You know, Ashley had high hopes for you.

DOUG: Yeah, well I had high hopes too. I was looking forward to a nice lunch with the one woman on ModernMingle-dot-com who caught my attention with her wit and wisdom and beauty.

Yet in a strange turn of events, I now find myself sitting across the table from someone who oddly can't seem to form a thought without input from her .... *Svengali* or whatever you are... and I suddenly feel the need to defend my own.... my...... *(He gestures to indicate his own body.)*

TERRANCE: Aaahhhh, so *that's* the real issue here. Your masculinity has been called into question. Could it be, Doug, that I've triggered some deeply suppressed ambiguity related to your sexuality that you haven't had the courage to explore until now? And, if so, shouldn't you be *thanking* me? *(leaning in to Ashley)* Pay attention, sweetie, I do believe we're making a breakthrough. *(He takes more notes.)*

DOUG: A breakthrough? What? No! There's nothing breaking through here. And there's definitely no ambiguity, I can assure you! I mean, I'm all for gender fluidity or whatever, but I don't actively participate in... I don't... I'm not ... *(He takes a stronger stand.)* I am *all man*... through and through... Is that not obvious? Would you stop writing please?

ASHLEY: I see what you mean, Terrance. And I have something else to contribute.

TERRANCE: Go ahead, sweetie. What've you got?

ASHLEY: Well, earlier in our conversation, before you got here, Doug asked if I was the type of girl who gets upset if a guy takes me places where he's already taken other girls.

TERRANCE: And?

ASHLEY: Well ... *am* I?

DOUG: Wait, are you asking *him* how you feel?

ASHLEY: Do you want to know the answer or not?

DOUG: I want to know *your* answer, not his version of your answer.

ASHLEY: But Terrance *cares* about me. He *respects* me. Who better to help shape my views than a man who looks out for my best interests?

DOUG: *(trying to keep calm)* Okay, Ashley, look, I'm sure you're a fine person, but I don't think this is working out.

ASHLEY: Oh my god. Are you breaking up with me?

DOUG: Breaking up? We haven't even.... look, I gotta be honest with you...

TERRANCE: Aha! At long last, *honesty!* See that, Doug? Doesn't it feel better to open up and dig deep inside to discover your own authentic self?

DOUG: As long as we're digging for truth, Terrance, why don't you tell us where it is you got your training?

TERRANCE: Which training is that now?

DOUG: Your life-coach training? Don't you need some sort of license for this sort of thing?

TERRANCE: Pfffft! There's no training for the kind of work I do. This is a natural god-given talent. In case you hadn't noticed, Doug, there's a pecking order in this world with men at the top of the food chain. And when we each play our proper roles as the creator intended, life works better for all of us.

DOUG: Wow, that just sounds so... shockingly ..... patriarchal!

TERRANCE: The word you're looking for is 'protective.' Clearly, you haven't given much thought to the concept of moral paternalism. If you had, you'd know it's our inherent duty as men to protect those less capable of protecting themselves, i.e., the lovely ladies in our lives. If you had even the vaguest sense of this, Doug, then you'd understand why my presence here is good for all of us.

DOUG: How do you figure?

TERRANCE: By working my magic to improve Ashley's dating skills, I'm making her a better person – and a better catch for you, I might add. *(He winks.)*

ASHLEY: Isn't he brilliant? I told you he was brilliant.

Ashley's attention is suddenly pulled toward an event happening at the next table.

TERRANCE: And the beautiful part is that if my input doesn't ultimately result in a better life for Ashley, well, that's not my burden to bear. As long as I've done my part. Because at some point, frankly, it's out of my control. I'm here to help her be the best Ashley she can be. The rest is up to her. Understand?

DOUG: I think I do. And frankly I find it all pretty revolting.

ASHLEY: Terrance, look! See that couple over there? He just showed her a ring. Ooh, they're going to get married. Just think, this is the beginning of their happily ever after. And here we are witnessing it!

TERRANCE: Look again, Ashley. The girl said no. Looks like their happy-ever-after is dead in the water.

ASHLEY: *(deflated)* But ... why?

TERRANCE: Who knows, sweetie. Maybe she's just not that into him.

ASHLEY: Aw, that is just so sad.

DOUG: Hold on a minute... did you just quote that pop psychologist guy? The one with the book deal and the movie and the talk show?

TERRANCE: I don't know what you're talking about.

DOUG: You just said she's probably *(air quotes)* "not that into him." Is that your professional diagnosis, doc?

TERRANCE: I never claimed to be a doctor. *(He smiles.)* I'm more of a life expert.

DOUG: And your expertise includes the inside track on whether or not people are "into" each other?

ASHLEY: It's okay, Doug-honey. You don't have to worry about that with me. I promise I will not say no when you ask for my hand.

DOUG: Your what?

ASHLEY: Now that Terrance has helped you open up and explore your sexuality... and your anger issues... and your inner authentic self, I will accept you unconditionally. As long as we both shall live. For better or worse.

DOUG: Hold on now! I don't know where you thought this was heading, but I have no intention of going down that path with you.

ASHLEY: No intention? What do you mean? Terrance, what's he talking about? Why is he sending mixed signals all of a sudden?

TERRANCE: *(He pulls a book from his satchel and quickly pages through it.)* I'm not sure, sweetie. It *could* be that he's dismissive-avoidant. Or it's possible he's just your run-of-the-mill commitment-phobe. Not willing to settle down... at least not with you.

>ASHLEY: *Not with me? (to Doug) So now I'm not good enough for you?*

DOUG: I didn't say that!

ASHLEY: So then you admit you're a commitment-phobe! *Nobody's* good enough for you, is that it?

DOUG: I didn't say that either.

ASHLEY: Because a commitment-phobe I can deal with. At least I know it's not something I did to push you away.

DOUG: Push me away? Look, we're not even ...

TERRANCE: Sweetie, listen to this. (he reads) "A commitment-phobe suffers from intense inner conflict and fear, often related to something he experienced in childhood, like a parental figure who was never there."

DOUG: Wow... okay, you're way off! I happen to be close with both of my parents. Dad and I play golf on Thursdays.

ASHLEY: Then why won't you marry me?

DOUG: *Marry* you? I barely *know* you! Why don't you marry your crazy love guru over here. You two seem perfect for each other.

ASHLEY: Aawww, baby, you're jealous! He's jealous, Terrance! Isn't that too cute?

>*As Doug launches into a rant, Terrance writes in his notepad, fast and furiously.*

DOUG: Look, for your information, jealousy isn't cute, nor is it an indicator of how much someone is "into" you. It's a symptom of neurotic insecurity and lack of self-esteem... neither of which I suffer from. I also don't suffer under some grand delusion that men need to protect women by controlling their behaviors or opinions or, god-help-us, their lives. *(Doug stands and addresses Terrance.)* And, by the way, the woman sitting next to you has a name. Regardless of how beautiful or kind or appealing she happens to be, you're not doing her any favors by referring to her as "sweetie." It demeans you both! Now if you'll excuse me ... *(He starts to walk away.)*

ASHLEY: Wow!

TERRANCE: Wow indeed.

DOUG: Oh that's nice. Now you mock me with a couple of parting *wows*. Just one last zinger for the road, is that it?

A transformation! Ashley drops the "helpless girl" act and reveals herself as a straight-talking intellectual, stopping Doug in his tracks.

ASHLEY: No, Doug. I meant *wow* in the sincerest sense of the word. In fact, it's the perfect word to punctuate my delight at your fascinating display of unmitigated equalism. I share your concern over women being prohibited from expressing original ideas, and I applaud your aversion to the concept of moral paternalism, *(She pages through Terrance's notepad to find a phrase she wants to quote)* citing it as... "shockingly patriarchal." Furthermore, you win big points for shunning the notion of unpremeditated matrimony, *and* for understanding that jealousy is a neurotic behavior and not something to be encouraged. I particularly enjoyed that you admonished Terrance for his use of the term "sweetie" in place of my name. Indeed, my name is not sweetie. *(beat)* But it's not Ashley either. It's Sydney. *(She extends her hand and a smile.)* And I'm very pleased to meet you, Doug.

DOUG: *(confused, he shakes her hand)* I'm sorry, what just happened here?

TERRANCE: Douglas, meet Dr. Sydney Gold, biological anthropologist, research fellow at The Gold Center for Genomic Studies, author of The Evolution of Humankind ..... and, as you've witnessed here today, woman in search of a date.

DOUG: But ... what happened to Ashley?

ASHLEY: Ashley is simply an alternative personality I adopt when conducting my social experiment, which is necessary to root out the less enlightened men on the dating horizon and establish a base line for potential interconnectedness. Most men will *say* they have progressive views. But unless they're put to the test, there's really no way to be sure. I've been waiting quite a while for a truly enlightened man to emerge. And by all measures, that appears to be you, Doug!

DOUG: So the approval you talked about earlier was never meant to come from Terrance. This was all about meeting *Ashley's* standards? ... or rather.... Dr. Gold's standards?

ASHLEY: Call me Sydney.

DOUG: *(to Terrance)* Okay, so then, who are *you?* Are you using an alias too?

TERRANCE: Me? No, my name really is Terrance. Terrance Baxter – union actor in search of a gig. You may have caught me as Rum Tum Tugger from the national tour back in the 90s? ... Remember me? *(He gestures with "Cats" hands.)* ...no?

ASHLEY: *(clearing her throat, a signal to Terrance)* So, anyway ...

TERRANCE: Yes anyway.... I *do* know when to make an exit. Au revoir you two... this cat is outta here!

> *Terrance gives his best "Cats" bows and exits, leaving Ashley at the table. Doug pulls out his chair and sits next to her. He smiles at her. She smiles back.*

ASHLEY: *(meekly)* Surprise.

DOUG: Wow, you're something else.

ASHLEY: Good something else? Or bad something else?

DOUG: Well now... that remains to be seen. *(beat)* And I do have one question for you.

ASHLEY: Yes?

DOUG: How *do* you like the view?

ASHLEY: It is truly spectacular.

> *Lights fade to black.*

HOME INVASION
Krista Knight

Produced by Actors Theatre of Louisville, Les Waters, Artistic Director, Kevin E. Moore, Managing Director, at the 2017 Humana Festival, April 8, April 9, 2017

Directed by Krissy Vanderwarker

Produced by the Actors Theatre of Louisville

The cast was as follows:

GHOST 1 – Andrea Syglowski

GHOST 2 – Kelly McAndrew

KATY – Regan Moro

TOM – Sam Breslin Wright

CHARACTERS:

    Ghost one

    Ghost two

    Katy

    Tom

SETTING:

    A fancy Tribeca Loft.

    There are jewels and phones placed about

Two ghosts in white sheets with eye holes in them.

GHOST TWO plays a snythy ghost riff on a keyboard.

GHOST ONE: It's not spooky enough.

GHOST TWO: Give me a second.

GHOST ONE: I'm looking for something 'bone-chilling.'

GHOST TWO: My hair is on end. Your hair isn't on end?

GHOST ONE: 'Bone-chilling' is the feeling we want to convey, I think.

GHOST TWO: Let it soak over you a little.

GHOST ONE: How about we add a little—

GHOST ONE joins ghost riff – maybe on some bongos.

GHOST TWO: Oh I like that!

GHOST ONE: getting into the 'spirit'

Yeah here we go.

GHOST TWO: You're feeling it.

GHOST ONE: I'm feeling it.

GHOST TWO: You're feeling spooky.

GHOST ONE: Very spooky!

GHOST TWO: I think we can kill them with fear alone this time.

GHOST ONE: Oh I don't know if we're there yet.

GHOST TWO: Your heart stops. It's science.

GHOST ONE: I don't know.

GHOST TWO plays some more on the keyboard.

GHOST TWO: How about now?

GHOST ONE: Oh I like that.

GHOST TWO: You like that.

GHOST ONE: We're good ghosts.

GHOST TWO: We make the heart muscles thicken.

GHOST ONE: The blood back up.

GHOST TWO: Tissue swell.

GHOST ONE: Breath get short.

GHOST TWO: Skin clam.

GHOST ONE: Lungs fill with fluid.

GHOSTS: Feet fill with fluid!

Sound of lock being picked.

GHOST TWO: Uhoh uhoh someone's here!

Home invaders in ski masks enter.

GHOSTS: Shhh shhh shhh shhh!

KATY: Wow!

TOM: Come on.

KATY: Look at this place!

TOM: 'In and out' what happened to in and out! ·

KATY: re: keyboard

I used to have one of these.

KATY plays some keys.

TOM: Be quiet – don't – don't *play* it!

KATY: There's nobody home. What part of "they're in Miami for the week" don't you understand?

TOM: Please don't be rhetorical, it's demeaning—

KATY: Yeah ok.

TOM: You should respect me enough not phrase things that way when I tell you I don't like it when you phrase things that way.

KATY: You sound just like my ex.

TOM: Did you rob houses with your ex? Hey. Hey. Hey. Did you rob houses with your ex? Hey. Which ex?

GHOST TWO sneaks up and plays a ghost riff.

TOM: What was that?

KATY: Did you hear an echo?

TOM: ….Maybe they have on a radio?

KATY: Yeah—Okay….

GHOST TWO: It's bone chilling – look look look – it's chilling their bones!

GHOSTS: Brrrrrrrrrr!

GHOST ONE: Adrenaline is starting to pump.

GHOST TWO: Heart rate is going up.

GHOST ONE: Blood vessels are dilating.

GHOST TWO: Pupils enlarging.

GHOST ONE: Breath quickening.

GHOST TWO: Muscles tensing.

GHOST ONE: Nervous system overstimulating.

GHOST TWO: Mania manifesting!!

GHOST ONE: We are such good ghosts!

> *GHOST ONE knocks something over or off.*

KATY & TOM: *startled* Ah!

GHOST ONE: Oops—got excited.

TOM: re falling object

> Geeze be careful!

KATY: What—I didn't do anything!

TOM: You're knocking things over.

KATY: I haven't moved!

TOM: You're being reckless!

KATY: Who cares what happens to this stuff—we're here to steal it, TOM.

TOM: SHUT UP SHUT UP SHUT UP what is wrong with you!? Don't use my name!?

KATY: What—they don't have a surveillance camera—I checked— I'M not an idiot—what's wrong with *you?*

TOM: Demeaning phrasing, once again! If there's no camera, why are we in ski masks?

KATY: Then take it off—

> *KATY goes for TOM's mask but he pulls back.*

TOM: No, I like mine! What if they come home early?

KATY: They are GONE. GONE. I'll show you on my phone how gone they are.

>*KATY takes out phone.*

KATY: See? Status after status of how they are in Miami until Weds.

>Tues, August 18: "Wow, I can't wait to have fun with Mario and the girls in the South Beach Four Seasons Penthouse."

>Friday: "I wish I could take all my jewelry but want to travel light so leaving most of it at home. Yacht emoii sad face"

>Sunday: "Oh my god—Mario just bought another iPhone for Deanna—how many expensive electronics can one apt. hold?"

>and this morning: "Uber X black escalade is here! Aug Vaycay 2K17 ALL SYSTEMS GO!"

TOM: Does any part of you think that might have been crafted // to attract us?

KATY: They're gone!!

TOM: You're not FB friends with them, are you?

KATY: What no.

TOM: Then all those statuses were public?

KATY: What I don't know.

TOM: Who goes to Miami in August?

KATY: Tom!

TOM: My name that's my name don't use my name!

KATY: *(wielding a knife hazardously)* Nobody is here.

TOM: Ok, Katy! Then put that away.

KATY: The knife is just for safe-zys.

TOM: OK!

KATY: Nobody is going to get hurt.

>*GHOST TWO grabs TOM's throat and starts choking him. KATY is looking the other way.*

GHOST ONE: Hey, hey! That's cheating.

GHOST TWO: Why?

GHOST ONE: Because you said we could do this on adrenaline, cortisone, and norepinephrine alone.

GHOST TWO: You're right.

GHOST ONE: You're a purist.

GHOST TWO: I'm a purist.

> *GHOST TWO releases TOM from the choke hold.*

TOM: *catching breath.* Oh my god what was that?!?

KATY: Let's just grab as much jewelry and Apple products as we can and get out of here.

TOM: HELLO WHAT WAS THAT?

KATY: What was what? I don't have any peripheral vision with this mask on.

Wait a second.

TOM: What?

KATY: Why *would* they be so obvious about their status updates?

TOM: Something feels like a trap.

GHOSTS ONE & TWO: chanting

> GHOST TRAP
>
> GHOST TRAP
>
> GHOST TRAP

GHOST TWO: I can't believe how well this is going.

GHOST ONE: I know!

GHOST TWO: Air B and B-ing a Tribeca loft is the best, one of the best, ideas you've ever had!

GHOST ONE: It would never have worked if you hadn't gotten the Facebook password from the dark web.

GHOST TWO: Thank you security bug Heartbleed.

GHOST ONE: We're gonna kill so many people!

GHOST TWO: Yay!

> *They high five.*

GHOSTS ONE & TWO: Ghost trap!

TOM: I don't like this at all—

KATY: Let's get out of here—

Ghosts touch KATY.

KATY: AH!

TOM: What?

KATY: I just felt something.

TOM: Good or bad?

KATY: BAD! Bad, Tom, Bad!

Ghosts touch KATY.

KATY: Ah! There it is again.

TOM: I don't like this I don't like this I don't like this.

One of the ghosts puts hands over TOM's eyes.

TOM: I can't see!

KATY: What?

TOM: I've gone blind – I can't see!

KATY: FOLLOW THE SOUND OF MY VOICE!

GHOST ONE: Katy….

KATY: Did you just say my name?

TOM: There's something in my mask – there is something moving my mask!

KATY: Oh god.

TOM: Oh god.

KATY: Oh god. Tom.

TOM: Katy.

KATY: Tom!

TOM: Katy! Am I the only one you've ever robbed with?

KATY: God dammit, Tom. Let's get out of here. Open the door.

TOM: I'm trying.

KATY: Open the door!

TOM: It's locked.

KATY: It can't be locked. How can it be locked? We picked the lock how is the door locked?

TOM: Hello? Hello!? Somebody?

KATY: Help!

TOM: Help!

KATY: Help! We're locked in!? Help!

KATY and TOM try in vain to pull it open.

GHOST ONE & TWO prance around them spookily, perhaps BOO-ing, perhaps poking.

KATY & TOM: *overlapping, much panic.* Help! No! No! Let us out! Help! Help! No! No! NO! Ah! Ah!

KATY: I think my heart just stopped.

KATY and TOM die of fear.

Jovial, celebratory laughter from ghosts.

Big musical send off where ghosts puppet dead bodies of KATY and TOM in choreographed dance number.

Just Desserts

David MacGregor

City Theatre (Miami, FL) – Summer Shorts XXII
June 1, 2017
Directed by David Nail

JOYCE – Irene Adjan

EVAN – Phillip Andrew Santiago

BECKY – Cassandra Zepeda

KRIS – Lindsay Lavin

SETTING

A company lunchroom.

TIME

Now and then.

CHARACTERS

JOYCE - Woman in her 20s-50s.

EVAN - Man in his 20s-50s.

BECKY - Woman in her 20s-50s.

KRIS - Man or woman in his/her 20s-50s. For the sake of consistency, male nouns and pronouns are used in the play, but these should be changed appropriately if a woman plays the part.

NOTE: References to the "Notorious Pig" can be pronounced as written or amended to "Notorious P.I.G." (a play on the name of the rapper Notorious B.I.G.) as desired.

(Two co-workers, JOYCE and EVAN, sit at a table having lunch. There is a refrigerator somewhere nearby.)

JOYCE: ...well, I've been feeling a little burned out and I was thinking of taking a few vacation days, you know, maybe go to Mexico or something, but I get the feeling they're going to send me to Akron next week.

EVAN: There's nothing quite like Akron, Ohio, in February. I'm just glad it's your turn to go.

(BECKY enters.)

BECKY: Hey guys...

(off JOYCE and EVAN's acknowledgement)

Okay, wish me luck. I'm going in...

(BECKY takes a couple of deep breaths, rolls her neck, and stretches her arms.)

BECKY: And...

(she opens the fridge door)

YES!!! My lunch is still here! Must be my lucky day.

(BECKY brings some Tupperware to the table and sits down with JOYCE and EVAN. They chat as they eat.)

BECKY: How'd you guys make out? Any casualties?

EVAN: Well, I thought I was living dangerously by bringing a fruit salad and a salami sandwich, but as you can see, they both made it through the morning unscathed.

BECKY: How about you, Joyce?

JOYCE: I lost a couple of brownies.

(EVAN and BECKY stop eating.)

BECKY: Brownies?

(to EVAN)

Did she say "brownies?"

EVAN: She said brownies.

BECKY: Joyce, what are you thinking? You put brownies in the fridge?

(off JOYCE's nod)

Well, of course they're gone! What did you expect with the Notorious Pig on the prowl! Those brownies probably didn't make it to nine o'clock.

EVAN: If that.

BECKY: If that! You might as well ask a pack of Dobermans to guard your cheeseburger.

EVAN: Are you feeling okay? Putting anything remotely resembling a dessert in that fridge is something no sane person would do.

JOYCE: I poisoned the brownies.

EVAN: You what?

JOYCE: Poisoned them. I knew they'd get ripped off, so I put poison in them. I even put a little sign on top--"Poison Brownies."

BECKY: Oh my God...but why the sign?

JOYCE: I wanted to be honest about it. But I figured the Notorious Pig would think the sign was a joke and eat them anyway.

EVAN: So what did you put in them? Like a laxative or something?

JOYCE: Nope. Straight up poison.

EVAN: What kind of poison?

JOYCE: I'm not really sure. It was a kind of a mixture of things. I found the recipe on the Internet.

BECKY: So, what does the poison do?

JOYCE: Well, at first, I guess it makes you feel really thirsty, you know, feverish? Then it starts to work its way through your system and it gradually paralyzes you. After that, you go into convulsions and die.

(JOYCE takes a bite out of her sandwich as EVAN and BECKY stare.)

I'm fed up, all right? It's ridiculous for us to put up with having our food stolen all the time. And if the company's too cheap to put a security camera in here, fine. Let's see how the Notorious Pig likes my special brownies.

(KRIS enters, looking flushed and frantic, and gulping water from a bottle.)

KRIS: Hey guys...what is the temperature in this place? Do they have the thermostat set at ninety?

(EVAN, BECKY, and JOYCE look at one another as KRIS opens the fridge in search of more water.)

JOYCE: Little thirsty, Kris?

KRIS: I'm dying out there!

(more drinking)

You guys aren't hot?

BECKY: We're fine.

EVAN: Say, Kris. You didn't happen to find a couple of brownies in the fridge this morning, did you?

KRIS: Brownies? No. Why?

BECKY: Because if you happened to take somebody else's brownies—

KRIS: Wait, what are you guys saying? I'm the Notorious Pig? You think it's me who's stealing food?

JOYCE: Is it?

KRIS: No! God, I'm thirsty!

(KRIS guzzles more water.)

JOYCE: You're thirsty because you stole my brownies and ate them.

KRIS: No, I didn't!

JOYCE: You did.

KRIS: That's ridiculous! You have no right to accuse me of anything! Besides, why would brownies make me thirsty?

JOYCE: Because I poisoned them. Just like the sign said.

(KRIS stops drinking, not quite believing what he just heard.)

KRIS: You're...you're making that up.

JOYCE: Are you feeling any abdominal cramping yet?

KRIS: *(as an abdominal cramp hits)* No...

JOYCE: Kris, you are the Notorious Pig and you've been stealing people's lunches for the past six months. Admit it.

KRIS: I'm not! I don't have to take this...you know what? Screw you guys! I don't feel well. I'm going home!

JOYCE: Suit yourself. But you'll never make it to a doctor in time.

KRIS: In time for what?

EVAN: The poison in those brownies is going to kill you—

JOYCE: --unless you confess to being the Notorious Pig. In which case, I have the antidote right here.

(JOYCE pulls out a glass vial and holds it up.)

BECKY: *(to JOYCE)* Nice. You really thought this out.

KRIS: But I didn't eat any...

(A spasm of pain hits KRIS.)

JOYCE: ...brownies? Then you don't need the antidote.

(JOYCE puts the antidote away and takes another bite of her sandwich. KRIS agonizes, until...)

KRIS: I found one of the brownies on my desk, okay? Somebody left it there and I ate it.

BECKY: That's a lie.

EVAN: Of course it's a lie.

JOYCE: Tell us what you are. Tell us you're the Notorious Pig.

(Another spasm rips through KRIS.)

KRIS: Oh my god...Joyce...please give me the antidote.

(JOYCE pulls out the antidote again.)

JOYCE: This? Only when you admit what you are.

(KRIS wobbles, grabs for the table, and drops to the ground, panic-stricken.)

KRIS: I can't feel my legs! Joyce...please...

(JOYCE holds out the vial, but when KRIS reaches for it, JOYCE pulls it back.)

JOYCE: Tell us what you are...say it.

KRIS: *(softly)*I'm the Notorious Pig.

JOYCE: I didn't catch that.

KRIS: I'm the Notorious Pig.

JOYCE: Louder. Like you're proud of it. Tell the world, Kris.

KRIS: I'M THE NOTORIOUS PIG!!!

JOYCE: Yes, you are. But I suppose even Notorious Pigs deserve to live.

(JOYCE holds out the vial. Just as KRIS is about to grab it, EVAN takes the vial.)

EVAN: I disagree. I don't think the Notorious Pig deserves to live.

BECKY: Evan! Give him the antidote! He's going to die!

EVAN: And what's the downside there?

BECKY: Death!

EVAN: So? People die all the time. I mean, seriously. Give me one good reason why he should live.

BECKY: You think he deserves to die because of a couple of brownies?

EVAN: It's not just a couple of brownies! He's been scavenging around here for months! It's like having a parasite inside your body. That's what we're looking at...a human parasite! I say, let's get rid of it while we can.

BECKY: But it's just some food—

EVAN: It's not just food! It's...let me tell you something. About a month ago, I knew I had a rough day ahead of me, so in the morning, I got up and made myself a sandwich for lunch. And not just any sandwich. I had some fresh sourdough bread, smoked turkey, a couple of slices of provolone cheese--and I made myself some guacamole to go with it, just the way I like it--nice and chunky, with some tomatoes, some lemon juice, and a little bit of garlic salt. And that day was the day from hell. Every phone call, every e-mail, I felt like my head was going to explode. But I kept telling myself, "Okay, this is bad, but you have the most kick-ass sandwich in the world waiting for you." But you know what? I didn't have it waiting for me. Because when I opened up the fridge at lunchtime, it was gone! And do you know what I ended up eating?

(shaking the vial in KRIS's face)

Some stale Fritos and a Twix bar from the vending machine!

JOYCE: I remember that day. I thought you were gonna stroke out on us.

(KRIS clutches at EVAN's pant legs.)

BECKY: But we can't just let him die! What are we, judge, jury, and executioner?

JOYCE: We don't need to be the judge or jury. He just confessed.

EVAN: And if he dies, he's his own executioner. He did this to himself.

BECKY: Give me that!

(snatching the vial from EVAN)

Honest to God...

(KRIS crawls to BECKY, hand outstretched, struggling to get a breath, as BECKY uncaps the vial. But just as KRIS gets there, BECKY pulls the vial away.)

BECKY: *(to EVAN)* But you know...you might have a point. Say we do give him the antidote. What then? I'm guessing after all this he would quit this job, but then he's going to go somewhere else and do the same thing all over again.

EVAN: Yep.

JOYCE: Well, we don't know that. Maybe he's learned his lesson.

BECKY: He's a grown man! And day after day, week after week, he has been ripping off his co-workers. What kind of person does that? And is this the kind of person we want in society? Do we want him to breed and have kids? No! Do we want him associating with other people and passing on his behavior? No!

EVAN: Exactly! Is the world a better place with him in it? I say no.

BECKY: Me too.

JOYCE: Okay, I see your point, but honestly, I never wanted to actually kill anyone. I just wanted to teach him a lesson. And if he dies, I might get into trouble.

EVAN: No, you won't! They were marked "poison brownies!" Can you sue a rat poison company if someone eats the rat poison? No! He knowingly ate brownies that were marked "Poison."

That's his problem, not yours. You're golden.

BECKY: Besides, none of us is talking, and when someone finds him dead in here, they're going to think heart attack or stroke or something.

EVAN: But you know, this really should be Joyce's decision. She's the one who cooked up the brownies, after all.

BECKY: That's true. Yeah, that makes sense.

(handing the vial to JOYCE)

Your call, Joyce.

JOYCE: Gosh, I don't know. This is America, right? A democracy and everything? Maybe majority rule is best.

(KRIS convulses violently, then goes still.)

JOYCE: Huh. That worked quicker than I thought it would.

BECKY: Well, what's that expression? "Death is what happens while you're busy making plans."

EVAN: I think it's, "Life is what happens while you're busy making plans."

BECKY: Oh. I guess they both make sense.

(EVAN stands up.)

EVAN: Well, I have a PowerPoint presentation to put together. I'd better get cranking on that.

(BECKY and JOYCE stand up as well. EVAN starts dumping the remains of his lunch into a trash bin.)

BECKY: And I need to start crunching some numbers for a certain somebody's trip to fabulous Akron, Ohio.

JOYCE: Dammit, are you kidding me?

BECKY: Sorry. You're up in the rotation.

EVAN: Hey, you know what? Take your vacation days. You deserve a a margarita or two on a Mexican beach. I'll go to Akron.

BECKY: Good call. I'll get started on the paperwork.

JOYCE: Seriously?

EVAN: Absolutely. You really went out on a limb taking care of this whole Notorious Pig business for everyone.

BECKY: And you know how they keep telling us we're a team and all that? Well, this is what teammates do.

EVAN: You had our back. We have yours.

BECKY: Damn straight.

JOYCE: Thanks guys! Hey, you know what? I'll grab some Mexican chocolate when I'm down there, and when I come back, I'm bringing in fresh brownies for everyone!

(They all high-five.)

ALL: Yes!...That's what I'm talking about!...Winner winner chicken dinner!

(They all start to exit, then pause to look back at KRIS.)

BECKY: It is a little sad.

EVAN: What happens to people?

JOYCE: I don't know.

BECKY: I just don't get it.

EVAN: Yeah.

JOYCE: Oh well.

(They all exit.)

END OF PLAY.

LORAX

Katherine Gee Perrone

Lorax was first produced by the Hub Theatre Company (Lauren Elias, Managing Director) in Boston, Massachusetts as a part of the Nineteenth Annual Boston Theatre Marathon on May 14th, 2017. It was directed by Rebecca Miller.

The cast was as follows:

CLARA played by Lauren Elias
PAMELA played by Zele Avrodopoulus
LORAX played by Robert Orzalli

CHARACTERS

CLARA: Female. Late 20's/Early 30's, A PhD Candidate in environmental science. Overwhelmed idealist.

PAMELA: Female. 50s/60s (any age, but at least a generation older than Clara). Clara's mentor and thesis advisor. Terse and a rule follower.

LORAX: Male. A popular Dr. Seuss Character. Clara's imaginary friend. Bright orange with an enormous yellow mustache and eyebrows.

SETTING

A University reception room. Present Day.

(Small reception room. There is a table with Starbucks coffee, a stack of Styrofoam cups, and a tray of store-bought cookies. A few chairs. Door off right. Pamela opens the door, holding it open for Clara, who enters, head down in shame. Pamela follows, enraged.)

PAMELA: I seriously hope that was a joke.

(Clara sits and buries her head in her hands.)

PAMELA: *(cont)* Pull yourself together, Clara. You were joking, right?

CLARA: Professor—Pam, I—

PAMELA: This isn't all about you today, Clara. My reputation is on the line here too, and if you want to compare what we do...to uh...to a *children's book*, then you can red fish blue fish all you want at home, NOT in front of your thesis committee.

CLARA: The Lorax isn't—

PAMELA: I don't even want to hear it. I am so embarrassed. Your thesis defense is not some therapy session about your childhood...get a PhD in shrinkage for that, or god forbid, *Humanities*, but don't bring that glop into the sciences. We are talking about four years of research here, Clara. *Real* facts that effect ecosystems, livelihoods, governmental policy!

(Pamela moves to exit, and then turns back.)

PAMELA: *(cont)* Maybe I can tell them you're high. Please tell me you're high.

CLARA: I'm not.

PAMELA: Agh!

(pause, referring to earlier)

Why did you have to say that?

CLARA: He was shouting and...

PAMELA: What?

CLARA: He was in the room.

PAMELA: Your...friend...was in the room.

(Clara nods. Pamela collapses in a chair, head in hands.)

PAMELA: I have been advising an insane person. My entire career, all my research, all OUR research...a load of crock. Because your primary source was the Lorax.

CLARA: No! He would just suggest things, like "look into the invasive species claims in California" or "take a look at the hydro electric plants flooding the Amazon"...

(Pause)

Stuff like that.

PAMELA: When you first became my student, I thought it was so cute, so cute that your imaginary friend had been the Lorax. I thought it was *so cute* that you ended up studying environmental science.

(She leans in)

It isn't cute when you're an adult and you tell everyone he's shouting things during your thesis defense.

CLARA: He just...never left.

(Pamela stands up and storms out of the room. She re-enters.)

PAMELA: I'm keeping them in the room for ten minutes. That's how long you have to come up with a convincing lie as to why you would talk about your imaginary friend from Dr. Seuss during your defense. Or you can kiss your degree, and your career goodbye.

(She exits. Clara sighs and sinks into her chair. Pamela reenters.)

PAMELA: *(cont)* Do not eat the cookies. Those are for PhD candidates who have earned the right to eat refreshments after a successfully defended thesis.

(Pamela exits. Clara watches the door, waiting, then sighs and puts her head in her hands.)

LORAX

(off)

Clara?

CLARA: (muffled, into her hands) No.

(Lorax enters. He is short, rounded in the tummy, bright orange with a full yellow mustache and eyebrows.)

LORAX: Clara?

(Clara lifts her head.)

CLARA: No!

LORAX: I came to speak for the—

CLARA: You aren't normal! You aren't a normal thing. You are a cartoon and you had no right to yell at me while I was defending my thesis, Lorax.

LORAX: When you talked about studies,
     they weren't about bees,
     they weren't about flowers,
     they weren't about trees!
     You were talking of egos,
     and other such stuff.
     What nonsense, what drivel,
     Academic white fluff.
     Talk of deforestation!
     Or fires! Invasive species!
     Why wouldn't you listen when I said,
     "Speak for the trees!"?

CLARA: Lorax, that is how a thesis defense works. We were getting to it, and instead you made me...Oh, I'm so embarrassed.

LORAX: Does embarrassment really matter, Clara?
     Who cares if I stopped all the prattle?
     Species are dying, going extinct!
     All to make room for farming and cattle!
     Earth could be losing the rainforest biome. And...
         (pauses, seeing the Styrofoam cups)
     Oh my, oh dear, what's this? Cups of sty-ro-foam?
         (Lorax marches over to the table and holds up the offending cup. Incredulous.)

LORAX: *(cont)*It doesn't degrade!
     It stays here forever!
     It's a carcinogen.
     Does it fade? Never!
         (Clara marches over to the table.)

CLARA: It's lightweight, and holds hot liquids very well.
         (Clara picks up a cup and pours herself a cup of coffee. She takes just a sip and lifts it up to show Lorax it's still full. She drops it in the trash can. Lorax gasps.)

LORAX: A waste!

CLARA: You know, sometimes, I want to waste! Sometimes, I want to eat and drink without thinking how every little thing I do is wreaking havoc on the environment.

(Clara pours herself another cup of coffee into a new cup.)

I want to go shopping without being told that the synthetic dye used in my red shirt is an Azo dye made with dioxin and formaldehyde, and that the dye workers in Japan are at a high risk of tumors and the American workers are at greater risk of cancer. I want to go on a road trip without a back seat driver reminding me that the longer we drive, the more carbon monoxide and nitrogen oxide is being emitted into the air, warming the globe, irrevocably changing the temperatures of ecosystems, increasing the lowest temperatures of the Rocky and Sierra mountains which means that the American Pika will probably go extinct because they can't survive greater temperatures then 77.9 degrees Fahrenheit.

(A breath)

I want to *drink a cup of coffee* without being told that it's going to end up as marine debris in the ocean!

(Clara throws another cup into the trashcan. Lorax walks over to trash and peers inside.)

LORAX: Then you're not unique.

And the future is bleak.

You want to be blind.

You want to not see.

You want to be human.

And forget about me.

CLARA: I just don't want to hear your voice in my head all the time. "I speak for the trees! I speak for the oceans! I speak for the bears!" I am wracked with guilt in everything I do because *I care.* You don't have to convince me to care!

(Clara pauses, and goes back to trashcan. She takes out the cups she threw away and stacks them.)

I can't enjoy life without worrying that I'm destroying life.

(Pause)

Of all the children you could have come to, you came to me...
and I've dedicated my life to the environment. I'm getting my
PhD! I'm speaking for the trees, Lorax. I'm doing the work.

LORAX: Pffh. Yes, how you "work",

> Hour after hour,
> in the quiet and peace,
> of the ivory tower.
> While outside such mayhem,
> such selfish enterprise,
> is churning and burning,
> before all your eyes.
> They slash, burn and choke,
> all for money and greed,
> they don't care about consequences,
> just filling their need.
> Their need for such fun,
> their need for the coin,
> so why do "your work",
> when you could just join?

CLARA: I know you're angry...

LORAX: I've spoken for years,

> all on deaf ears.
> Then you came along,
> you listened, remember?
> That cold winter day.

CLARA: In the tree house.

LORAX: December.

> *(Pause)*

> I found you dear Clara,
> with such passion and grace.
> I knew you could help me
> speak in Earth's place.
> When nature and creatures are voiceless, you see.
> They need people like you.

They need people like me.
If you are done listening,
and speaking their woes,
then I'll go away,
where someone else knows.
That the earth is in danger,
that the earth needs a voice,
if you want to be silent,
then that is your choice.

(Clara walks around the room while the Lorax watches.)

CLARA: Orphans.

LORAX: What?

CLARA: Rape. Poverty. Disease. Domestic abuse. Crime. Terrorism. Homelessness.

LORAX: What?

CLARA: Dwindling water supplies. Famine. Hurricanes. Corruption. Tyranny. Racism. Civil war. Infanticide. Genocide.

LORAX: Yes...

(Clara sighs.)

CLARA: I haven't slept...really slept...in years.

LORAX: If—

CLARA: This Earth is in danger. From so many, so many things. It does need a voice. But it needs more than one person shouting. Life simply isn't long enough for me to solve every problem. I can't do it, Lorax. And I can't be overwhelmed because of it. But...I can start by not being selfish. I can do one thing. I can do one great thing. And hopefully enough people elsewhere will do one great thing. I can't cure poverty or racism, or prevent wars or disease. I can't remove trash from the oceans, prevent pollution in the dye factories, or stop people from driving cars. But I can research "The Patterns and Projections of Species Loss Due to Deforestation for Agricultural Use in the Amazon River Basin."

(Pause)

I can do that.

(Lorax pauses for a long moment.)

LORAX: So goodbye, Clara.

CLARA: So goodbye, Lorax.

> *(Lorax exits. No sentimentality. Clara sighs. Quiet. Pamela pokes her head in the door.)*

PAMELA: Ready?

CLARA: Yes.

> *(Clara stands and starts to leave, pauses, then grabs the Styrofoam cups off of the table and carries them with her offstage. The end.)*

MEN ON THE MOON

David Folwell

Men on the Moon premiered on June 1, 2017 at the Playroom Theater in New York City. It was produced by New Circle Rep Theater as a part of their Inferno Project: Limbo, and was directed by Randy Noojin.

CAST:

David Arrow - NEIL
Robert Tekavec BUZZ
John Richardson BRIAN
Wyatt Ash-Milby MATTHEW

CHARACTERS:

    NEIL - White male in his 30s
    BUZZ - White male in his 30s
    BRIAN - Navajo man, 60s and up
    MATTHEW - Young Navajo man, 17

TIME AND PLACE:

    New Mexico desert, 1969

Special thanks to Michele Kiser and her students at the Navajo Technical University for their help with the translation.

*In the dark, we hear the howl of the wind. Center stage,
we see a small SPARK popping. The warm glow of a fire
pulses to life. We see the silhouette of two shivering men
crowd around the make-shift fire on their knees, blowing.
BUZZ and NEIL, two healthy American males who are
not dressed for the desert at night.*

NEIL: Blow on it.

BUZZ: I'm blowing on it.

NEIL: It's going to go out and my lighter is almost dead.

BUZZ: I'm blowing on it, Neil.

NEIL: Not when you're talking to me you aren't. Blow.

They both blow until the fire finally takes hold and glows steady.

BUZZ: Ah, thank god.

NEIL: Pile some stuff on it.

BUZZ: No. Not yet. You gotta let it breathe a little bit.

NEIL: I know how to make a fire.

BUZZ: So do I! Jesus, it's cold. It was burning up an hour ago.

NEIL: Yeah, that's how the desert works, Buzz.

BUZZ: I know how the desert works okay, Neil. You don't think I
know how the desert works?

NEIL: Okay, tell me how it works.

BUZZ: The absence of cloud cover in the evening allows the heat
to escape into space.

NEIL: Good. That's basically it. Do you know how fire works?

BUZZ: Of course, Oxygen-fuel-heat.

NEIL: Good. Go get some fuel.

BUZZ: Wait, why do I have to get fuel? Why can't *you* get it?

NEIL: Because I have to tend the fire.

BUZZ: Well, I want to tend the fire.

NEIL: But, I have the poking stick.

*Holds up the stick he is using to poke at the fire. Buzz
looks out into the darkness and turns back to the fire.*

NEIL: Well?

BUZZ: We have plenty of fuel.

NEIL: No we don't. We don't know how long we are going to be out here. The wind could kick up and--

BUZZ: I don't like snakes.

NEIL: Nobody likes snakes! It's a human instinct. Anyway, we were just walking around out there. There were snakes everywhere. What's the difference?

BUZZ: The difference is, they have the advantage now. Ya know what, gimme the stick.

Buzz lunges for the stick.

NEIL: No! Get your own.

BUZZ: Gimme the stick and you look for fuel.

> *He lunges again and they start to wrestle. Suddenly, they hear a "RATTLE". They stop and listen.*

BUZZ: Shit.

NEIL: Snake. It's okay. Snakes are cold blooded animals. It's cold out so they move slow.

BUZZ: It rattled! That means it's pissed.

Another rattle.

NEIL: Shit. It's pissed.

BUZZ: Gimme the stick and I'll kill it.

NEIL: Get your own god-damn stick!

> *Another rattle. This time, we see an old Navajo Man, BRIAN, barely visible at the edge of the light, holding a rattle in his hand.*

BUZZ: It's closer! Give me the fucking stick!

NEIL: NO! Get your own!

BRIAN quietly sneaks directly behind them. He rattles and yells, scaring the shit out of the two men.

BRIAN: You're gonna need a bigger stick.

NEIL: Where the hell did you come from?

BRIAN: This is my desert. Where did you come from?

BUZZ: The base. We went for a hike and-

BRIAN: You don't know how to walk in the desert?

NEIL: No, we... a sand storm kicked up and we lost our bearings and we--

BRIAN: You got lost.

NEIL: Well, no. We know exactly where we are. We were following the north star back to base.

He points up to the sky.

BRIAN: That's not the North Star. That's So' Tsoh. The Big Star of the morning.

BUZZ: Venus? That's Venus, Neil!

NEIL: No, Venus is over, wait-- hold on.

BUZZ: Shit.

NEIL: Okay, then where is Polaris?

BRIAN: Follow the leg of the great bear.

Brian draws across the sky and lands on the North Star.

NEIL: Ah, okay. Yeah. You're right.

BUZZ: *(furious)* We've been out here for god knows how long because you are were following the wrong star?

NEIL: Technically, it's not a star. It's a planet.

BRIAN: It's actually a coyote. When the holy people were planning the world, they left the coyote out of it because he was such a pain in the ass. The coyote asked them what they were doing and they told him to fuck off. The coyote angrily ran off. So the holy people made the first man and the first woman. They made the sun and the moon and hung them in the sky. Then the coyote came running back and grabbed the buck skin that the stars were laying on and shook it. The stars scattered randomly in the sky. The holy people were angry and asked the coyote why he did that. He said because you left me out! Coyote was an asshole.

BUZZ: Why is Venus named after the coyote?

BRIAN: Because it fell back to earth and the coyote took it as his own. You were following that piece of shit coyote.

The fire starts to die. Brian snatches the stick away from Neil. Buzz looks at Neil like - "why did you give HIM the stick." Brian works on the fire and brings it back to life.

NEIL: So, uh... what do they call you?

BRIAN: People call me Brian.

BUZZ: Brian?

BRIAN: Yeah. What do they call you?

BUZZ: I'm Colonel Buzz Aldrin, United States Air Force.

BRIAN: Do I have to call you all that?

BUZZ: You can just call me Buzz.

NEIL: I'm Neil Armstrong.

BRIAN: Armstrong? You have a more Navajo name than I do.

NEIL: Okay, well. Do you have a car or something? Maybe you could help us get back to base.

BRIAN: What do you do at the base?

NEIL: *(a little reticent to say)*Well... We are training for a mission.

BRIAN: What kind of mission?

BUZZ: *(enthusiastically)*We're going to the moon!

> *Brian starts to laugh. Neil looks embarrassed. Buzz is bewildered. He thought Brian would be impressed.*

BRIAN: You can't find your way to town. How are you going to get to the moon!?

NEIL: Well, we are going to have lots of help.

BRIAN: Good, you will never make it on your own.

NEIL: So, do you know where we could find a phone? We really need to call the base. I'm sure they are concerned--

BRIAN: Why do you want to go to the moon? What is up there that they don't have down here?

BUZZ: Well, it's... It's the moon. Nobody has ever been.

BRIAN: That's not true. My people have ancestors on the moon. They went hunting there and they never came back.

NEIL: We want to go there because we want to learn more about our planet.

BUZZ: And, we want to get there before the Russians get there.

NEIL: Well, no. That's not the main--

BUZZ: That's a big one!

NEIL: No, look... we need to know more about ourselves. We need to explore. We can't just live on this planet forever. There are an infinite number of livable planets in the billions of galaxies in the universe! Can you imagine what there is to see?

BRIAN: What if you can't see?

NEIL: What do you mean?

BRIAN: Why do you think you can see these things with your puny little eyes? The bat thinks he sees, but we call him blind. Maybe you go to the moon and just see a big grey rock. But my ancestors have better eyes and they see you bumbling around like idiots.

BUZZ: Well... we have to try.

BRIAN: Not really. How are you going to get there?

NEIL: A rocket is going to shoot us into the space.

BUZZ: It's like a huge fire wagon that carries us into the sky.

Neil looks at him disapprovingly.

NEIL: It's a rocket. We orbit around the moon and drop down in a landing craft.

BRIAN: Hmm. Sounds expensive.

NEIL: It is, but it's for the good of all mankind.

BRIAN: Except for the Russians.

BUZZ: RIGHT!

NEIL: No. It's good for them too.

BUZZ: They just won't be first.

Brian pokes at the fire.

NEIL: So, maybe a payphone, or-

BRIAN: When you get to the moon, can you give my ancestors a message?

NEIL: Um... Sure.

BRIAN: Do you know Navajo?

NEIL: No.

He looks at Buzz.

BUZZ: No.

BRIAN: Okay. Repeat after me. "T'aadoo"

Buzz and NEIL: "T'addoo"

BRIAN: " nihaaíínîléhé "

BUZZ AND NEIL: " nihaaíínîléhé"

BRIAN: " Kéw'é"

BUZZ AND NEIL: " Kéw'é"

BRIAN: "nihikeyah"

BUZZ AND NEIL: "nihikeyah"

BRIAN: "nihaa"

BUZZ AND NEIL: "nihaa"

BRIAN: " noó iil"

BUZZ AND NEIL: " noó iil"

BRIAN: "biniina neiikai"

BUZZ AND NEIL: "biniina neiikai"

BRIAN: "T'aadoo nihaaííníléhé.Ê Kéw'é nihikeyah nihaa noó iil biniina neiikai."

BUZZ AND NEIL: "T'aadoo nihaaííníléhé.Ê Kéw'é nihikeyah nihaa noó iil biniina neiikai."

> *They repeat it until it flows.*

BRIAN: Okay. My son will take you back to the base.

BUZZ: Your son?

BRIAN: Yes. We live right there. You are in my front yard. *(calls off stage)* Matthew!

> *Brian starts to exit.*

NEIL: Wait. What's the message?

BRIAN: That is between me and my ancestors. Just give them my message.

> *Brian walks off. Neil watches him go. Buzz looks around.*

BUZZ: Holy crap. We are in his front yard... There's a swing set! How'd we miss that!?

NEIL: Because we're blind, I guess. I wonder what the message is.

BUZZ: I don't know. But we can't say that stuff when we get to the moon. They are transmitting everything. People will think we are crazy.

NEIL: He's a very wise man. I'm going to take his message to his ancestors. I don't care.

BUZZ: Okay. I just hope they don't scrub the mission because they think you are O2 drunk.

> *A young Native American man enters, MATTHEW (17).*

MATTHEW: Hey, you guys ready?

NEIL: Your grandfather is a very wise man.

MATTHEW: Yeah, he's a trip. My trucks over here.

NEIL: Is he, like a shaman for your tribe, or something?

MATTHEW: Pops? Nah. He teaches at the rez school. Math and science. Why? What did he say?

BUZZ: He wants us to give a message to his ancestors on the moon.

MATTHEW: Yeah. What's the message?

NEIL: T'aadoo nihaaííníléhé.Ê Kéw'é nihikeyah nihaa noó iil bi-niina neiikai.

Matthew starts to laugh hysterically. Neil and Buzz are bewildered, but can't help but to join in the laughter too. Then...

NEIL: Wait. What are we laughing about?

BUZZ: Yeah? What's the message say?

MATTHEW: The message is, "Don't trust us. We're here to steal your land."

Blackout.

END OF PLAY

New York City Girls Will Kill You

Graham Techler

Produced by New Jersey Rep, SuZanne and Gabor Barabas, Producing Directors, All About Eve Festival of the Arts, Saturday, October 8th, 2017

DIRECTOR:
Ashley Marinaccio

CAST:
Larissa Marthe Jeanniton (Amy)
Rachel Schmeling (Karen)
Katherine Wadleigh (Christina)
Juliet Kapanjie (Jessica)

CHARACTERS

AMY, Female, 20s
JESSICA, Female, 20s
CHRISTINA, Female, 20s
KAREN, Female, 20s

SETTING

A bathroom, some club, New York. As far as set elements, let's pretend.

(Some club somewhere. Maybe in the financial district. The bathroom. AMY and JESSICA, both in costume, apply makeup in the mirror.)

AMY: God it's hot in there.

JESSICA: God it's FUCKING hot in there.

AMY: I'm sweating.

JESSICA: I'm sweating so bad. "It's Eden, baby!"

AMY: Some guy tried to grab my ass in there and he slipped and fell.

JESSICA: I feel like if you tried to wring me out into a bottle you couldn't bring that bottle on an airplane no way.

AMY: I think he cracked his collarbone, I hope he's okay.

JESSICA: Some rave guy with glowsticks keeps throwing baby powder off the balcony and the second it hits my skin it just evaporates I'm so sweaty.

AMY: God, it's hot. It's like they want us to be hot in there or something.

JESSICA: I'm starting to feel like you're exactly right. You're so right, Amy.

AMY: Hey. Jessica. Have you made any progress with (*the sound of a colossal fucking trainwreck blasts as she speaks*)? You know, out on the dance floor?

JESSICA: No. He's dancing with some girl by the shark tank.

AMY: God, I can't believe they have a shark tank. That's so fucking hot. Imagine grinding with a guy on one side of you and a real full-on shark on the other side. And the guy is like "uhhhhng" and the shark is like (*makes the silent sounds of a shark in ecstasy*). God, that'd be hot. She must be so pretty.

JESSICA: Oh who cares, there's a whole sea of sharks in there.

(JESSICA is satisfied with herself. Pause.)

AMY: What?

JESSICA: Sharks are a metaphor for guys, Amy.

AMY: Oh, *nice.*

(CHRISTINA bursts through the bathroom door, also in costume.)

CHRISTINA: God, is it FUCKING hot in there or is it just me?

JESSICA: Oh hey Christina.

CHRISTINA: Oh hey Jessica.

AMY: Oh hey Christina.

CHRISTINA: Oh hey Amy. What are you two dressed as?

AMY: (*sexy*) I'm the snaaake!

JESSICA: (*sexy*) I'm the Aaapple! You?

CHRISTINA: (*sexy*) Bitches, I'm Jiva, the bird version of Eve who represents the individual soul and by eating fruit from the tree of Atman and Jiva was therefore responsible for the fall of that same soul into this material world of birth and death as written in the Vedic scriptures that predate both Hinduism and the book of Genisis, sluts!

(A long pause.)

JESSICA: That's kind of off theme, Christina.

CHRISTINA: No, I don't think it is, Jessica. It's better than Biblical, it's pre-Biblical.

AMY: I guess she's kind of right, Jessica.

JESSICA: What's wrong with being Eve, Christina? You just had to glue a few fig leaves around and about and boom baby that's you're costume. Half the girls in there did it.

CHRISTINA: Exactly, it would be like showing up to prom in someone else's dress. How embarrassing. So I had to pick between Jiva, or Embla, the first woman of Norse mythology, created alongside Ask by the powers of Villi, Ve, and Odin from a tree, or, if I was feeling fucking scandalous I could have been Mashyana, the first woman according to Zarathustra, but I went with Jiva because my mom always said I was like her little bird.

JESSICA: Whatever. Christina, just don't bum us all out. We're here to have fun, we're here to live our lives and fuck tomorrow and be our best selves with no regrets! Let's commit some original sins out there tonight, ladies! "It's Eden, baby!" Woooo!

CHRISTINA: You guys want to commit some original sins out there tonight?

AMY: No.

JESSICA: No, not really.

CHRISTINA: Exactly. So I don't wanna be an Eve, I wanna be a cool bird spirit.

JESSICA: Eve was the original bad bitch, Christina, what's your problem?

CHRISTINA: No, I get it, it's just that a lot of the time I kind of feel like I'm already the cause of all the world's problems and even if I wake up feeling okay and then go outside I just sort of get the sense that I'm the root of all evil who is to blame for the fall of mankind, and then when I think about how even Paul was forgiven for what he did in ignorance and disbelief, how he was granted ministry after his crimes against God, and still that forgiveness and ministry is denied those who carry the weight of the original sin alone, so basically when the guy at the corner deli already gives me that classic look that says "you are the sole architect of wickedness" then I end up not really wanting to glue fig leaves hither and thither and go out dressed as Eve.

(Long pause.)

JESSICA: Oh.

AMY: Yeah.

CHRISTINA: Plus, original sin doesn't even mean fucking so I think everyone looks a little silly out there.

AMY: I feel sober.

(KAREN stumbles out of a stall.)

KAREN: I feel sick.

(The other girls overlap.)

JESSICA: Oooh, Karen, oh no! Are you okay, Karen?

AMY: Karen, are you okay? Do you feel alright, Karen?

CHRISTINA: Karen, sweetie, do you feel not at all very good right now?

(KAREN cuts them off.)

KAREN: No, I feel sick.

(The girls cradle her head by the sinks and wash some stuff out of her hair.)

JESSICA: Well, at least you look fucking hot tonight, Karen. You know that?

CHRISTINA: You do, Karen, you look fucking hot and everyone knows it.

AMY: (*sexy*) Who are *you* dressed as, Karen?

KAREN: Oh, that's so sweet of you guys. I'm just, um, Lilith? Adam's first wife, who was born from the Earth as he was instead of from his rib, so they fight a lot especially because she doesn't want to "submit" to him, which is like a fancy Bible way of saying that she wants to ride that dick like a kween and he's more into missionary so, um, she leaves him in order to go have sex with some demons and terrify pregnant women and also murder infants? Then I guess in some other stories she is regarded primarily as the mate of Samael, archangel of death, or even as the snake -- like the one Amy is dressed up as so sexily and hotly -- who seduces Eve before she sleeps with Adam and then also, um, rapes Adam and bearing more demons from him, which then -- I mean, I guess -- kind of implies that Eve's menstrual impurity is Lilith's seed within her. Also the Zohar claims that she skips around at night giving men wet dreams and the Greek

KAREN: *(cont.)*concept of Lamia connects her with O.G. vampires, so she may also be a cannibalistic snake woman who sucks the blood from men and devours little baby children?

> *(Pause.)*

Does anyone have a tampon?

JESSICA: Karen what the shit is going on with you right now.

AMY: You too, Christina-bird-spirit. What the shit is going on?

KAREN: Those are just the traditions I'm most familiar guys.

JESSICA: If you keep talking like that, Karen, there is no way you're going to get with (*the sound of an airplane exploding into the side of a mountain as she speaks*) tonight. No way.

KAREN: That's okay. His breath kind of smells like a barrel.

> *(Silence. They shiver.)*

CHRISTINA: God, it's fucking cold in here.

JESSICA: Yeah it was so fucking hot in there but now it's so fucking cold in here.

AMY: I feel like if you tapped me with a tiny little pick-axe I'd just totally explode into a million tiny pieces.

CHRISTINA: God, I thought I had more blood than this.

JESSICA: My veins feel really small.

KAREN: That's so funny, my veins also feel very small.

AMY: All my little blood cells just feel so petite.

JESSICA: Was Eve petite, Christina?

CHRISTINA: (*teeth chattering*) Well, according to the Saudi Arabian archaeological site that's known to scholars and travelers of distant lands as the Tomb of Eve, she would have been around eight feet tall. One statesman thought it was "as well, therefore, that she had not survived to welcome us in the flesh, for although it is rumored that we men have an eye for ladies of heroic proportions we draw the line at the titanic."

(Pause.)

JESSICA: Oh. Did he say that in the 1400s?

CHRISTINA: No, the 1900s.

JESSICA: God. Fucking. Dammit. Fucking dammit.

(KAREN begins to cry, softly. The four girls huddle together for warmth.)

KAREN: I don't want to suck blood, I don't want to eat anyones babies. I didn't. I never ate even one baby. Not one baby.

JESSICA: I know, Karen. It's okay.

AMY: Yeah, Karen, we know you didn't. It's okay.

(A pause.)

CHRISTINA: I've got another story if anyone wants to hear it.

AMY: Okay.

JESSICA: Yeah, just don't bum us out Christina, we're here to party.

AMY: Yeah, as long as you don't bum us out, Christina.

CHRISTINA: Karen?

(KAREN nods.)

In the tradition of the Gnostics, they do not call the artisan who fashioned and maintain the physical universe "God." They instead call him the Demiurge. Or else... Yaldabaoth.

(Pause.)

AMY: Cool.

CHRISTINA: The Demiurge wasn't God. Insofar as the material world is evil, and God is good, the Demiurge is at the very least... bad. And when Eve ate from the apple of the tree of the knowledge of good and evil they were granted knowledge so that they may escape the Demiurge. And Adam thanked Eve, and together they thanked the tempting snake, for then they were free of him.

JESSICA: Where did you hear that one, Christina?

CHRISTINA: Some chick mentioned it in the other bathroom.

KAREN: Does anyone have that tampon?

JESSICA: Yeah.

>*(She hands KAREN a tampon.)*

KAREN: Thank you, Jessica.

>*(They lie there. It seems a little warmer than it was.)*

AMY: I don't feel like going back out there.

JESSICA: Yeah, I don't really feel like going back out there right now.

CHRISTINA: Neither do I. We can just stay in here.

>*(KAREN squeezes them.)*

KAREN: We can stay in here as long as we want.

>*(Blackout.)*

No Time For Baby

Susan Eve Haar

NO TIME FOR BABY was produced by the Manhattan Repertory Theater, directed by the author, April 29-May 1, 2017

CAST:

MRS: Olivia Stoker
MR: Matt Stanger
NANNY: Esme Boyce

CHARACTERS:

MR: Age flexible. A new but older father. 40-55

MRS: A smidge younger than her husband. A woman of ambition.

DOLLY: An elective mute with impeccable nannying credentials. Extremely polished and kempt.

TIME:

The present

SETTING:

An Upper East Side New York apartment. Tastefully furnished by a decorator.

MRS and MR are interviewing DOLLY for a position.

They are both dressed in exquisite taste. MRS is perusing an extensive interview form, flipping the pages. MR looks a little bored.

MR: It says here, you are legal, a U.S. citizen, that you pay your own social security, can drive a car, cook and play badminton.

DOLLY nods vigorously.

MRS: *(continuing)* You don't smoke, favor classical music, and you like to play with sculpty...What is sculpty? Oh! You can't answer! How silly of me. *(to MR)* Sweetheart, what is sculpty?

MR: You play with it? Why, it must be some kind of a game!

MRS: Of course. You are too clever!

(To DOLLY)

Your credentials are impeccable, but it's a little difficult conducting an interview with an elective mute! Do you do use sign language? No. But, it says here, you speak French and Spanish.

(to MR)

She is very accomplished.

MR: She is very expensive.

MRS: It really doesn't matter, does it?

(to DOLLY)

We want the best care for Baby. I mean you must be so careful these days. Baby could end up with one of those island accents, or eating only rice and fried bananas!

MR: Will she cook for us too? I mean at that price she should be able to manage the cooking too!

MRS: Well it says here, that she cooks with imagination, flair, elan.

(to DOLLY)

So many kind words for a woman who is so quiet!

MR: Quiet does have its advantages.

MRS: He likes the help to be unobtrusive. I like them to be part of the family. It definitely, definitely appeals to us both that you have elected to be mute.

MR: You are an elective mute.

(DOLLY nods, emphatically)

Which means, you could start to talk at any time?

(DOLLY nods)

That could be useful in emergencies. But I can't say I'm altogether happy about it. There's something so appealing about a silent woman.

MRS: Well I'm sure that, if it's all that important to you, she could agree not to talk for, say the first eighteen months?

(to DOLLY)

Would that be O.K.?

(DOLLY nods)

MRS: You see how accommodating she is. No kind of attitude. And so accomplished. So, what about stimulating Baby? Baby isn't doing much now, but after all, Baby is just two weeks old!

(laughs)

Have you had any training in development? No?

(DOLLY pantomimes reading, then wiggles her fingers. MRS wiggles back)

MRS: (CONT'D) Oh, so you read. Well, that is a terrific way to keep up with your profession. And I do regard what you do as a profession. I have the highest regard for women who have the capacity to stand against the current, to make child-care a career!

(DOLLY nods and smiles.)

MRS: I can tell already how warm you are. That in your own quiet way you would be devoted to Baby. That you could give Baby the kind of attention--even love--that we all need to achieve our highest potential. Of course, you would in no way interfere with *our* relationship to Baby, in the hours that we are home. You wouldn't be one of those selfish nannies, alienating Baby, keeping Baby all to yourself because you have nothing else. Though I expect you to be on call, nights. We are in very demanding jobs and we need our sleep! I can assure you, the last two weeks would have been a complete nightmare without nurse. But now, it is time for nurse to go.

MR: Nurse is a boozer and a snorer. If it weren't for Baby's excellent disposition and innate good health it would certainly never have survived.

MRS: Baby is really no trouble at all. Just wash Baby once a week. And skip all the creams and powders they burden you with in the hospital. As if Baby needs all those things, why Baby is absolutely new! Baby is very understanding and so are we. Which brings me to the rules. Your eye shadow is most becoming. But in my house no makeup, except for me. Do you find my husband attractive?

(DOLLY shakes her head vehemently no)

Well, of course not. I also notice that you have very lovely breasts. Would you consider breast reduction? It would be fully covered, as part of your compensation package. Of course, it is not a job requirement.

MR: Did we get the results of the fingerprint check? Or does the agency do that?

MRS: *(flipping through the form)* It doesn't say. Look, is this really necessary? She's a lovely woman.

(To DOLLY)

Your own room, though you will, of course, respect the fact that it's our house. TV, cable, cell. Oh, I suppose that doesn't matter to you! Every other Saturday off.

MR: Aren't we being a little hasty, sweetheart? I mean, did you check her references?

MRS: Her agency has the highest reputation! I apologize for my husband's rudeness. Fingerprints indeed!

MR: This is our only child.

MRS: Baby is perfect. Baby is sufficient. Don't get carried away by paternity.

MR: It's not that. It's just, well, we are entrusting Baby to this complete stranger.

MRS: So?

MR: Will she love Baby, will she teach Baby kindness to others, will she teach Baby how to whistle?

(he demonstrates)

MRS: That is definitely outside of the parameters of the form.

MR: *(to DOLLY)*How do you discipline a Baby?

(DOLLY shrug)

MR: I see.

MRS: What was that? A trick question?

MR: I was just hoping...

MRS: Do *you* want to stay home with Baby? Cleaning up little pukes, grinding up sweet potatoes, or whatever they eat? Learning to babble?

MR: No.

MRS: No.

MR: I had a nanny.

MRS: Why sweetheart! I thought I knew all your secrets. You see Nanny is a family tradition already!

MRS nods encouragingly to DOLLY.

MR: I had a Nanny with long slender calves; a Nanny who painted her toenails red then topped them with crescent moons. I screamed and screamed for her when they took me out of her bed.

MRS: You see how dear a Nanny can be? Precious, beloved even treasured.

MR: But then there was the angry Nanny. She ran the tub scalding hot and she would never make me turkey sandwiches.

MRS: Our Nanny is so very kind.

MR: I wanted my mother.

MRS: I know, dear. But that's another conversation, and we've already had it.

MR: Why did we want Baby?

MRS: Because everybody wants one. Baby, Mother, Father equals family. It is the cornerstone of civilization.

MR: And Nanny? What is she? Crown molding?

MRS: Don't be such an idiot.

MR: While we're at work, what will you do? Sing silent lullabies, teach Baby Jihadist propaganda? What do we really know about you? Though my wife is correct, you do have very lovely breasts.

MRS: Let's get back to the form, dear.

MR: So, missy, do you believe in one God? Or are you going to start burning incense in the sconces and teaching Baby to worship some pot bellied elephant god with a ruby on its forehead?

MRS: I've gotten to the written references sweetheart. Impeccable!

MR: I must tell you, by the way, your base salary requirements are outrageous.

MRS: Honey, you are such a joker. We can't afford *not* to have Nanny. We can't care for Baby! No. Nanny will raise Baby; we will be the parents. It's very simple. Nanny is human, we are human, it will all work out. Just put a lid on it.

MR: No time for Baby.

MRS: We will have quality time with Baby, special time. Otherwise it's just time, stretching forward remorselessly, gripping you in its coils and crushing you mercilessly. You'd have to give up golf entirely.

MR: Well I can't stay home with Baby. I can no more nurture than nurse.

MRS: I told you he was clever.

MR: *You* should stay home.

MRS: How dare you? I can only assume you've confused your medications today.

(to Dolly)

Please excuse him.

(to MR)

We are a pair, a couple in stride, and we cannot break that stride, dear, or we will be plunged into the abyss. And Nanny is here to rescue us before my ten forty-five. She is an angel sent to rescue us and to rescue Baby. Who could we be to Baby but the only parents we know--our parents!

MR: Our parents? Like our parents? No!

MRS: Yes. It's inevitable. I'd play your father and you'd play my mother--or, maybe, it would be the other way round. But either way it would be a painful disaster.

MR: Baby would be emotionally maimed.

MRS: Endless therapy sessions and ten to one Baby ends up at the Betty Ford clinic by sixteen.

(shaking it off)

So do *you* want the job?

DOLLY nods. MR and MRS collapse onto each other with relief.

MRS: Well that's done then. Congratulations. And goodbye. We both have urgent meetings. Can you drop me in your car, darling?

MR: My car only has one charger.

MRS: *(dialing)*Hello, Jack. Send a car. Now. Here. The usual. Manicurist. No waxing today. Well, enjoy Baby! Baby eats...well I think nurse made a list before she stumbled out of here. If not, well, whatever babies eat! You're the professional!

(DOLLY holds up two tiny blankets, one pink, one blue)

MR: She's asking about the nap schedule.

(DOLLY shakes her head emphatically no.)

MRS: Perhaps she wants to know if Baby is a boy or a girl. Well really it is unimportant. We don't want Baby raised in a gender-prejudiced way. After all, it is these early expectations which shape us, whether that tiny fist is given the hammer or the dolly. So we'll just let you guess.

(DOLLY shakes her head again.)

MRS: Not it. This really is difficult. Could you give us a clue? You know. Sounds like...

(DOLLY is stumped. Then she gets a sudden idea. She pulls a small, raggedy teddy bear out of her purse)

MR: Toy, boy, Roy?

(DOLLY shakes her head. Again she points to the bear.)

MRS: I believe I mentioned I have a ten forty- five meeting? All right. Hairy.

(DOLLY excited, motions her on)

Hairy, Harry, Harry was Hairy...ladies run down fire escapes to get away from hairy apes. What? The bear. Bear, tear, wear it is all one long weary--no that's it. Bear. All right.

(DOLLY, excited urges her on)

MR: Grin and bear it. Bare your chest. No, that couldn't be it. Stock advice?

MRS: Where.

(DOLLY jumps up and down with excitement)

Where is what? The emergency phone numbers are by the phone; the take-out menus are in the drawer. There are extra rolls of toilet paper under the sink. Where is what?

MR and MRS: Baby!

MRS: How silly. We forgot to show you Baby!

They drag a bassinet out from under the table. They coo at its inhabitant.

MRS: Baby is a sunbeam in our life and Nanny… well you are a ray of hope.

Exit waving.

END OF PLAY

ONE ANOTHER

Cindy Turner & Jon Tuttle

One Another premiered on August 17, 2017, at Tapp's Art Center in Columbia, South Carolina, as part of Syzygy: The Solar Eclipse Plays, an event sponsored by the Jasper Project (Cindi Boiter, propr.). Project Director was Patrick Michael Kelly. The play was directed by Bakari Lebby; the cast included Akida Lebby (Lavon); Jason Stokes (James) and Avery Bateman (Celia).

CHARACTERS

LAVON: Male, black, a teenager.

JAMES: White, going on 40 or just past it, a little rough around the edges.

CELIA: Black, in her 30's, plainly dressed. Wears an ankle monitor.

SETTING

In the present: the porch, front door and front room of a small, older frame house in the country.

A bit of grass in the corner of the stage is part of the adjoining yard. The house is gray and run down. The screen door swings freely and has a big hole in it. In the living room there is very little furniture—an old couch, an old TV, a table maybe. It looks unlived in.

ONE ANOTHER
SCENE ONE

> *At rise: Mid-day. The yard. LAVON, a teenager, black, is on one knee, fiddling with a lawnmower. He's got it on its side, looking at the blade. He rights it, pushes the choke a few times, stands and tries to pull-start the engine. It won't turn over. Frustrated, he unscrews the cap to the gas tank and sniffs the gas. He's puzzled. He sniffs it again, puts his finger in, and tastes it. Lights to black.*

SCENE TWO

> *At rise: Late evening. A driving rain. Thunder—terrible thunder. Out of the rain and onto the porch runs JAMES, white, around 40, carrying a gas can and shielding himself from the downpour. He stamps his shoes and raps on the door.*

> *In the house, CELIA appears from the kitchen, drying her hands with a towel. She's black, in her 30's, and wears a skirt, so we can see the conspicuous black monitor around her ankle. She looks at the closed door, hesitantly. He raps again and calls through the door:*

JAMES: Ma'am? It's me. The fella borrowed your gas can.

> *Pause. No answer. He raps again.*

…Ma'am? It's me. I'm just bringin' your can back. …Hello?

> *Pause. He starts to rap again—doesn't.*

…I'll just leave it out here on the porch. Thanks for the help. I 'preciate it.

> *At this he starts off, but she rushes toward the door and opens it—then backs away.*

…Oh hey—there you are. Sorry to bother you again. I'm just returning your can. Got my car going, so….

> *She offers no response, seems skittish, so:*

…Well, again. I 'preciate your help. I didn't mean to scare you before. I know you ain't supposed to open your door to a stranger nowadays. …Sooooo…you have a nice night.

CELIA: Thank you.

JAMES: You're welcome. You take care now.

CELIA: Umm, wait. …What's your name?

JAMES: …James.

CELIA: …James what.

JAMES: Hartshorn.

CELIA: James Hartshorn. …I never heard that name around here.

JAMES: My people are from Georgia. I'm on my way north, see about a job. Think I might have to wait the night, though, the way it's coming down out here. There a Shoney's or something around here I can maybe get some coffee?

CELIA: Not the way you're goin'. We don't have much out here. You're kinda off the beaten path.

JAMES: Yeah, I know. I don't much like the interstate. Makes me nervous.

CELIA: Are you hiding?

JAMES: …Ma'am?

CELIA: Hiding. From the law. …Are you wanted by the law.

Lighting, followed closely by thunder. Several more strikes may follow.

JAMES: Well no ma'am, I'm just—

CELIA: *Indicating her ankle bracelet* I am. See this? Know what that is? That's a monitor. I'm a convicted criminal.

JAMES: …Yeah I saw that.

CELIA: I ain't afraid to shoot nobody. Just so you know. Already done it once.

JAMES: …Well I'm just gonna leave you alone. Thanks again for letting me use your—

CELIA: I can get you a Co-Cola or something. For the road, I mean. If you want.

JAMES: Ma'am you've done enough. I'm just gonna—

CELIA: Wait! …Truth is I didn't think you'd bring that can back. Thought you'd be long gone. I don't mean 'cause you're white. I don't mean that. I just mean: that's what most men'd do, isn't it? Just got to grab and go without a mind for anyone else. But I couldn't stand there lookin' at you and say no I don't got no gas can. You look like a decent man. …And you were in a bind.

So I took a chance. My mama'd say I'm a fool.

JAMES: Well. Again, I—

CELIA: Don't need to keep thanking me. Folks are supposed to be nice to one another. Don't you think? Folks are meant to care about one another, that's how I was raised. You were raised that way too, I bet.

JAMES: …Well yes, yes I was.

CELIA: You probably think it's strange for a woman been to prison to talk like that.

JAMES: You been to prison?

CELIA: See that hole in the screen? I did that. With a shotgun. … You wanna know why?

JAMES: …Uh. Sure.

CELIA: 'Cause my husband was sitting right there where you are.

Pause. He nods, sizing up the situation.

JAMES: …You git him?

CELIA: *giggling, feeling a bit ridiculous now* …I tried! I tried, mmm-mm. But I missed. Spent almost two years in prison, my mama died while I was in there, couldn't even be with her. Got house arrest until October, can't go across the street, can't even mow my own lawn, gotta have the neighbor boy do it. Then a whole year parole. Ain't nobody ever gonna hire me. I was taking classes to be a paralegal. Now I'm a convicted felon. Probably stuck here the rest of my life.

JAMES: …Ma'am, I'm real sorry.

CELIA: …I don't know why I'm tellin' you this. You probably think I'm crazy. I'm afraid of thunderstorms, if you want to know. Loud noises and the dark, ever since I was a little girl, like to scare me to death.

JAMES: Well, I…I think this one's probably—

Boom! A flash of lighting and thunder very nearby— and the lights blink out. The stage is now mostly dark. Both react.

CELIA: Oh God! Oh Jesus!

JAMES: Holy—! That was a close one! …You okay?

CELIA: …Yes I'm—*no!* I don't know. The lights went out.

JAMES: I got a flashlight in the car. I'll get it for you.

CELIA: You can't go down there you'll get killed.

JAMES: I'll be happy to get it for—

CELIA: No no I'm—. Just. …Would you…would you like to…I probably oughta let you come in.

JAMES: Well, ma'am, no, I'm…you don't even know me, and I'm soaking wet and, I don't know if it's—

CELIA: You're a good man, aren't you? James Hartshorn? Aren't you a good man?

JAMES: …I guess, ma'am. I try.

CELIA: You brought my gas can back, that's a small thing, but you didn't have to, most men woulda kept on goin', I know that. So I'm thinkin' you're a good man, and I think it'd be okay if you come in. …So… come on in, if you want to.

She holds open the screen door.

…I got a towel. Here. Take it.

She holds it out to him. He reaches for it and takes it— and enters the house.

We see them as shadows. She'll back away and watches him.

JAMES: Thank you. …This storm ain't so bad, ma'am. It gets a lot worse in Georgia. We get tornadoes there. I think this one's gonna blow over pretty soon.

CELIA: My dog Cash used to sit with me on the floor when it came down like this. I don't know who was protecting who.

JAMES: Where is he now?

CELIA: Husband took him while I was in prison. Took most of the furniture too. Come home to a empty house. You can sit on that couch if you want.

JAMES: I'll just stand right here, ma'am.

Pause. She watches him wiping the rain from his clothes, drying his hair.

CELIA: …You got a family, Mr. Hartshorn?

JAMES: …Well I used to.

CELIA: Used to?

JAMES: Wife run off.

CELIA: Oh....

> *Pause. He hands her the towel.*

...Why'd she do that? Meet somebody else? ...I mean if you don't mind my asking.

JAMES: No, no, nothing like that. ...It was probably my fault.

CELIA: You hit her?

JAMES: Did I--?

CELIA: Did you hit her? Beat her up?

JAMES: No ma'am, good Lord. I been a drinker and a liar. But I never once hurt a woman, not like that.

CELIA: ...Well then what'd you lie about.

JAMES: ...Well, you know: all the usual little lies. Like I don't know where that money went, so on. Told her I never been to jail, but I had.

CELIA: You been in jail too?

JAMES: Petty theft. Twice actually. And yeah, I remember once I did lay my hands on her, after a fight. She was bad for fighting. I pushed her into a chair. Fell over backward, Lord she gave me an earful... So there's the truth. I been to jail and yes, I have hurt a good woman.

CELIA: ...Bad for fighting. Just like my husband. Some folks are just mean.

JAMES: No, no, she had a good heart.

CELIA: ...You do too, though, don't you. You're a good man in your heart. Or you try to be.

JAMES: ...I guess everybody tries to be good. In their heart.

CELIA: I don't. I'm tryin' to be as hard as I can. I want to be evil as a snake. I want to hurt someone so bad.

JAMES: Now, you don't mean that.

> *She sits—maybe on the floor, her back against the wall.*

CELIA: Yes I do.... I don't understand what's goin' on inside me anymore. 'Fore he came along, I was different. I was happy, I was real pretty too, gonna get myself established, you know, be self-sufficient like my mama. But I got greedy. I got greedy and I started wanting a man, and I didn't even care what kind. That's when he came along. And he was all charm and politeness, bring a shy girl out her shell with pretty words and sweet gestures. You know the kind.

JAMES: ...You got to be careful, that's true.

CELIA: He was a white man like you, actually. I mean I know all white folks ain't the same, but my mama, she said you can never trust any of 'em.

JAMES: ...I don't know 'bout that.

CELIA: His people said the same thing 'bout me. They all blamed me for all the bad that happened. Couldn't keep a job, couldn't have a child. The races ain't meant to mix, that's what everybody says, don't they?

JAMES: ...Yeah they do.

CELIA: ...I tried to make him happy. Like it was when we started, tried to do everything the same way. ...But it didn't last long. ...He come in one night. I was boilin' eggs 'cause I know he likes egg salad, see. 'Starts in 'bout *mayonnaise*, 'bout there being Hellman's instead of Duke's, whoever heard of such. He wasn't drunk, either, he was just *mean*, that's all, just, just—. ...Well so he takes my arm, see, and he twists it real hard until I'm down on my knees, and he takes that boilin' water and he pours it on me, he pours a whole pot of scalding hot water all over me. And I was screamin' but he just held me down with his boot until he was done, and then kicked my twice right in my face. ...Broke my nose and two teeth.

JAMES: ...Jesus, ma'am, that's...hard to hear.

CELIA: I laid on that floor I don't know how long. When I finally opened my eyes and came in here, he was sittin' out there on the porch, just...starin' out down the road.

JAMES: I'm so sorry.

CELIA: You don't need to keep apologizin'. Not your fault. You been nothing but good to me. I been sittin' here alone for four months, nobody to talk to, nowhere to go. It's all my fault.

JAMES: ...So why'd they send you to jail?

CELIA: Oh. 'Cause I went in and got his shotgun and cocked it back and I stood right here and aimed it right at him, right through that door. I say *turn around* but he wouldn't. I say *you look at me* but he wouldn't. He say: you ain't gonna do it. You ain't got it in you. And he was right. ...I don't.

JAMES: But that doesn't...I mean... they don't put you in jail for shooting out your screen door.

CELIA: Oh, apparently they do. Apparently , if he says terrible lies in court, they give you twenty-two months plus house arrest, and it doesn't matter that you show 'em your burns and your busted face. ...So here I am. No job. No money. Didn't get to tell Mama goodbye. ... I don't even have my dog.

The lights abruptly come back on. She is sitting, her eyes closed, head bowed. Now she opens her eyes and finds him. An awkward pause.

...Well. ...Nice to meet you. ...James Hartshorn from Georgia.

JAMES: I never caught your name.

CELIA: Celia. That means sky. Mama named me that 'cause I was born on a bright sunny day.

JAMES: Well that's very pretty.

Now she stands, somewhat self-consciously, and smooths out her clothes.

CELIA: Sounds like it's slowin' down out there.

JAMES: Told ya it wouldn't last long.

CELIA: Bet you ready to bust on outa here. Probably think: this Celia woman: she got me held hostage. Gonna tie me up and keep me for company 'til Christmas comes.

JAMES: No ma'am. ...I just. Well there's just something I need to—

CELIA: Been sittin' here alone so long she can't hardly help herself.

JAMES: No...no I—I just need to tell you something. Before I go. There's something I need to say to you.

CELIA: ...Well, alright. I guess it's probably your turn, isn't it. You want that Co-Cola?

JAMES: No I—just-just...listen for a minute. It's about that gas can.

CELIA: ...Okay.

A difficult pause. James looks at her standing there— expectantly, hopefully

JAMES: ...I—

CELIA: But you better not be thanking me again. I think I made myself clear about that. There's such a thing as basic human decency and I'll take all a' that I can get.

A long, awkward pause. He can't complete his thought.

JAMES: ...Yes ma'am. I guess so. ...So I...I probably oughta get going.

> *She holds out a hand, which he takes, and gently shakes.*

...You take care, Celia.

CELIA: Goodbye James. You drive careful.

> *James nods, pulls away, and exits to the porch, where he picks up the gas can.*

...You can just leave that right there. I'll take it out to the shed.

> *He pauses, a pained look on his face, then puts it down—and exits.*

...Thank you, James.

> *This last softly, to herself. She smiles now, looking out through the door as he walks away. Then she goes onto her porch, picks up the gas can, feels that it's full and heavy, smiles, and watches him disappear. Lights to black.*

SCENE THREE

> *At rise: Mid-day. The yard. LAVON is on one knee, fiddling with the lawnmower as before. He has unscrewed the cap to the gas tank and is sniffing the gas, puzzled. He puts his finger in and tastes it. Realization dawns. He tastes it again, stands, walks to the front door of the house, and knocks. Celia appears inside—hopefully:*

CELIA: ...Who is it?

LAVON: Miss Celia, it's Lavon. I think we got a problem.

> *Celia opens the door. Through the screen.*

CELIA: What's the matter, honey, the grass too wet?

LAVON: Nah. The problem is I was trying to get your lawnmower started—

CELIA: My God, it musta growed three inches, look at it! We sure needed that rain, didn't we?

LAVON: Yes, ma'am. And the part you wanted me to reseed? By the fence? It's coming in already, but I can't mow any of it. Did you leave your gas can out?

CELIA: …What you mean, leave it out.

LAVON: …'Cause it's full of water, Miss Celia. You can't put water in an engine or it gets ruined. I didn't know it was water. …I'm really sorry.

> *Long pause. Celia stands stunned.*

…Miss Celia? I'm really sorry. But I think I ruined it.

CELIA: …No no. That's alright, Lavon. …Thank you. …That's… that's my fault.

LAVON: But…Miss Celia?

> *But she has already pressed the door closed. Pause. Lavon exits. She leans against the door, whispering to herself:*

CELIA: …It's alright. …It's all my fault. …It's my fault.

> *Pause. End play.*

PROTOCOL

Brenda Foley

Protocol premiered on May 14, 2017 at the BAC Stanford Calderwood Pavilion in Boston as part of the 19th Boston Theater Marathon, produced by Boston Playwrights' Theatre and Kate Snodgrass. It was directed by Liz Adams. The cast was as follows:

ELLIE: Jen Alison Lewis
MARK: Alan R. White
URIAH: Kim H. Carrell
PARROT: Alisha Jansky

CHARACTERS
    ELLIE – 30s/40s
    MARK – 30s/40s, married to ELLIE, a teacher
    URIAH – 40s/50s, works at the lab with ELLIE: PARROT –
    heard, not necessarily seen

TIME
    Now

PLACE
    The home of ELLIE and MARK:

Brenda Foley

Lights up as MARK is typing on the computer at a table that has a potted geranium on it. ELLIE enters, flinging about a briefcase, coat, hat. There are two chairs (one with a blanket over the back), some kind of side table with the wine bottle and glasses, and US a birdcage.

ELLIE: *(Frazzled)*WORST day, EVER. Prize-winning, terrible, worst day.

MARK: *(Not looking up)*That guy from the lab called.

ELLIE: *(Disrobing for comfort, jacket, shoes, etc., whatever, leaving puddles of clothing.)*What? Which guy?

MARK: The guy you don't like.

ELLIE: You're going to have to be a little more specific. That description fits very nearly all my colleagues. *(Moves to the birdcage onstage)* And how is my pretty? Can you say "Hello?" "Hello." "Helloooo" --

MARK: *(Typing and not really engaging)* The one you think is smarmy. You know, the one you said is Uriah Heep reincarnated – unctuous, I believe, was the descriptive used for him. And you know that bird is never going to talk to you. The store lied. It's probably not even a parrot.

ELLIE: *(Stops and turns)*Please tell me you are making that up.

MARK: Well, I'm not. He hasn't said a word in two years. Why would he –

ELLIE: No, not that. What you said about Uriah. Tell me it isn't true.

MARK: You think I would come up with a word like "unctuous" on my own? That's got you all over it.

ELLIE: Oh, my God. Could this day get any worse? What did he want? What did you say to him?

MARK: I told him you'd be back later this evening –

ELLIE: You didn't! Jesus Christ, Mark. Why would you do that?

MARK: Uh, because it bears resemblance to truth? *(Taking her in)* What exactly is the problem here?

ELLIE: The problem is you giving out personal information about me over the phone to smarmy colleagues.

(MARK gets up from the table and crosses to her.)

MARK: Really, that's the problem? Why don't you sit down? *(She starts to object but he cuts her off)* Please, sit down. I'm going to stop my grading, pour us some wine, and we're going to back up three minutes to you coming through the front door.

ELLIE: (*Sitting at the table*) It's too late.

MARK: *(Getting wine and glasses)*For what? You're not giving me much to work with here, El. I know there are some things you can't disclose but what happened? Give me something. (*Pours.*)

ELLIE: There was a bit of an accident at the lab.

MARK: *(Sits)* Ok, good, let's start with that. What kind of accident?

ELLIE: A protocol breach.

MARK: Is that bad? It doesn't sound that bad.

ELLIE: I would characterize it as very bad.

MARK: Oh, sorry, ok. (*Drinks*) So, was it you? The breach. Was it your accident?

> *(ELLIE stares at him weighing what and how much to tell.)*

MARK: (*Cont'd*) C'mon, you can tell me, whatever it is, you know you can tell me.

ELLIE: I made an error. In judgment. And because of that, something leaked out. Was released.

MARK: Like what? Information?

ELLIE: *(With difficulty)* Something toxic. And possibly dangerous. (*They both drink.*)

MARK: *(Starting to feel uneasy)*Well, how bad can it be? You came home; they let you leave. It must have been…contained? The toxin…

ELLIE: I thought so. I thought it was. Right up until you telling me Uriah Heep called. He's not really my boss, more like a handler.

MARK: His job is to "handle" you? I'm not sure I like the sound of that –

ELLIE: His job is to ensure proper procedures are followed and that there are no breaches. That no contact is made.

MARK: Contact with what? How is it I'm only now hearing about this part of your job? This apparently dangerous part of what you do every day?

ELLIE: Because I signed a non-disclosure agreement.

MARK: You what?! Alright, I can feel myself getting irritated and I

---

don't want to do that. But this is very *Three Days of the Condor* and that opening scene had some unfortunate -

ELLIE: Which one am I?

MARK: What?

ELLIE: Which character in *Three Days of the Condor*? Because you probably want me to be Faye Dunaway but I think my situation is much closer to Robert Redford's role –

MARK: Ellie –

ELLIE: As long as you aren't Max Von Sydow trying to kill me, I don't care which --

MARK: For God's sake, Ellie! Please, just state in a straightforward way what the hell happened today.

ELLIE: I accidently released a toxin from one of the controlled environments. The team immediately initiated emergency protocol and we thought it was contained. I wrote up the report and filed it. But if Uriah is looking for me, that means there has been contamination.

MARK: What kind of contamination? Are you saying you have been contaminated by some toxic accident? Ok, I'm calling the hospital –

ELLIE: That isn't going to help –

MARK: Then what? The CDC? I don't know! As it would appear I have no idea what it is you really do at your job, how are we supposed to –

> (*Her cell phone rings. They stare at it and ELLIE answers.*)

ELLIE: "Hello?" Yes, I know. I'm sorry. (*Beat*) I don't think that's necessary – alright. I understand. Yes, he's here (*she looks to MARK*) but there's been no contact. Ok, we'll wait. (*She hangs up.*)

MARK: What was that about? Was that him? Uriah?

> (*They overlap.*)

ELLIE: Look, we don't have much time –

MARK: What are you –

ELLIE: Please, Mark, listen carefully –

MARK: You're freaking me out –

(There's a knock at the front door. They freeze.)

ELLIE: *(Taking control)* Stand on the other side of the room, away from the door. And let me do the talking.

(MARK does as she says and moves across the room. Ellie opens the door and URIAH enters.)

URIAH: Good evening. I'm terribly sorry for the disturbance. (*Looks to ELLIE*) Are you alone?

MARK: No, she's not –

ELLIE: *(Jumping in)* Yes, we're alone. There's been no contact.

URIAH: You realize that contact is inevitable?

ELLIE: I thought the containment –

URIAH: No. It failed. *(Beat)* It's coming for you.

MARK: Ok, that's enough –

ELLIE: Don't, just –

URIAH: *(Overly polite)* Hello, Mark.

ELLIE: He should go. He has no part in this and has time to get away. There has been no contact –

(We hear a growing storm. MARK rushes to protect ELLIE.)

URIAH: Too late. It knows you're here. Prepare –

MARK: What the hell –

(The door blows open, there's general tumult, flashing lights, maybe fog, etc., whatever your tech can accommodate.)

URIAH: *(Beat)* Now there's contact.

(As the tumult ceases there is, apparently, nothing there.)

MARK: I don't see anything. Should I be seeing something? Do you? Because I don't –

URIAH: Stop talking. And don't move.

MARK: You know I'm getting a little –

(Suddenly MARK begins to spasm and contort, flailing, and then becomes very still. ELLIE and URIAH watch in horror.)

ELLIE: Mark? Honey, are you ok? Can you hear me? (*She moves toward him.*)

URIAH: Don't get too close!

ELLIE: You're scaring me. Can you speak?

MARK: *(Turning to ELLIE and fixing on her)* But I do love thee. And when I love thee not, Chaos is come again --

ELLIE: What? I don't understand. *(Turning to URIAH)* What is that?

URIAH: Shakespeare. It's using Shakespeare to communicate with you.

MARK: Make me a willow cabin at your gate and call upon my soul within the house -

ELLIE: You're joking. Are you saying he has a, a what, a Shakespeare infection? That he's been infected by a toxin obsessed with Shakespeare?

URIAH: Don't be absurd. Did you read Shakespeare to it in the lab? It's using that to communicate. The toxin thinks that's how we speak.

ELLIE: Is that contagious?

URIAH: Only if he touches you. Be careful it wants you.

> *(ELLIE places a piece of furniture between herself and MARK.)*

ELLIE: But how do we get it out of him? How do we quarantine it?

URIAH: There is no way to contain it, other than giving it another host. It can only reside in one host at a time.

MARK: *(A little more forcefully)* Why then, can one desire too much of a good thing?

ELLIE: You, you just stay back. Until we can think what to do next. *(To URIAH)* But what does it want? How can we get it to leave if we don't understand what it wants?

URIAH: Well, clearly, it desires you.

ELLIE: But why?

URIAH: *(Unhinged)* Because you reached out to it, in the lab! You touched it. And that touch released it. If you had followed the established proto –

ELLIE: I didn't touch it! I just talked to it, was nice to it, let it know we didn't want to hurt it –

URIAH: But you didn't consider what *it* might want or need -

MARK: This hot desire converts to cold disdain -

URIAH: It's getting angry. (*To ELLIE*) That's not a good sign. You obviously transmitted something vocally. Communicated with it. Something you said, or the tone. You aren't supposed to communicate with the other beings. It's why the protocol stipulates silence.

(The following exchange between MARK and ELLIE overlaps and escalates.)

MARK: Does Rosalind lack then the love which teacheth thee that thou and I am one -

ELLIE: No, look, no we aren't. You and I are not one. I'm sorry if I misled you, thee. I'm not Rosalind and, honestly --

MARK: Say that I love you and say you love me not –

ELLIE: Yes, that's right, I don't mean to be harsh but I don't love you. I accept that I'm responsible because I reached out to you, initiated contact but -

MARK: If you poison us, do we not die?

ELLIE: Wait, what? Look, I made a mistake, interfered with your state of being, or whatever, but we can fix it –

MARK: If I must die, I will encounter darkness as a bride, and hug it in my arms – *(goes toward her.)*

ELLIE: *(Moving out of its reach)*Hey, pal, there's no hugging and nobody's going to die here –

MARK: (*Building with fervor*) And if you wrong us shall we not revenge? Blood will have blood.

ELLIE: Now you're really creeping me out -

MARK: *(All puffed up and angry)*Blow winds and crack your cheeks. Rage, blow --

ELLIE: *(Frantic)*Just settle down. No one is cracking or blowing anything --

MARK: What's done is done.

ELLIE: NO! Nothing's been done, we're all very much undone –

(He moves towards her as if to overpower or transform her. She suddenly throws the geranium from the table at him, knocking him down. There is a brief, silent stillness.)

MARK: *(Shakily, stands up)*Ellie? I feel a little woozy -

ELLIE: Oh, thank God, it's you (goes to him). But, wait

(They both look with trepidation at URIAH.)

URIAH: NO, no, it isn't in me. But, where -

> *(All three turn and stare at the geranium. ELLIE walks over to it.)*

URIAH: *(Cont'd)* Don't touch it!

ELLIE: *(Taking a step back)*Did you see that? It moved. I'm pretty sure it moved.

> *(She goes to the chair to get the blanket to throw over the plant. Suddenly from the birdcage we hear:)*

PARROT: To be or not to be...

> *(They look at each other.)*

PARROT: *(Cont'd)* When in disgrace with fortune and men's eyes *(They turn to stare at the birdcage)* I all alone beweep my outcast state.

> *(They move slowly up to the cage.)*

PARROT: *(Cont'd)* Thou knowst 'tis common, *(lights start to fade)* all that lives must die, passing through nature to eternity...We cannot hold mortality's strong hand...Like as the waves make towards the pebbled shore, So do our minutes hasten to their end...

> *(They stare at each other. Blackout.)*

Silo # 3

Kate McCamy

Originally produced by the New Circle Theatre Company & LIU Post, performed at the Playroom Theater, 151 West 46th Street, New York City. June 1- 17, 2017. It was part of the Inferno Project: Limbo.

Directed by – Melanie Sutherland

CAST:

    KATH – Alice King
    DICK – Tom Bozell
    CARL – Mark Austin Merman

CHARACTERS:

KATH; A wealthy woman anywhere between the ages of mid 40's to late 50's.

DICK; A wealthy man, 50's plus.

CARL; A congressperson's son, 20's.

TIME:

In the near future.

Place:

A survival Silo, formerly a nuclear missile silo, somewhere deep underground.

Lights up. A sparse impersonal room with fancy but tacky furniture. KATH sits on a chaise lounge, has on a mud mask and wears a robe. She has a drink and stares ahead. DICK, also in a robe, is semi asleep holding a phone like device. The sound of chirping birds turns into a static garble.

KATH: Pookie the view has gone all pixilated again!

DICK: Here Lovie, I'll switch to the ocean, you like that one.

(He uses the device.)

(The sound of ocean waves.)

KATH: Ugh, it reminds me of the Hamptons.

DICK: You love that house...

KATH: Yes I did.

DICK: Then why not the ocean?

KATH: Those waves constantly crashing, gives me a headache.

DICK: I'd say that's the vodka...

KATH: You hear that?

DICK: What?

KATH: That, that wave!?

DICK: It's a wave.

KATH: One, two, three. There! That one! Hear that? That third wave! Sounds the same. It's a loop! How cheap can you get? Only three waves.

DICK: What do you mean? Waves do that, they crash. It's water.

KATH: How is crashing soothing? This is supposed to soothe us right? Like in the spa, they play those atmosphere things to you know, calm us. I don't know why they think the ocean is relaxing, I mean Christ, the ocean is taking over. Remember the Brockmans? Hurricane Donald? Destroyed all five floors of The Brockman's house!

DICK: Then here, the city-scape, you like the central park view.

(They both stare ahead.)

(The sounds of Central Park.)

KATH: Hey. It's the same dog! Look, look close you see the same damn dog chase the same damn ball the same damn way.

DICK: What?

KATH: Look! Look. In sheep's meadow. It's brown. And the Dakota is smack dab in the middle.

DICK: Dakota? It's a labrador.

KATH: Oh come on Dick! THE Dakota. Where John Lennon got shot, hello! ?

DICK: *(chuckles)* John Lennon. You'da thought the President got shot and it was the end of the world.

KATH: What's so funny about that?

DICK: The guy who preached peace and love got murdered in front of his home.

KATH: Yea well because of John Lennon daddy made us have our own bodyguards. Who is gonna shoot a rich girl? Mine looked like Vin Diesel. He had a scar across his face. He scared me more than getting shot at.

DICK: There's no end to violent nutjobs. He was right to get bodyguards.

KATH: I had curfews! I couldn't shop! Not with that big goon. Really screwed up my teens.

DICK: I thought you were in Switzerland for your teens?

KATH: That was after Reagan got shot. I went through puberty locked up in a penthouse!

DICK: Then the Alpen chalet?

KATH: Yea, lucky me! I learned to yodel. That really helped promote my branding!

(pouring the last of the bottle into her glass)

I need more, put in an order.

DICK: I need more patches anyway.

KATH: More patches? Dick. Already!?

DICK: They're better than drinking all day. You should go back to them...

KATH: And be numb? No thanks! Who knows what they put in them.

DICK: They're time released. Very safe, effective, no side effects. The miracle drug of the future. They thought of everything. Worth every penny.

KATH: Millions of dollars to stay alive for what? Huh? Dick? For what? It's all dead, dead up there. Maybe we should be too.

DICK: No, survival gangs are up there scraping by on what's left. Skin falling off, really disgusting.

KATH: *(seductively)*So, you're going to save me from some Mad Max with spikes sticking out of his neck?

DICK: *(ignoring her seduction)*You're funny, we're safe in our condo.

KATH: It's a fucking silo!

DICK: Nuclear missile silo. Impenetrable. Bomb proof. It's safe. Just like being on a cruise ship that....

KATH: Yeah yeah yeah.

DICK & KATH: That won't sink.

KATH: I'm sick of that slogan! I'm sick of all the passengers on this dumb boat! I wanna jump overboard! They're all so dull. The one person who was entertaining disappeared. What ever happened to him?

DICK: The gay guy?

KATH: Well duh! He was entertaining? He got kicked out because he was gay?

DICK: He was old, maybe he passed away?

KATH: What do they do with us when we die?

DICK: Look in the brochure; I'm sure there is a section somewhere.

KATH: That brochure is a liar!

DICK: It's a brochure. It can't lie, it's informational.

KATH: Well it lied! It said we'd be with our families! I haven't seen the kids since... The Event!

DICK: Sure we have, skype, we skype all the time.

KATH: How do I know it's really the boys? Not some pre-taped video 3 D virtual hologram ?

DICK: Oh come on Kath, it was the boys. You asked very specific questions, believe me.

KATH: Like what?

DICK: You asked Trent about his butt acne! That's pretty specific.

KATH: And he didn't answer me!

DICK: Why would he do that in front of his friends? You're being paranoid again.

KATH: Paranoid! Look at us, we're underground! I was right! They were doing what, the fake or real fake news was saying..

DICK: Hey, hey, we're fine. The kids are in Silo 32, they're fine. They're vaping medical marijuana and playing video games as usual.

KATH: I regret having children. I really do.

DICK: They probably don't even notice the difference.

KATH: What kind of life is this? For them, for us? The future is so, uncertain, but certain that it'll be the same thing! Over and over and over...

DICK: And we're the lucky ones.

KATH: Hah!

DICK: We're safe, like being in a gated community.

KATH: It's all gates! We're locked in a sealed tank! Like fish, swimming in the same stupid fish tank pointlessly blooping around and around!

DICK: It's safe, like the fifties?

KATH: The fifties? What are you talking about?

DICK: Everyone loves the 1950's? Big cars, gas was cheap, Rock n Roll? Cocktail hour, nostalgia, what we all voted for...

KATH: The fifties? Fuck the fifties! I wasn't even alive for the fifties, what do I know from the fifties!? I'm alive now! I wanna be in my own home!

DICK: Which one Hon?

KATH: The one with the Picasso!

DICK: The Hamptons.

KATH: Yes the Hamptons! I had a lover! Dick. Did you know that? That's kinda fifties right? Wife swapping, car keys in the bowl... Repression!

DICK: Kath? What are you saying?

KATH: You heard me. Renaldo! The pool guy? The Mexican!

DICK: Pool guys were Guatemalans.

KATH: Whatever! He loved the Picasso too. And he loved me, like you never did.

DICK: The Picasso was a fake.

KATH: Sotheby's sold us a fake?

Kate McCamy

DICK: No insurance company covers artwork in a beach house.

KATH: He would FUCK me, not just wet noodle around and then fall asleep! I mean really take me! From behind and in the pool, the water slide, up against the cabana! I had orgasms, yes orgasimS!! Multiple, I could fill a bucket! While you were on one of your 'business' trips, I was getting my plumbing plunged by a bad hombre! Can you dig that Dick?

DICK: This isn't... come on now, Kath.

KATH: You! You're a doped up dead man, in your multimillion-dollar silo coffin! Pathetic! I hate this!! This is soo, so...

DICK: You need a patch.

KATH: I'd rather be ripped apart by a zombie than be one!!

DICK: Kath, now... Kath please...

(She finds his patch and rips it off him.)

KATH: You need to FEEL something!! Look around you, this is our reality! They may as well have killed us Dick! We ARE the walking dead.

DICK: Who is They?

KATH: I don't know, Them, who ever caused the "event'. Probably Ted and those jerks. They're the real problem!

DICK: Ted? He worked for me....

KATH: They are the real horsemen of the apocalypse! They did this to us! To Everyone! They lied and took everything from me that was fun. For what? Money? What good is it if you can't buy things! I hate them all! I hope they're all dead! No, worse, I hope they're out there crawling in the wreckage with their faces falling off! I want, I need fresh air, real sunlight, to shop for new shoes!

(The doorbell rings.)

KATH: Get the door.

(She runs off. CARL enters.)

CARL: Your order sir. One bottle of vodka and of course, these.

DICK: Thank you. You sure are quick.

(He takes the bottle and package from him and stands uncomfortably close.)

CARL: Faster than Amazon prime!

DICK: Yes you are...

KATH: *(VO)* You guys are the best. Thank you so much Carl darling. See you later.

CARL: Yes, see you tonight. It's going to be a lot of fun. Bingo night!

DICK: Ah Wednesday. Bingo. How terrific!

(Pause)

CARL: If you need anything else don't hesitate to ping us upstairs.

(He tries to leave.)

DICK: I will. And how are things upstairs?

CARL: Fine, sir.

DICK: Good.

(awkward silence)

I'll see you later, Carl? Is it?

CARL: Yes, sir. It is.

(He backs out of the room. KATH comes back in without the mud mask. She pours herself a healthy drink.)

KATH: How come we have servants?

DICK: What do you mean? We have to have servants.

KATH: I thought we had limited resources.

DICK: Yes and?

KATH: They're rationing Botox for Godsake! There's limited food and stuff, why do we have servants? Aren't they taking up oxygen?

DICK: I think he's the kid of that congressman who couldn't afford the full package. Has to earn his keep.

KATH: Hah, I guess his daddy didn't take enough bribes!

DICK: Only the privileged could do that, believe me. WE are the privileged!

KATH: Yes we are darling.

DICK: I saw the writing on the walls, hell I wrote that writing. I predicted the up tick that made a ton of money, for me and a few of us. I predicted the... flip thing.

KATH: Yes you did.

DICK: You, you don't know how hard it is to get ahead. You never had to scramble. You had a daddy!

KATH: I watched daddy...

DICK: I tripled your daddy's fortune remember that!?

KATH: Yes how could I forget?

DICK: I figured it out, on my own! Me. My deals. Very big deals. I'm a big, very big deal Kath. Don't you forget that! You don't get HERE by letting people shit on you!

KATH: Richard...

DICK: Power, isn't that attractive?

KATH: Uhm.

DICK: Power and money. And I got both. You should be happy to lick my balls! To be in the same room as my balls!

KATH: Honey, put on a new patch. You're scaring me.

DICK: Renaldo?! That isn't even a Mexican name. Who knows where he was from or what kind of diseases! What a sad nobody!

KATH: Finally you have some feelings and they're shitty ones!

DICK: All I've done for you and the kids! I've had my things too you know. And I can tell you Nadia and Kelly and whatever her name was, they certainly didn't think I was a 'wet noodle'!!

KATH: Yeah, well ain't lust grand?

(She slaps a patch on DICK.)

DICK: Renaldo is dead now!

KATH: And so is Sharon. That was her name, Sharon! And don't forget the nannies!

DICK: Uppity little... how dare he touch what's mine! That's why it was time to purge the planet of people like Renaldo.

KATH: Rid the world of pool guys?! What the hell were you thinking?!

DICK: To stop the infiltration of the white race. We were getting muddied up as they swirled into our gene pool damn it! Weakening our DNA! Dumbing us down. Making us hard to recognize. I could see it. We could see it. It was there. Spreading their brown tentacles into everything that I ... that was mine damn it! I owned it all.

(She puts another patch on him.)

KATH: And look where it got you.

DICK: I don't know why... why you want to hurt me after all this time. It's you who I chose for eternity.

KATH: Eternity? Lord help us!

DICK: I didn't like that feeling...

KATH: Because you were actually feeling. I'm going to change for dinner.

DICK: I don't know why you bother?

KATH: Because if we lose our social decorum then we're truly lost Goddamnit!

DICK: No one seems to care anymore.

KATH: It's all I have.

(She leaves. Pause)

DICK: The view is pixilated, you'd think at these prices they'd fix that...

(Black out)

END OF PLAY

SOME PEOPLE SAY

Mark Saunders

Some People Say premiered as part of the 2017 Source Festival in Washington, D.C. Performances were held on June 13, June 18, June 23, June 24, June 30, and July 1. It was directed by Rebecca Wahls. Cast: Amanda — Zoe Walpole, Janet — Carol Spring — Dylan Hares, Zach. Props Design by Kyla Duff; Costume Design by Jeffery Peavy; Light Design by E-hui Woo; Sound Design by Bob Pike. Sara E. Cohen was the Dramaturg; Tori Ujczo was the Stage Manager; Carissa Gilson was the Assistant Stage Manager. Jenny McConnell Frederick, Artistic Director; Lee Cromwell, Associate Producer.

CHARACTERS

JANET: Attractive mother in her late 40s, dresses prim and proper

AMANDA: Janet's pre-teen daughter, also neatly dressed

ZACH: Janet's twenty-something son recently discharged from the military; he's disheveled and walks with a slight limp, perhaps a war injury

SETTING

City apartment, cramped quarters. Dark but not messy.

TIME

Late in the afternoon, middle of the week.

At Rise: Kitchen table is covered with papers and books. Although it's daytime, lights are on everywhere because it's a dark apartment. Heavy, black curtains are pulled shut on two windows. A child's backpack hangs over a chair. Nervous, Janet paces. Amanda is at the table writing in a notebook.

JANET: He should have been back two hours ago. Where is he?

(Amanda stops writing and looks up.)

AMANDA: Do the Bavarians or the Elders of Zion run the banks?

JANET: Elders.

AMANDA: Will the Elders give Zach the gold?

(Janet moves next to Amanda, looks over her shoulder.)

JANET: They better. It's all we have left of the insurance money.

AMANDA: Why do we need gold?

JANET: In three days the entire world economy is going to collapse and the only thing that will have value will be gold.

AMANDA: And food.

JANET: Your brother's not been right in the head since coming back. They did something to him over there. I swear to God they did something. Those people brainwashed him.

AMANDA: Maybe he's on his way.

(Janet continues to pace.)

JANET: Two hours! I should have gone instead. If you want something done right, you do it yourself. Remember that, Amanda. Don't trust anyone. Do it yourself. In this world, you can't trust anybody.

AMANDA: Maybe it's taking so long because he's bringing dinner back with him, like you asked?

JANET: Anything but K-F-C. What does K-F-C fried chicken do to men?

(Ah, a learning experience.)

AMANDA: Some people say it can make them sterile.

JANET: That's right, dear. It'll make them sterile. Do you know why it will make them sterile?

AMANDA: It's part of the New World Order.

JANET: Good. And where did we get AIDS?

AMANDA: The government. Also part of the New World Order.

JANET: Did we land on the moon?

AMANDA: Some people say facts suggest otherwise.

JANET: What do we know about fast food chicken?

AMANDA: It can make men sterile. *[beat]* I thought that was only black men? Zach's not black.

JANET: Remind me some time to tell you about your great-great grandmother.

AMANDA: What's sterile mean?

JANET: Never mind. If they don't give him my money, they'll have a fight on their hands, I can tell you. I know people. I know people who make bombs. Your father died for that money. That's blood money and they're not taking it away from me.

AMANDA: I'm hungry.

> *(The phone RINGS. Janet stares at the phone, but doesn't pick it up. She lets it RING. Amanda stares at it.)*

AMANDA: Aren't you going to get it?

> *(Amanda goes to pick up the phone.)*

JANET: Don't answer that. We don't know who it is.

AMANDA: It might be Zach.

JANET: What's the readout say?

AMANDA: It's an eight hundred service number.

JANET: Do not pick up that phone!

> *(The ringing stops and there's a KNOCK at the door. Janet leans into the door.)*

JANET: Who is it?

ZACH: *(O.S.)* It's me.

JANET: Who's me?

ZACH: *(O.S.)* Zach. Your son.

JANET: How do I know it's you?

ZACH: *(O.S.)* Who else would it be? Come on, open up.

JANET: What's the password?

ZACH: *(O.S.)* Lizard.

JANET: Wrong.

ZACH: *(O.S.)* Lizard People. Now open the door.

(Janet fiddles with several locks in opening the door.
Zach enters and before he can settle down, Janet gets
in his face.)

JANET: Did you have any problems at the bank?

ZACH: No. No problems.

JANET: Did you convert the money like I asked?

ZACH: Yes. It's been converted.

JANET: To gold?

ZACH: To something better than gold.

(Zach removes his backpack and sets it on the table.)

AMANDA: What's better than gold?

JANET: Good question, dear. Yes, what's better than gold?

(Janet grabs the bag, hefts it.)

JANET: Whatever it is, it's awful light.

(Zach unzips the bag, reaches in and pulls out what looks
to be a piece of paper currency, cut to the normal size
of American currency. It has a photo image of Zach in
the center. He hands the paper to Janet. She stares at
the currency, confused.)

JANET: "In Zach We Trust?" … Is this a joke?

ZACH: You always said the only person you can trust is yourself.
I made our own currency. If governments can print their own
money, why can't we?

JANET: I asked for gold Krugerrands. Or bars. Where's my gold?

ZACH: I gave it to the printer that printed up our money.

JANET: You gave our money to Kinko's!!!?

ZACH: Look, there's all sorts of denominations in there. Your
picture's on the thousand-dollar bill. Amanda's is on the five
hundred-dollar bill. I'm the lowest, the one hundred. Well, technically it's not a "dollar." We need to come up with a name for
it. You know, like pound, yen, peso, whatever we want to call it.

JANET: Were you followed? Did anybody follow you? Omigod, it
just hit me. You're a counterfeiter. They could put us all in jail.
This is how they're going to finally catch me.

ZACH: Counterfeiting is faking somebody else's money. This is
our own money.

(Janet reaches into Zach's backpack and grabs a hand full of the paper money. She studies it.)

JANET: This isn't money, you moron! This is. This is. This. I don't know what this is but it's not money. It's useless scraps of paper with family photos on it.

(Janet holds up a piece of the "currency" and turns it over.)

JANET: And you only printed one side!

ZACH: I was running late.

(Janet throws the paper money at her son. She SLAPS Zach on the cheek. He doesn't react.)

AMANDA: Mom!!!

(Janet SLAPS Zach a second time.)

JANET: You were supposed to come back with gold. Instead, you came back with this worthless shit. Who do you think you are, Jack and the Beanstalk? What am I supposed to do now? What will I do?

(Janet grabs Zach and shakes him.)

JANET: What am I supposed to do, you idiot? You stupid idiot. That's all we had left. Don't you realize the end is coming? We're out of time. We're ruined.

(Janet sits down. She puts her head in her hands. Zach walks over to his mother. He pulls a business card from his pocket and hands it to her.)

ZACH: You'll find it here. Our money.

(Janet clutches the card, stands and runs to the door. She turns and looks at Zach. She speaks calmly, in a measured voice. Back in control.)

JANET: Keep the door locked. Don't answer the phone. And try and do something useful for a change. Watch your sister.

(Janet sighs, puts on sunglasses, exits.)

AMANDA: Mom? Mom? Wait for me.

(Zach restrains Amanda. She struggles.)

AMANDA: Let me go.

ZACH: Listen to me. Mom's not right.

AMANDA: What do you mean not right?

ZACH: She hasn't been right since Dad died.

AMANDA: She is too right. She's always right.

ZACH: She's not right. She's not right about so many things, I don't know where to begin. She needs help.

AMANDA: Where'd she go? Where'd you send her?

ZACH: I'm taking you to live with Aunt Sarah. Until Mom is right again.

AMANDA: Where'd Mom go?

ZACH: A place where she can get help. Some good people are expecting her.

AMANDA: I want to go with Mom.

(Zach gently grabs Amanda by her shoulders and makes direct eye contact.)

ZACH: Look at me, Amanda. There's no such thing as Lizard People. Shape-shifting Lizard People do not rule the world. George Washington was not a space alien. The diary of John Wilkes Booth did not predict 9-11. Area Fifty-One is just a bunch of sand. The moon landing wasn't faked. AIDS wasn't created in a lab as an experiment. And you really want to know something else? Big Foot doesn't exist, either. Grizzlies, yes. Big Foot, I don't think so.

AMANDA: But Mom said --

ZACH: -- I know what Mom said. But there is no grand, horrible world-wide conspiracy. There is no New World Order and there is no Old World Order. No conspiracy, just people. A bunch of confused, frightened people trying to explain their own lives. That's pretty much it.

AMANDA: Some people say ....

(Amanda doesn't finish her thought.)

ZACH: I'm sorry, not all dots in life are connected. And not everything is a dot. Life's just not that simple. In fact, if you want to know the real truth, life is pretty complicated and mostly random. That's the one thing I learned over there. Why does one man survive and get to go home while the man next to him gets his head blown off? Nobody knows. Do you think the dinosaurs wiped out by that asteroid thought they were victims of a conspiracy? One moment they're munching on leaves, the next moment they're gone for good. It just happened. That's all. Nothing they could do about it. Nobody to blame. Chance is the world order. It's not new. And it's certainly not something called the Bavarian Illuminati. Or the Rosicrucian. Or whatever group of people some whackjob loves or hates that day.

AMANDA: Mom's not a whackjob. She's not. Take it back.

(Zach up his backpack, slings it over his shoulder. He hands Amanda her backpack. They move to the door.)

AMANDA: Are we broke?

ZACH: You mean Dad's insurance money? It's still there, in the bank. I didn't take any of it.

AMANDA: What does "In Zach We Trust" mean?

ZACH: It was a joke. I also had "In Amanda We Trust" and "In Janet We Trust" printed.

AMANDA: I'm hungry. You were supposed to bring something to eat.

ZACH: We can catch a bite on the way to Aunt Sarah's.

AMANDA: No K-F-C.

ZACH: I know. Mom's afraid I'm going to become sterile.

AMANDA: She was gonna tell me about our great grandma.

ZACH: It was your great-great grandmother. And that story Mom tells about her? That story is true.

(Zach out the lights as they exit their basement apartment.)

End of Play

That Night "Butcher" Pete Wilcox Got Knocked Out By Jessie "The Cannon" Tesori

Jonathan Cook

ORIGINAL PRODUCTION:

THAT NIGHT "BUTCHER" PETE WILCOX GOT KNOCKED OUT BY JESSIE "THE CANNON" TESORI was originally produced by Le Chat Noir Theatre (Augusta, GA) April 14-22, 2017 as part of their annual Quickies Play Festival.

CAST:

"BUTCHER" PETE WILCOX: Tom Colechin
JESSIE "THE CANNON" TESORI: Annaleesa Rogers
MIKEY B: Robbie Cook

Directed by Jonathan Cook

CHARACTERS

"BUTCHER" PETE WILCOX: Male boxer in his 30's. British accent.

MIKEY B: Male in his 50's or later. Pete's trainer. He is stern, but should never come off as mean to Pete.

JESSIE "THE CANNON" TESORI: Female boxer in her 20's. Should have some attitude.

TIME

Present Day

PLACE

The locker room of an arena in some place called Mayor's Income, Tennessee

Jonathan Cook

(In BLACK, we hear a roaring crowd. An arena bell rings and then we hear the announcers along with the sound of boxing gloves landing hits. *For convenience, the announcer lines below can be prerecorded and played along with the boxing match sound effects.)

ANNOUNCER 1: The Champ doesn't look to good going into round two, Jim.

ANNOUNCER 2: Well, that first round was brutal. I've never seen anything like it.

ANNOUNCER 1: And look at that! Jessie is completely unstoppable right now! Oh, did you see that hit! The Champ's dazed. Look at his face!

ANNOUNCER 2: And DOWN he goes!

ANNOUNCER 1: He's not getting up from that one.

ANNOUNCER 2: There it is. The ref has called it! Your winner ladies and gentlemen, Jessie "The Cannon" Tesori!

ANNOUNCER 1: UN-believable!

(The sound of the crowd fades out as the lights fade in to reveal "BUTCHER" PETE WILCOX in an arena locker room. He's wearing ring attire and looks exhausted as he puts on a t-shirt. He slowly sits on a nearby bench and stares blankly into the air. Some bruises on his face – mainly in the lip and left eye area.)

MIKEY: *(ENTERS with a small towel over his shoulder.)* Alright. Let's see the damage.

PETE: Just go on, will ya.

MIKEY: *(Inspecting Pete's face.)* Busted lip. That'll be swollen tomorrow for sure. Probably gonna have you talkin' funny for a few days. We'll get some ice on it. Hematoma around your left eye. You got clocked pretty damn good.

PETE: Jesus, Mikey. You come in here to rub it in?

MIKEY: Come on. No fighter can go undefeated forever.

PETE: Are you kidding me? A bleeding loss on my record by that lightweight Jessie Tesori.

MIKEY: Jessie "The Cannon" Tesori is one of the best.

PETE: Not even in my league, Mikey!

MIKEY: It was only an exhibition match. Just something they felt the fans would get a kick out of. Think of it like a scrimmage. You still have your title.

PETE: This will be the fight everyone remembers. It doesn't matter if it's official.

MIKEY: What do you want me to say, huh? Ya want me to sit next to you and cry about it? Hold your hand for a while? Wipe away the tears and join you for a verbal rampage on Tesori?

PETE: Just tell me this is a dream. Tell me I'm gonna wake up in that ring again ready to fight.

MIKEY: Yeah, maybe that's it. Maybe you're just having a little dream right now in the ring. Either way, it still means you got knocked the fuck out.

PETE: I can't show my face in this circuit anymore. I've never lost a match and that little shit gets my number with a couple of lucky punches.

MIKEY: You sound like a bratty child. You wanna quit and move back home to mommy in Bristol just cause you lost *one* fight? You're the heavyweight champ. You can't quit.

PETE: They're gonna be showing that knock out on every channel for the next year. I know it.

MIKEY: Oh, that doesn't matter. It's already all over the internet, kid.

PETE: What? It's only been about a half hour…

(burst of rage)

Cor Blimey! Fuck technology! Fuck computers and fuck all these arseholes with their stupid little smart phones! It should be illegal to put that shit on the internet.

MIKEY: Technically it is. The league owns the televised footage and the "no filming" policy was supposed to take care of all the amateurs with their "stupid little smart phones".

PETE: I want them arrested, Mikey. All of 'em. Lock 'em all up at Her Majesty's pleasure.

MIKEY: Come on, Butcher! Get your head straight, will ya. You're up against Sanchez right after the New Year and I don't need you psyching yourself out with this one lousy defeat.

PETE: Sanchez. God damn it. That bloke is gonna throw this in my face every chance he gets. He'll be dishing out insults in every interview. Gonna do his best to embarrass me. I'll never be able to live this down.

MIKEY: No. You won't. And you may as well start looking for a new trainer cause you threw everything *I* taught you straight out the window tonight.

PETE: You don't mean that.

MIKEY: The hell I don't. I could see it all over your face. You thought this was gonna be a gimme match against Tesori and you got too cocky out there, kid. You were leaving yourself wide open. What do I always tell ya, huh? Hands up, elbows down. Every time, Butcher. It was bad form all around. You left your face wide open and your feet... they were all over the damn place. It looked like someone had placed hot coals under 'em or something.

PETE: It felt like I had control the first round.

MIKEY: Your feelings don't make it fact.

PETE: I did get some solid hits in.

MIKEY: You call those hits? I've seen kittens do more damage to a ball of yarn. Do you even remember anything from the second round?

PETE: Yeah.

MIKEY: Yeah? All sixteen seconds of it?

PETE: Right outta the gate that rabid slag launched at me.

MIKEY: Yeah, like a *cannon*. Blasted ya with the one-two.

PETE: This is a career ender. It is, Mikey. One night of hard lines and I bet half my sponsors are gonna sack me after this.

MIKEY: Alright. Enough. Have a drink. Sleep on it. There's nothing to do now but get over it. You're "Butcher" Pete Wilcox. The Pistol from Bristol. A legend among men. Even with this loss, no one else has a record like you. And no one has a coach like you. I like to rattle your cage a bit, but I'm through listening to you derail yourself. Call it an off night. Call it a stroke of bad luck. Call it bad karma catching up to you for snubbing that Wyoming kid's "make a wish". Call it whatever you want, but you're gonna get your ass back in that ring when the time comes.

(JESSIE TESORI, a small-framed female fighter, EN-TERS. She's dressed in her fighting shorts with top and has no visible bruises on her.)

MIKEY: Evenin', Jessie. I think you may have taken a wrong turn.

JESSIE: Hey Mikey B. Can I speak to the Butcher for a minute?

MIKEY: Uh yeah, he's right here.

JESSIE: In private please.

MIKEY: Oh. Sure thing.

PETE: What for?

MIKEY: Take it easy, kid. I'll go get you that ice pack. Nice fight, Tesori.

(He exits.)

PETE: So, what brings you here? I can't imagine there's anything important for us to chat about.

JESSIE: I know what you did.

PETE: What on Earth are you on about?

JESSIE: Tell me why.

PETE: Why what?

JESSIE: How much money was in it for you to fall in the second round?

PETE: What… ? You think I… ?

JESSIE: Don't act brain dead with me, pal. I barely tapped you and you went wobbling like a toddler learning to walk.

(PETE turns his back to Jessie. His facial expressions indicating an idea is forming.)

JESSIE: What? You don't have anything to say?

PETE: *(takes a confident stance)*You know I would have destroyed you if I'd gone full force.

JESSIE: That's bullshit. Are you just saying that because I'm a girl?

PETE: You have less experience. Your winning streak has been against less than formidable opponents. And yeah. You're a girl.

JESSIE: I'm not going to accept a win that's handed over this way.

PETE: Take it and clear off.

JESSIE: I would have won that match with or without you taking a dive.

PETE: In your dreams, love.

JESSIE: I want a rematch.

PETE: A what? Come on. You won. Victory is yours. Congratulations on defeating "Butcher" Pete Wilcox. You'll be a legend by tomorrow morning. Someone may even write a song about ya.

JESSIE: When I called you out, it was for a legit challenge and you've turned it into some petty game. I figured the highest rated fighter to ever brandish the title of heavyweight champion would take this seriously.

PETE: My six-year-old ankle-bitin' nephew called me out last week. And guess what? I let him win too.

JESSIE: Alright, hotshot. Next time, I'm gonna tell the conference to make it official. No more of this showcase exhibition bullshit. I bet you'd take it more seriously then.

PETE: That'll never happen. This was a one off event. Just something to entertain the fans.

JESSIE: I promise you I'll make it happen. Being a woman doesn't make me handicapped against you. I train ten times harder than you and no one comes close to my stats in my division.

PETE: Right. *Your* division. The lady's division. It doesn't matter how much you fancy my title, you don't have a chance. They won't allow it.

JESSIE: You're such a little pussy, you know that?

(JESSIE quickly steps into him to be face to face and PETE momentarily breaks character and flinches, scared she's about to hit him. He immediately recomposes himself and plays it off.)

PETE: Excuse me?

JESSIE: You heard me. Put on your big boy pants and bring me a real fight. I'll murder you.

PETE: You gonna bring out the "cannon", love? Is that the right or the left? I couldn't tell. They both felt like sweet kisses from your mum.

JESSIE: Go screw a goat, you fuckin' Irish prick.

PETE: I'm British.

JESSIE: Whatever.

PETE: Settle down, will ya. I'm only taking the piss outta ya. Just having a bit of fun, that's all. Look, you connected some good shots. Gave a nice right knuckle to my jaw here. Eye is feeling a bit numb as well. And no doubt you're definitely faster than most opponents I've faced. You were striking like a bloody rattlesnake out there. You got a lotta bottle, sure, but you're far from perfect. You got flaws just like the rest of 'em. If you ever want to swing by my gym and join a session with me and Mikey B., you got an open invitation.

JESSIE: Is it the building with the sign out front that says "Chauvinist Dickhead Training Camp"?

PETE: *(shocked again at her foul mouth)* I invite you to get some pointers from a World Class trainer like Mikey B., and you go and say something like that?

JESSIE: Your hubris becomes you.

PETE: Listen. A lady has no place in the ring against a man. I know you don't want to hear it, but that's the blunt truth of the matter. We're built differently. And that's just how things are. Oh, but we're living in this feminism generation where the female is this symbol of strength and power. So, yeah, I decided to give the World a little taste of entertainment. You know that's all they really wanted, right? The underdog victory. The iconic courageous woman overcoming the testosterone driven male. Samantha beating Goliath. And just like that the sport gets a bump in ratings. And you gain the respect of new fans that'll be at your next match, pulling for you and all your glory. Don't let 'em down is the only advice I have for you.

JESSIE: And what about you? What respect do you gain?

PETE: One loss in an exhibition match ain't gonna break me, love. I've already shown my worth over the years.

JESSIE: I don't know why you consider that to be honorable. You think you're doing some kinda good for women by letting me win? I don't want your charity. I want you back in that ring and I'm gonna give 'em all an honest knock out, you sorry sonuvabitch.

(MIKEY enters carrying an ice pack.)

MIKEY: Woah. Settle down. The match is over.

JESSIE: I'm meeting with Jimmy first thing tomorrow. I'm gonna petition for a rematch, and if there's anyone that will be able to make it official, it's Jimmy. Don't think you've seen the last of me in the ring.

MIKEY: Rematch? You already won.

JESSIE: Did I?

> *(She exits.)*

MIKEY: Butcher, what was that all about? What'd you say to her?

PETE: Holy shit, Mikey! That bitch thinks I threw the fight.

MIKEY: Threw the fight?

PETE: Yeah. She says the punch that ended the match was barely a jab.

MIKEY: Butcher, come on. Tell me you didn't take a dive.

PETE: Jesus Christ, Mikey, you know me better than that.

MIKEY: Well, I'm going to set all this straight. We don't want her damaging your credibility by spreading rumors about you faking the knock out. That would be a P-R nightmare.

> *(pulls out a cell phone about to make a call)*

PETE: Yeah…I don't know though. Maybe that's the kinda thing I need.

MIKEY: Have you lost your mind? You want bad rumors floating around about you?

PETE: Think about it. Rumors are neutral. It's all about the perception of the audience. Rumors can be more exciting than the truth. If we let something like this get out, then people may think I was doing her a favor. Ya know? Just helping her out with her career. My title wasn't on the line, so in their eyes, they'll see that I had nothing to lose. They'll say, "Oh, there's Butcher, giving that little lady his full support. We all know he could annihilate her if he was really giving her a go." And then it's all Chinese whispers from there.

MIKEY: *(puts the phone away)* You *want* people to think that you threw the fight?

PETE: Yeah, but here's the thing. If I ever get asked about it directly, I just tell the complete truth. I gave it my all – one hundred per cent. I'll talk about how great of a fighter she is and that sorta thing and then Bob's your uncle! They'll eat it up, Mikey. And rumors have power. Sure, many will accept the truth, but in the back of their minds there will always be some doubt. And no matter what I say...

MIKEY: They'll always wonder if you faked the knock out to make her look good.

PETE: I'll be a walking conspiracy theory!

MIKEY: I don't know, Butcher…

PETE: Come on. It's brilliant.

MIKEY: Well, at least you're not moping around anymore. And what about this rematch? What did she mean she wants to make it *official*?

PETE: She wants to be the champ. Who doesn't?

(off Mikey's look)

But surely they'll never cross the men and women's division. Not for a valid title match anyway.

MIKEY: I've seen crazier things happen in my day. You gonna let her schedule if they allow it?

PETE: Fuck no. That lady has pit bulls for hands. Look at me. I haven't been this bruised up since that time I went five rounds with Ol' Looney Blythe.

MIKEY: Pit bulls, huh? I thought you called them lucky punches.

PETE: Well, in the end, luck is always to blame, isn't it?

MIKEY: You are a piece a work, you know that?

(gives Pete the ice pack)

Here. Get some ice on that lip. I'll tell them to pull the car around.

(exits)

PETE: *(look of achievement)* "Butcher Pete the Walking Conspiracy"…

END OF PLAY

THE NIGHT OF ALL NIGHTS

Elayne Heilveil

First performance at At Rise Players, Los Angeles CA
July 16, 2017.

Produced at Theatre 40, Beverly Hills, CA.
Dec. 2, 2017
Produced by Ernest McDaniel
Directed by Elayne Heilveil

CAST :

    RHODA: Anne Leyden
    KARL: Bill Sehres
    PRETTY GIRL: Kira Brannlund

CHARACTERS:

KARL: (50's -60's) Husband. Married to Rhoda…for years.

RHODA: (50's- 60's) Wife. Married to Karl…for years.

PRETTY GIRL: (20's) Doubles as News Girl and Receptionist. Young and obnoxiously pretty.

(Note: Actors should be able to play with a stylistic flair.)

AT RISE: Karl, in a bathrobe, is seated Stage Left, on a couch watching 'TV'. RHODA, in a bathrobe, is seated beside him eating chinese food from a carton. She picks at the food with chopsticks and stares straight ahead. There is a flatness to their speech.

RHODA: Do you love me?

KARL: (*Staring at TV*) I love you.

RHODA: Do you want me?

KARL: I want you.

RHODA: … you're watching the news.

The Pretty Girl ENTERS as NEWSGIRL. She stands, poised as if in the TV.

KARL: Shhhhh.

RHODA: Do… you… want…?

NEWSGIRL: …Blind trusts…? Conflicts of interests? Or…! (*She winks*)

RHODA: (*Makes a face about the 'Pretty Girl'*) me….?

KARL: (*Still watching; annoyed*) Honey…!

She looks at the carton, stabs the chopsticks in, and swallows a chunk. Suddenly she holds her stomach, groans, and doubles over.

RHODA: Ohhhh….

BLACK OUT. In the darkness they slip off their robes; underneath is evening attire – Karl, in a dapper suit and tie, Rhoda an evening dress. As the lights come up he takes her arm and they cross, like regal dancers, to a row of chairs and sit, upright, alongside each other. (We may hear forties style music as the scene changes. When they speak, it is like a forties ROM COM, think Rosalind Russell and Cary Grant or a Nick and Nora Charles, with a snappy repartee.). Across from them is a table set as a counter where the PRETTY GIRL , now A RECEPTIONIST, sits. She is somewhat bored, filing her nails. Karl is brousing a sheetlike MENU.

KARL: …A Petite Filet?

RHODA: What was that, my love?

KARL: With extra… béarnaise…

RHODA: A Petite Philly, you say?

KARL: What? No, Lovling. You asked what I wanted. (*Louder*) A *Filet.* With extra béarnaise.

RHODA: No need to shout. But when we were young, that's what you said, you wanted a friskie Philly. With a petite little shape. Like mine.

KARL: I never said that.

RHODA: You just don't recall, is all. A Freudian slip.

KARL: Well then, it looks like I'll have to settle for a dreaded vegetarian burger on a lettuce leaf -- without the bun, if that's not slipping too much? (*He chuckles.*)

RHODA: It's our memories that are slipping, my love. We've forgotten our dreams.

KARL: Well, I never dream of bunless burgers, I can tell you that.

RHODA: Am I that kind of burger now, my love?

KARL: (*Staring at menu*) Yes, dear.

RHODA: Is that the truth? Or the news of the day?

KARL: We hear what we want, wouldn't you agree? (*Looks around.*) What kind of world are we in?

RHODA: It IS our anniversary you know. Or did you forget? Our 'night of all nights,' you'd say.

KARL: And how did it come to this? (*He looks down at his suit and tie.*)

RHODA: I thought we could use a bit of a lift?

> They both sit up stiffly. He checks the menu.

KARL: And a burger wrap with a side of…(*Stares at menu more closely.*) …wax? One of the choices of side dishes, Lovling, is a chest hair wax for guys and a bikini for dolls. Huh. A waxful of guys and dolls. (*He chuckles again.*)

PRETTY GIRL: (*SINGS 'Guys and Dolls' song while filing nails.*) "…That's a guy only doin' it for some doll, some doll, some… (*Notices them watching; Stops, speaks…*) …doll."

KARL: How tasteless and rude…

RHODA: She's just showing your age with our antiquated songs, my Love.

KARL: I'm sorry, Lovling. It's just that you know how I get when my stomach growls.

RHODA: It is I who is hungry too. Do you want *me*, as a *dish…* anymore?

KARL: Hmmm… (*Checking menu*) If you were the fruit plate, with the added cottage cheese…?

RHODA: (*Somewhat insulted*) …and you were the lettuce leaf…?

KARL: …I suppose we could share.

RHODA: (*Pointedly*) Unhappily, of course. As your TRUE desire was the Petite Philly Filet, (*Snidely.*) …with the béarnaise sauce oozing out of the side of your mouth.

KARL: Well, now, that would be messy, indeed. Even for a Freudian dream, don't you think? (*He chuckles.*) Where the hell are we, Lovling, my dear?

RHODA: (*Annoyed at interruption*) I was trying to tell you, in the midst of the bills and (*snidely*) *alternative* tweets or twits or twots of the news, it came!

KARL: (*Suspiciously*) What came?

RHODA: The Invitation! To the party, my Love. With drinks and hors d'oeurves.

KARL: (*Checks menu; squints*) Ahhhh. At (*Reads*) "The Second Chance Spa?" "Where one can grow older while looking… younger." (*Smirks*) Hmmm.

RHODA: It's so hard to resist when one is hungry, my Love. Would you want me again? A second time around?

The PRETTY GIRL SINGS softly, from "The Second Time Around."

PRETTY GIRL: "Love is wonderful, the second time a… round."

They give her a dirty look. She abruptly stops.

RHODA: (*Annoyed; repeats*) Would you want me again…a… (*Smiles, avoiding a song.*) …at another stage?

KARL: (*Checks menu*) Well, to be perfectly honest. Lovling…

RHODA: (*Politely sarcastic*) Please.

KARL: I'd prefer not to get anything waxed but my car.

(Rhoda gives him a look. He checks his watch.)

And it's getting quite late. For this kind of date. Don't you agree?

PRETTY GIRL: (*Checking her watch*) Tick Tock. Tick…

They both turn to look. She shrugs.

KARL: And if we rush like a bunny we can catch the news. Or was it a snooze?

RHODA: Curled up on the couch, with a sick little tummy, on this night of all nights?

KARL: (*Checking watch*) Perhaps it was the chicken my Lovling, that had done you in.

RHODA: Perhaps it was *you*, the chicken, my Love, who done the trick.

PRETTY GIRL: (*Escalates louder*) Tick Tock… TICK TOCK.

Annoyed, they speed up the conversation and 'lines'.

KARL: Is THAT the truth? It is I who makes you sick?

RHODA: (*Dramatically*) I'm dying! Can't you see it, my Love?

KARL: Crying you say?

RHODA: And you're dying too!

KARL: Oh dear, not that communicable thing again?

PRETTY GIRL: (*Filing her nails*) TICK TOCK!

RHODA: Our coupons are running out!

PRETTY GIRL: (*Nonchalantly*) Between seven and nine. Tuesdays and Thursdays the doctors are in.

RHODA: But we have a chance. WE could be young and great again!

KARL: Why Lovling, I don't know who you are.

RHODA: The girl over there? Would you like *her*, my Love?

KARL: …For what?

RHODA: For any young thing you'd want. The truth, my Sweet.

KARL: At the moment, I'd settle for the big, fat whopper at McDonalds down the street.

RHODA: (*Delicately cries*) Her, instead of a… a fat whopper like me?

KARL: But dear, she's like… twelve!

RHODA: All right, all right. If she weren't…twelve. Be honest, my Love.

KARL: (*An aside to himself*) I fear this won't go very well. Historically speaking, I mean.

RHODA: If we didn't look like us, if we all could be pretty and young and...blonde...

KARL: An alternative way of seeing...*us*, you mean?

RHODA: What if I could be her? Or you could be...

(Rhoda turns towards the Pretty Girl. She quickly holds up an 8x10 Glossy of a handsome young man.)...him.

PRETTY GIRL: Or...?

The Pretty Girl holds up another photo of handsome young guy.

RHODA: What if we could have our pick, look like any young thing, or... cop a feel of any fresh meat?

KARL: Why we could be arrested, for arrested development, my Lovling. We could.

RHODA: Without a blemish or frown?

KARL: (*Considering*) The loving....and hating...?

RHODA: ...And sameness of things?

KARL: Alternative...facts?

RHODA: You and I. You and...me? I   and...?

KARL: ...her? Hmmmm.

RHODA: This is our chance. Our Spa of a Second Choice.

He checks the Menu for the name, confused.

KARL: The...the Second Chance...Choice...my Love? Or, is this... where we dance?

Rhoda looks towards the Pretty Girl. Who suddenly becomes alert.

PRETTY GIRL: Now?

(She pirouettes over and stands before them with a clipboard and brochures.)

Can I help you?

RHODA: Are you the pretty girl I spoke with on phone?

PRETTY GIRL: QVC? ABC? CNN?

RHODA: I RSV...P'd? With the coupon codes?

PRETTY GIRL: And the gifts of youth? (*Checks clipboard.*) Ah, yes, and the nuclear peels?

KARL: And food. Meat and potatoes at least?

RHODA: My husband, Karl. Of twenty, no thirty, or could it be... forty? wonderfully imperfect years.

PRETTY GIRL: Oh, how terribly...awfully...sweet. And 'cute'. He must have been a looker in his day.

> *(She winks at him. Then winks again. Eye stuck. And smiles.)*

RHODA: Once, he was a looker...at me.

PRETTY GIRL: Well, we can fix that up with our super duper Great Again specials of the day.

KARL: And the food and the party is...? (*Looks around*)

PRETTY GIRL: ...You! We have cucumber slices on gluton free cracked wheat crumbs and sparkling lime juice for the guests.

> *Rhoda groans. Holds her stomach.*

KARL: My love has a bit of a tummy bulge, tonight of all nights.

PRETTY GIRL: Don't you worry, we're just a nip and a tuck away with (*checks clipboard*)... Dr. Wing and Dr. Woo! And with the double coupon Tuesdays if you both agree...and sign on the dotted line...

> *She holds out the papers as they lean in to see...*

KARL: The print is quite miniscule, my Love, don't you agree?

PRETTY GIRL: (*Like a naughty boy*) Just for those mature little eyes. But lucky you! Dr. Wing specializes in lids and Woo in the feet of the crows! (*She winks again at Karl. This time her eye is stuck shut.*) May I read it for you then?

KARL: (*Shrugs to Rhoda; flattered*) She said I was cute. And a looker, she said.

RHODA: They say babies are cute. And old people are cute. And we're not the babies anymore, dear. So, it seems to be our day. Or... our night of all nights...is here? Now?

PRETTY GIRL: (*Reading with fluttering eye*)We have Juvederm, Sculptafirm, Gaspertane, Ultravain, and... Nuclear Silk! Which will peel all that sagging sadness away. And, because of your invitation to the special party...

KARL: (*Looks around.*) The party...?

PRETTY GIRL: The *Botox* Party! Yes, with the double coupon deal, it's only ninety-nine dollars a vile!

(She hands him receipt.)

KARL: *(Squints and reads)* So that would be… 10 viles…each? Of… Oma..bo..tulin…um…toxin… A?

(To Rhoda; concerned.) It's… a vile…*toxin*, my love?

PRETTY GIRL: We did have an issue with the type B cow but A was quite clean.

RHODA: *(To Girl)* Have you tried any of these treatments yourself? You're so pretty and young.

PRETTY GIRL: Oh, I've tried them all. If you won't tell…I'm *(whispers)* sixty-three.

RHODA: No!

KARL: No.

She starts winking again -- fluttering her eye.

PRETTY GIRL: Of course not. It's just…fake news! I'm really… sixty *one!*

(She opens her mouth to laugh… and her lips get stuck.)

Ha ha ha… ha HAAAA!

(She tries to stretch them out and like a bad opera singer with a stiff, distorted mouth her HA HA HA's turn into grotesque musical scales.)

Ha Haaaaah… Ah AHHHHHHHHH….!

And with her eyes wide in shock and arm raised like a Diva's, she jiggles her underarm skin in horror, and rushes OFF.

Rhoda and Karl back away. RHODA YELLS… "NO…. NO…!" as the LIGHTS DIM. In the BLACK OUT they rush back to their original seats. And slip back into their robes. As LIGHTS COME UP Rhoda shoots up in her seat, awakened from The Dream.

RHODA: *(Cont.)* No…! NO…..!!!!

KARL: Honey….!? Honey!

She looks around, now fully awake. Her attitude shifts from the beginning, now more present and alert.

RHODA: Do you… love me?

KARL: *(Staring back at TV)* …I love you.

RHODA: (*Really asking*) Do you want me?

KARL: (*Not paying attention*) I... want you.

> *She looks down at her ratty robe. Decides to be proactive, and slips it off—now, down to her slip. She crosses in front of him, blocking the 'TV'.*

RHODA: Do... you... want...*me*?

> *She poses in her slip, maybe drops a strap. Maybe jiggles her underarm flab, as a memory of The Dream, and shrugs sheepishly, like 'This is it...'Me.' He laughs. Shrugs sheepishly back. Switches OFF (imaginary clicker) TV.*

KARL: Honey. (*Beat*) Come here... My Petite Philly.

> *And he opens his arms. And as they embrace we may HEAR the forties Dream MUSIC once again as it swells to...*

> *THE END.*

THIS QUINTESSENCE OF DUST

Cory Hinkle

This Quintessence of Dust was commissioned by Pavement Group (Chicago, IL) and performed at the Den Theatre April 14 - 16, 2014 with the following cast:

Jane: Yunuen Pardo
Chip: John Zinn
Henry: Brian Stojak

It was directed by Tyrone Phillips.

The play was subsequently produced at the Humana Festival of New American Plays at Actors' Theatre of Louisville April 9 - 10, 2016. The cast was:

Jane: Kelly McAndrew:
Chip: Todd Lawson
Henry: Pun Bandhu

It was directed by Les Waters.

CHARACTERS:

Jane: She's caustic and funny, a survivor.

Chip: He's vain, but lovable.

Henry: He's like a little boy – sensitive, naïve, wide-eyed.

All characters are in their late 20's to early 30's.

SETTING:

The future. Los Angeles, California.

A light rises on Jane.

JANE: I don't really miss how everything used to be.

Like

Not at *all*

Yes, in many ways things totally *suck* now

Like I can only eat *canned goods*

And not having the possibility of any sort of medical attention if you like cut off a finger is kinda *scary* and my hair is all ratted up like dreads cause I haven't washed it in ten months

BUT

What did I give up?

I was always stressed and depressed and moody and bitchy

Due to *social networking*

And *you-tube-ing*

And *upworthy-ing*

And *netflix-ing*

I don't miss it!

> *(Admittedly, I really liked (and miss) Orange Is The New Black, not the main character, but the secondary characters? Like a LOT)*

But I was always seeking adoration and LOVE and now I realize

OH MY GOD

I don't need it!

All of that love I thought I wanted?

I DON'T NEED LOVE

> *(Though I've lost my family and most of my friends, but the thing is when I really think about it, you know, I was never that close to any of them anyway, not really)*

I like the quiet ... The quiet is soooooo nice ...

I watched the sunset last night.

(It was kind of hard to see, due to a weird dust storm?)

But I have an appreciation now for the *light* here in California

(How did I *never* look at a sunset before?)

And, yes, I feel sorry for all of the "island peoples" that no longer have homes and the cultures that have been LOST and the languages that are now DEAD and you can't swim in the ocean anymore due to all the JELLYFISH

But on the other hand

I won't ever have to LIKE one of your STATUSES ever again

And I won't have to watch videos of your kids.

Because ...

You're dead.

And your kids are dead.

> *Small pause.*

JANE: Aaaanyway, everything would be fine

I would totally really be digging the apocalypse right now

Except that

Here I am trapped inside this tiny little super hot dank dirty apartment cum shelter that isn't even MINE, hiding from bands of cannibals

(Cormac Mccarthy was totally right on that)

And I just happened to get trapped with

My ex, Chip.

It's like I'm stuck inside a sit-com from the nineties

Except, you know,

This sit-com is set – at the end of the world?

> *Chip suddenly enters.*

CHIP: It's funny actually

Because we *did* date in the 90's

And then I broke up with her //

JANE: //No, not true

CHIP: And we both went our separate ways

And I was "doing my thang" in Hollywood

And she was out here visiting a friend

Even though there was this whole water shortage thing

And like people were dying, like, totally all over

It was super ugly

JANE: I should've stayed in New York.

CHIP: And then we had one of those "catch up" coffees

JANE: How are you?

CHIP: I'm great.

JANE: Yeah? What's new?

CHIP: Oh, national commercial for Ray-Ban you know what about you?

JANE: The usual. KILLING IT.

CHIP: And that's when –

JANE: The shit –

CHIP: Hit –

JANE: The fan. Los Angeles went DARK.

CHIP: Dark as Mumbai had been for months.

JANE: And Cape Town.

CHIP: And *so* many other places.

JANE: But America was different.

CHIP: Or so we thought …

JANE: And then …

CHIP: In order to survive, I killed someone, which I *still* feel really kinda bad about? And for like *weeks* my right hand smelled like Intelligentsia coffee (from our catch up date) –

JANE: It wasn't a date.

CHIP: And my left smelled like, well, human blood?

JANE: The strange thing is – Everything got *so quiet in this world* that I actually started to see things clearly for *the first time in forever* and I was just, like, living in the present, in the *now*, in my *body*, not needing love or adoration from anyone, *one* with the world, the animals and the *plants* (well the plants and the animals are mostly all dead, except for the jellyfish)

CHIP: So you were one with the jellyfish.

JANE: I was one with *myself.*

CHIP: I think you might have like PTSD from everyone, you know, *dying?*

JANE: NO! I'm happy.

CHIP: Anyway, now we're living in my neighbor's apartment?

He shows us physically in space –

CHIP: *(cont'd)*There's a wall here

And it's completely covered floor to ceiling with canned goods.

My neighbor was like a Boy Scout when it came to the end times.

JANE: He's the guy Chip had to kill?

CHIP: *(through clenched teeth)I still feel bad so please don't bring it up.*

JANE: There's a bottle of whiskey.

And we get *SO* drunk and it's *SO* dark

CHIP: It turns out, the end of the world is dark and QUIET

JANE: Which is good for me because I can finally hear myself THINK

CHIP: But not for me because, actually, I kind of hear VOICES?

JANE: We get drunk and Chip likes to talk about his ex-girlfriends –

CHIP: It's just so WEIRD (you know) to think

    that all of these girls I broke up with

    they're all DEAD

    and here I am ALIVE

    and they won't ever see me again

    well, except for YOU.

JANE: *(through clenched teeth)You didn't break up with me.*

CHIP: And then …

    From off, a loud knocking.

    They stand completely still.

    Another knock … And another …

CHIP: What do we do?

JANE: Shh!

    More knocking.

CHIP: It's the cannibals, isn't it?

JANE: Shut, up.

    Henry enters.

HENRY: I come in

    Through an open window

    My leg's broken

    A bunch of cannibals like nearly killed me and –

JANE: Henry!?

HENRY: Jane!?

    YAAASSSS

    Jane!

    HERE IS HOPE

    Here's a ray of LIGHT –

CHIP: Who's this guy?

HENRY: I dated Jane in Brooklyn

    We were SOOOOO into each other

JANE: No, YOU were into ME.

HENRY: JANE!

    She was like

    The most unattainable girl I ever dated.

JANE: What are you doing here!?!

HENRY: All of this end-of-the-world-stuff went down during pilot season, I was gonna do a thing with Shia LeBeouf?

CHIP: *(suddenly angry)* Whatever, man!

HENRY: I'm sorry?

CHIP: She was waaaaaaaaaaaaay into me too.

HENRY: She was?

CHIP: She like TOTALLY dug me

    We dated in college?

    She had to go to the hospital once for

    Like um

    HER WRIST?

CHIP: *(cont'd)* Cause she like

    BROKE IT from giving me HANDJOBS.

    Jane and Henry both stare at him.

CHIP: Yeah I made that up I don't know why I'm sorry but she loved me, she did.

JANE: I don't love people.

HENRY: How can you not love people? They're awesome.

JANE: Because when I finally *truly did love someone*, this guy in New York named Rich, less than a month after we got together he turned REALLY COLD FOR NO REASON and said he NEEDED SPACE and so I came out here to hang out with my friend, Stacey, so she could *console me* because my heart was broken! And in a moment of desperation I got a cup of coffee with Chip and THEN THE *WORLD ENDED!?!*

 Jane and Chip bicker as Henry confides in us.

HENRY: They're *screaming* at each other
 And I think I'm going to *die* from loss of blood
 (which actually I *do* die later, but for a different reason)
 But anyway, because of their screaming
 I never get to tell them what happened.
 See, I went out looking for food
 Something
 Anything!
 A squirrel
 Or I would have eaten a rat I was so hungry
 And I see this group of cannibals
 Heads shaved
 Long black fingernails
 Their clothes *black* from dried blood
 And I run!
 But I'm so fatigued
 Delirious
 Malnourished
 That I can't get away!
 I beg for mercy
 And I can't believe it!
 They actually give it to me!

 Henry (cont'd)

They take me in, as their slave, for a time
 I work for them
 Boiling human scalps and turning them into candle wax
 (Very interesting process, actually)
 But, still, I'm – I am *hungry* … I have to *eat … Something …*
  Pause.

HENRY: What else was I supposed to do?

I know! I know!

But honestly … ?

It was delicious.

I've always loved people, people are awesome, but never this much.

CHIP: He *cannot* be here.

JANE: He's my ex.

CHIP: He may also be a cannibal.

JANE: Your breath does smell like human flesh.

HENRY: I can't leave.

Now that I've found you Jane!

I've been with *a lot* of women

And I never wanted to stay the whole weekend with any of them except *you*

I never wanted to shower with them

I never wanted to rub their feet with oil

Or watch movies in the afternoons

Or read yesterday's New York Times even though it's old, but we're too lazy to go out of bed and get today's paper? Or do crafts remember THAT?

JANE: Not REALLY

HENRY: My mom LOVED you

I NEVER introduced women to my family, like, ever

But you were different

You were my friend

Henry (cont'd)

You know how they say you, like, fall in love with your best friend?

Pause.

HENRY: I always loved you.

Long Pause.

JANE: Later, that night …

HENRY: I lie down to sleep in the quiet darkness of the apocalypse

And it's the last time I do.

I don't know if it's because I told her I loved her, or because she intuited I now have an insatiable taste for human flesh?

JANE: Little bit of both.

HENRY: But she killed me, in my sleep …

> *Pause.*

JANE: I won't tell you how I did it because it was quite gruesome

And sometimes I feel, like, a little pang of guilt?

Because actually I think I took a lot of my anger toward Rich out on Henry?

But …

It's almost like I can feel Henry from beyond

Sending me these little, like, pings

Little messages?

I'll be sitting eating some canned beans

Trying to make out the sunset behind the orange dust

And I feel almost, like, like I want to respond to him in some way.

Like if I was still on Facebook?

I mean I AM ON IT

There's just no power right now to boot all the systems up

But If I *could* post something

I would post a really cool and poetic quote on Henry's wall.

Like, um, I don't know something from Shakespeare?

Do you know any Shakespeare, Chip?

CHIP: To be or not to –

JANE: Not that!

Something moving!

Like a picture of the earth with a quote from Shakespeare superimposed

Something about

How we had something we could really love, but we didn't care about it, you know?

No, you know what?

Like Hamlet! (I read that in college)

What's that quote?

Oh shit, *what is it?*

He's talking about how beautiful the world is and he talks about the sky, how it's a golden roof – yeah! "fretted with fire," though actually, maybe that's a different part (whatever) and he says something about the "paragon of animals," just how *incredible* it all is!

Everything, you know?

But when Hamlet looks at all that beauty?

He's just all like, "What is this quintessence of dust?"

Like he looks at everything and all he sees is *dust*

Which is

Just kind of … How I feel about people?

You know?

How Hamlet feels about the earth is how I feel about people.

Aaaaanyway

Enjoy it while you can, I say.

I mean there's still the sunset right?

Look at that sunset!

Wow!

You can barely see it, but you can *just* make it out …

> *Small Pause.*

JANE: I wouldn't trade the sunset for anything.

> *The lights begin to change*
>
> *And they all watch the sun set*
>
> *Then lights fade.*
>
> *End.*

Three Anne Franks

Maya Macdonald

Produced by Oye Group

Cast:

PROPS MISTRESS: Molly Bernard
ANNE THREE: Gabby Beans
ANNE TWO: Sarah Baskin
ANNE ONE: Dee Hamid

Playwright: Maya Macdonald
Director: Jaki Bradley
Producer: Oye Group

CHARACTERS:
  PROPS MISTRESS
  ANNE THREE
  ANNE TWO
  ANNE ONE

TIME:
  Current day, but everything is trying to be 1942, if not always so successfully so.

PLACE:
  A sort of in-between world where we are all waiting to see who we will become.

  An in-between world where we are all trying to recreate someone we didn't know.

  Someone who has been reinterpreted so many times that we can never really know who she was or how to be her, become her. We are in the process of becoming in someone else's image. It's a waiting room, a purgatory, and how we get out of this space is someone else's decision.

(A tight, enclosed space. Lets call it a waiting room outside of an attic.

The space looks like a confused period piece, except for one very modern plastic

table center and three uncomfortable, equally modern chairs arranged around a table)

(After a beat, PROPS MISTRESS enters carrying a large cardboard box, a roll of blue tape around the top of one arm and a clipboard nearly glued to one side of

her. She places the box down and begins to unroll the blue tape onto the table.

After a beat, we see that she is creating boxes on the table top with tape. After this

is done, she begins unloading objects from the box onto the table. First is a deck of cards. She looks at a clipboard.)

PROPS: *(muttering under breath)* playing cards

(She places the cards in one of the squares and writes "playing cards" on the tape.)

(She looks at a clipboard and checks it off the list, then goes on to the next on the list.)

PROPS: *(continued)* candle & match book

(She retrieves items from the box, places them on the table, labels them, checks off list)

(ANNE TWO enters. She is dressed in a classic button-down collared shirt, plaid shirt, simple shoes. She holds two stapled pieces of paper, slightly worn, with a few markings as well as a 8 by 10 headshot. She has her movements down to a t, all professional. She greets PROPS MISTRESS, who glances at her and then looks down at her clip-board and flips the top page to look at the one below it.)

PROPS: *(continued)* Name?

ANNE TWO: Anne.

(PROPS finds and checks off her name. Then goes back

to the box. ANNE TWO: takes her seat. She lifts up her headshot and looks at it. Then looks at the first page of the sides. Turns to next page. Places them on her lap. Takes a breath. Begins a vocal warmup. Simultaneously, PROPS continues to set up, going to her original list, etc.)

PROPS: Sack of Potatoes & Peeler…

> *(She retrieves an enormous sack of potatoes from the box and places them on the table. She goes back to search for the peeler. She searches for a bit until she finds it.)*

ANNE TWO: …

Dear Kitty

Deeaaaar Kittty

Dear Ki-tt-y

> *(PROPS finds the peeler, places it on the table, marks down the name, etc.)*

> *(ANNE TWO continues to warm up. Her movements eventually take her to her feet. She reads from the sides, practicing, mostly to herself.)*

ANNE TWO: *(continued)*July 6th

1942

Today, Father said that we might have to go into hiding.

Today

Father said

> *(She looks at the sides.)*

> *(As she continues, PROPS continues.)*

PROPS: *(Looking at list)* Cigarettes…

> *(She begins looking through the box.)*

ANNE TWO: TodayFathersaidthatwe…

Today Father Talked about going into hiding.

I was stunned.

> *(Simultaneously, PROPS cannot find the cigarettes in the box, then remembers she has them in her own pocket. She takes out the pack, takes the cigarettes out of the pack and places them onto the table and labels them.)*

ANNE TWO: *(Continued)* Stunnnned

A call-up: everyone knows what that means.

(Suddenly, with a frantic, disorganized energy, ANNE ONE enters. ANNE TWO: notices her and stops abruptly. They make brief, vaguely piercing eye contact.

> *ANNE ONE is dressed similarly to ANNE TWO, but a bit more modernized. Her plaid skirt has suspenders. There is a sense of irony to it. Like if Zooey Deschanel were Anne Frank, ya know? If anyone is to wear a Star of David on their chest it would perhaps be this Anne, but it might be the wrong choice. She looks urgently through her bag. PROPS sees her and flips to the other page in her clip board.)*

PROPS: Name?

> *(ANNE ONE continues to look frantically through her bag, not responding to PROPS.)*

…

NAME

ANNE ONE: Oh, right, sorry

Anne.

> *(PROPS looks down the list. Then up the list. There she is. She checks her name off.)*

PROPS: You can take a seat.

> *(ANNE ONE takes a seat, continuing to look through her bag, eventually finding two crumpled up pieces of paper and a marred, but usable headshot and resume.*
>
> *ANNE TWO watches her as she smooths out her head-shot and sides against her lap. ANNE ONE looks up to find ANNE TWO staring at her. ANNE TWO: immediately looks down, raising her sides up.)*
>
> *(Simultaneously, PROPS continues to set up.)*

PROPS: Silverware.

> *(She takes silverware out of the box and drops it on the table. It makes a loud noise. She labels it. Checks it off the list. Goes onto the next.)*

PROPS: Fountain pen…

(She goes to her hair, where the pen is tangled, takes it out and places it on the table, labels it, checks it off the list.)

ANNE ONE: *(to ANNE TWO)* Excuse me?

(ANNE TWO doesn't look up.)

…

Excuse me, did they ask you to do a-

(Suddenly, ANNE THREE enters. She is dressed similarly to the other two, but her clothes look like perhaps they truly belonged to someone in the 40's. ANNE TWO: looks up at her. ANNE ONE does the same. ANNE THREE walks over to PROPS.)

ANNE THREE: Hi, I'm Anne.

(PROPS lifts up the sheet, searches up, searches down, and then up again. She finds her.)

PROPS: Got you.

(She checks her off the list and goes back to the box. ANNE THREE finds her seat. The three Anne take turns taking secret looks at one and other. Whenever one is caught by another, they look down back at their sides.)

PROPS: Diary.

(When they hear this word, all three ANNES look up and watch as PROPS makes her way to the box of props, retrieves a well wore prop Diary. All their eyes follow as she brings it to the table, labels it.)

ANNE ONE: *(to Anne Three)*Are you going to-

Did they ask you about the accent?

ANNE THREE: My agent mentioned something.

She said it was optional.

ANNE TWO: Optional.

Definitely.

It's definitely optional.

…

ANNE ONE: But isn't that always code for it's definitely not optional?

(ANNE TWO doesn't answer.)

ANNE ONE: *(To ANNE THREE)* I like your necklace.

(ANNE THREE touches a Star of David necklace)

ANNE THREE: Thank you!

My mother gave it to me.

Love your skirt.

ANNE ONE: Ha, thanks.

It was literally a piece of my school uniform.

(ANNE TWO clocks this.)

PROPS: Hello, Annes, thanks for coming in.

You all look great. Really period.

I want to just say, you should feel really honored to be here.

You're all here because you have a little piece of something special we want our Anne to have.

But only one of you can-will be the next

Anne Frank

…

(Beat)

I fell in love with Anne when I first read her diary years ago, and have been obsessed with her ever since.

ANNE TWO: Me too!

This is actually the eight time I've auditioned for Anne Frank.

PROPS: I was up to ten.

…

I myself was almost an Anne

(She pauses for effect.)

They said I was too much of a Margot.

And too much of an Anne

to be a Margot.

…

So

Now I do props.

…

exclusively for productions of *The Diary of Anne Frank*.

(*Beat.*)

Always the props mistress, never the Anne

...

what are ya gonna do

...

> (*She fails at laughter. In fact, she doesn't move her face at all.*)
>
> (*Beat.*)

Sorry if my default facial expression is confusing.

Some people have Resting Bitch Face.

I have Resting Anne Frank Face.

> (*Beat.*)

This production of The Diary of Anne Frank is a little different.

The Anne Frank Foundation only licenses certain quotations from her diary. Things like, "In spite of everything I still believe that people are really good at heart" and "Paper has more patience than people."

ANNE ONE: I have that tattooed on my lower back.

> (*Everyone looks at ANNE ONE. Beat.*)

I'm Anne Frank OBSESSED too.

PROPS: So, long story short, the producers on this project couldn't get the rights to a single word that Anne actually said, so we will not be doing the sides you prepared today.

> (*The ANNES take this in.*)

Alternatively, they want everyone to do a series of improvisations as Anne Frank.

A recreation, if you will.

While this may not be historically accurate, it will prevent potential law suits.

> (*PROPS flips to a third page on the clipboard.*)

You've all been assigned props to work with.

...

Anne?

(ANNE TWO immediately knows this is her and gets up.)

Potato and peeler.

(She gestures to the table. ANNE TWO looks disappointed.)

ANNE TWO: Do you mind if I take the cigarettes?

I really feel like my Anne would smoke.

(PROPS looks her up and down.)

PROPS: You look more like a potato peeling Anne.

(Beat. ANNE TWO picks up the potato and peeler, sits down, and begins peeling her potato. PROPS looks back at the clipboard.)

Anne?

(ANNE ONE immediately knows this is her and comes forward.)

Cigarettes and lighter.

(ANNE ONE takes the cigarettes and lighter. ANNE TWO watches her. ANNE ONE sits down, takes a cigarette out, lights it and begins smoking.)

Anne?

(Immediately, ANNE THREE knows this means her.)

You can take the playing cards.

(She gestures to the table. ANNE THREE goes and picks up the cards.)

They'd like you all to practice your tasks with a penetrating gaze.

(PROPS exits. All the ANNES practice their respective task. A beat of the three ANNEs all doing their tasks. It almost morphs into a play in and of itself.)

ANNE TWO: *(To ANNE ONE)* You know, Anne didn't really say "Paper is more patient than people."

ANNE ONE: Yeah she did. It's one of the most famous things she said.

ANNE TWO: She was just mentioning a common saying. It's not like, something she wrote.

ANNE ONE: I know, it just felt like it really captured who she was, so that's why I got the tattoo.

I just wanted her to be close to me at all times, ya know?

ANNE TWO: Well, I guess since you can't be buried next to her.

ANNE ONE: What?

ANNE TWO: …um. you know that if you have a tattoo you can't be buried in a Jewish cemetery, right?

ANNE ONE: I'm Catholic, actually.

ANNE TWO: Of course you are.

ANNE ONE: But I've loved her my whole life!

She was the theme of my sweet 16.

I feel like I *am* her.

ANNE TWO: Well, it wouldn't be the first time I was the only Jewish girl in callbacks for Anne Frank.

ANNE THREE: I'm Jewish, actually.

(ANNE TWO looks at ANNE THREE. ANNE TWO starts to laugh in what she thinks will be with ANNE THREE, but ANNE THREE stays serious. Beat.)

I wasn't joking.

I am Jewish.

ANNE TWO: Right.

ANNE THREE: I'm also black.

Which obviously you already noticed.

(They all go back to their respective tasks. Beat.)

(PROPS enters.)

PROPS: Anne?

(ANNE THREE immediately knows that that means her.)

Lets have…

Saturday, January 22nd 1944.

(ANNE THREE gets to the center of the room, taking the cards with her.)

ANNE THREE: Hello Kitty,

It's me, Anne.

I looked at the reflection of my face today.

I hadn't looked since we arrived in hiding.

I can see myself.

I can see my eyes are clear.

Why do we hide?

I don't mean hiding, but I mean like our real selves.

Mother asked to read my diary again today

I told her never, I can't stand to see her most days-

PROPS: Sorry, we can't have Anne saying anything bad about her mother.

THREE

But didn't it say in her diary that she and her mother didn't get along?

PROPS: That is true, but her Father, the only family member who survived cut all of that out, and the Foundation has the rights on lock.

Trade the cards for the silverware.

We'll circle back.

> *(ANNE THREE takes the silverware and sits down again.)*

Anne?

> *(ANNE TWO immediately knows this is her.)*

September 10, 1942.

> *(ANNE TWO comes forward, furiously peeling potatoes.)*

ANNE TWO: Hey Kitty Hello

It's me Anne

I've been peeling the potatoes all morning

As planes screech back and forth

I haven't slept a wink

But I dreamt of how lucky I am

And I thought about how God is really great

I thought about how everything probably happens for a reason

and there was no blackness in my heart

PROPS: Great

On a good track

Now they'd like you to try it with a British accent.

TWO

...
A British
Accent?
PROPS: Can you not
Do
A British accent?
TWO
Of course
Yes, I can
Do
A British accent but that's not
That's not the point
(Beat.)

...
Um
You know that Anne Frank wasn't British, right?
PROPS: My grandmother survived Auschwitz, actually
So yeah
I know Anne Frank wasn't British
TWO
Well, than you should understand
How incredibly
Offensive
I mean if she were British she wouldn't even have had to go into hiding.
If Anne Frank were British she would have survived.
PROPS: They like Anne to have a British accent cause it helps an American audience understand that she's foreign, while still relating to her.
TWO
So they can't relate to her in say, Yiddish...
PROPS: Can you not do a British accent?
TWO
It's on my special skills.

PROPS: So that means, no?

TWO

(In a horrible British accent)

'Ello Kitty Dear,

Haven't slept a wink!

Dreamt of Hitler finding it in his heart to forgive me

Talked to God, he says 'ello.

PROPS: Yeah, that means no.

…

Why don't you take another potato and sit down.

(ANNE TWO does, discouraged.)

Oh, also we can't mention "Hitler."

Or "concentration camp."

(PROPS goes back to clip board.)

Anne-

ANNE ONE: I can do a pretty good British accent.

(ANNE TWO looks at ANNE ONE.)

PROPS: Great, lets have Valentines Day, 1943.

(She comes center stage.)

ANNE ONE: Dear Kitty,

Today is Valentine's Day and I'm alone.

So much has changed, but I'm the same person.

I saw my reflection today and I thought to myself, I don't know, you tell me.

PROPS: Thanks.

That accent really made her feel more accessible.

Now lets take a quick three and circle back.

(PROPS goes back to the table, consults on a headset, etc.)

(The ANNES continue with their respective props. We stay with this for a beat.)

ANNE ONE: *(To ANNE TWO)* Why would Anne Frank have survived if she was British?

(ANNE TWO doesn't answer, or ANNE THREE cuts her off.)

ANNE THREE: Because England was never occupied by the Nazis.

ONE

Oh.

TWO

Yeah.

(Beat.)

THREE

(To TWO)

What was your bat mitzvah theme?

TWO

…

Oh

Actually, I didn't have a bat mitzvah.

THREE

...

Oh.

TWO

I was really

Culturally

Jewish, though

I grew up in New York

So

THREE

Is your Mom Jewish…

Or your Dad?

(Beat)

TWO

…my

Dad, actually.

THREE

Oh.

My Mom is Jewish
So I guess I'm actually more Jewish than you.
ONE
Why…?
THREE
In Judaism-
(ANNE TWO cuts ANNE THREE off.)
TWO
In Judaism
Technically
You go by the religion of your Mother
But
I mean, if you *identify* as Jewish than…
THREE
Right

…

My bat mitzvah theme was Magic
We had a magician and everything
(PROPS enters.)
PROPS: And we're back!

So lets talk about what we talk about when we talk about Peter, the boy who lived upstairs from Anne in the secret Annex. Anne?
(ANNE TWO comes forward. She's probably still peeling that potato, lets be real.)
TWO
Heyhi Kitty
I noticed
To my flabbergast
That Peter looked
At me
I know what you're thinking

before I got here "it" was only spoken about in a whisper and was a disgusting secret now the secret is pretty cool and it's mine I tried talking about sex with Dad He just said "you are too young to understand that kind of desire."

PROPS: Our Anne can't say anything about "desire."

ANNE TWO: Why?

PROPS: People like their Anne to be pure. Angelic.

And they want their Anne and Peter to just be friends.

ANNE TWO: But she was 15 and locked in an attic for two and a half years, you don't think she hit that?

PROPS: I don't make the rules, I just do the props.

...

Go ahead and take another potato.

(ANNE TWO does.)

Anne?

(ANNE THREE knows this is her.)

Tell me a secret.

ANNE THREE: Kitty, guess what?

Today I saw a white smear on my panties and-

PROPS: Nope.

No.

Anne Frank doesn't have panties.

ANNE THREE: She mentions them right before she gets her period for the first time.

ANNE THREE: She said it was like she was carrying around a "special secret."

PROPS: Stop quoting things she actually said.

We want our Anne to make us feel better

They don't wanna see all of that

All that gook

Up in your Anne

They want her to make them feel okay about what was done to her.

(ANNE THREE picks up the candles and matches and sits down.)

Anne?

(ANNE ONE gets up. She leaves all her props behind.

A long beat.)

ANNE ONE: Hey Kitty,

> It's me
>
> Anne
>
> Anne Frank
>
> Just in case
>
> Anyone asks
>
> I want you to know that I think I'm probably totally cool with being dead and stuff
>
> Just in case people feel really sad and guilty
>
> Tell them it's all good
>
> …
>
> I think
>
> I think about reaching out my arm
>
> To touch you
>
> I mean, just someone
>
> Anyone
>
> But it's just the thought
>
> I'll never actually do it
>
> I never even lift my hand
>
> I always have the thought
>
> But I've been trained never to reach
>
> My desire is not your problem
>
> I am not real
>
> Not anymore
>
> Now, I'm whatever you need to hear
>
> I'll be whatever gets you through the night
>> *(A long beat. Something in ANNE ONE has shifted. She takes her seat.)*

PROPS: I'll be right back with the decision.
> *(PROPS exits.)*

ANNE TWO: I don't think Anne would have said that.

ANNE ONE: You have no idea what Anne Frank would have said.
> *(PROPS enters. She goes to the table and picks up the*

diary and fountain pen.)

PROPS: And the diary goes to

…

…

Anne

(ANNE ONE immediately knows this is her, as do the others. ANNE ONE comes forward and takes the diary as if it is a rose on the Bachelor)

ANNE TWO: I can't believe this. She's not even Jewish.

ANNE THREE: You're only half.

ANNE TWO: So are you!

ANNE THREE: Yeah, but the right half.

(Something shifts in PROPS.)

PROPS: Both my parents are Jewish.

My grandmother was born the same year as Anne Frank in Berlin and survived Auschwitz.

I didn't have a Bat Mitzvah theme.

My Bat Mitzvah theme? Was Hebrew.

And I've never been an Anne.

Anne Frank is no longer about what she *said.*

Anne Frank isn't even about Judaism anymore.

Anne Frank is a symbol with all the things that are scary stripped away.

Anne Frank is all the things we should have remembered by now.

(PROPS shifts back to her clipboard and goes to the last page and reads from it.)

On August 4th of 1944, in the morning, Anne Frank

As well as the other members of the Secret Annex were arrested and taken to Aushwitz.

Later, Anne and her sister Margot were taken to Bergen-Belsen where she died of Typhus.

We don't know much else, because she never wrote another entry.

Yet in the many of the depictions words have been put in her mouth about what final entry she might have written on the day she was taken.

(She looks up from the clipboard and speaks.)

Because it makes us feel better to put words where there are none.

…

Anne?

(She looks at ANNE ONE.)

Go ahead and give us a final entry.

(A long pause. ANNE THREE struggles with this, then something changes.)

ANNE ONE: Dear

…

Dear…

Dear Anne Frank,

Hey, it's me.

I have a tattoo of something you said

On my lower back?

Or something you didn't say, but a saying you quoted

"Paper is more patient than people"

I just wanted to ask you…

Did you still think paper was patient when you no longer had any?

…

(ANNE TWO stands and addresses ANNE ONE.)

ANNE TWO: Anne?

Are you okay with who you've become?

Who we've made you into.

We want you to give us hope, okay?

But also…

We just can't imagine what was done to you…

We don't

want

to imagine

I

I don't want to imagine

…

Anne, did you still really believe people were really good at heart when they were killing you?

(ANNE THREE stands and addresses ANNE TWO.)

ANNE THREE: Anne? Who are you now?

Are you a 12 year old Syrian writing a blog?

Anne

Is it okay that I need you to tell me that it's okay?

I need you to tell me I'm okay

I need you to tell me that it's okay that you're dead.

ANNE TWO: Anne, I just want you to forgive me.

Anne?

ANNE THREE: Anne?

Would you forgive us, do you think?

PROPS: Anne, will you forgive me?

END OF PLAY

A VISIT TO THE RUST BELT

Jenny Lyn Bader

The play was developed for and first presented at School-house in the City: a series of short politically charged pieces, at the Dramatists Guild Fund Music Hall, on February 5, 2017, curated by The Schoolhouse Theatre (Bram Lewis, Artistic Director; Janice Maffei, Literary Manager).

The cast was:

NORA: Meghann Garmany;
CHRIS: Matt Biagini;
JD: Vince Trani

An earlier, shorter version of the play was written for and presented at the "Our Response/Our Country" One-Minute Play Festival (Dominic D'Andrea, Producing Artistic Director; Caitlin Wees, Associate Producer) in November 2016, where it was directed by Pete Boisvert at the Brick Theatre in Brooklyn, NY.

CHARACTERS:

    NORA, a twenty-something who rarely leaves Brooklyn

    CHRIS, a twenty-something who works in the high-tech industry in California

    JD, forties or fifties, a Trump voter from a rural area in the rust belt

A note on casting: while the cast as written is 2M/1W, the play can alternately be performed by three women (where Chris and JD would be played by women) or three men (where "Nora" could become "Noah.")

SETTING:

    The front door of JD's house

TIME:

    November 10th, 2016. Afternoon.

(NORA and CHRIS are outside a house. CHRIS rings the doorbell then knocks tentatively. They wait a moment.)

NORA: You're being too soft.

(NORA knocks louder. Then tries knocking in a rhythm. They wait a beat.)

CHRIS: I guess no one's home. We should go.

(They start to leave. NORA spots something on the floor.)

NORA: Wait.

CHRIS: What?

(NORA points to the floor.)

NORA: Look at their newspaper.

(They both crouch down, reading the headlines)

CHRIS: Oh my god.

(CHRIS takes out his phone and takes a picture of the newspaper.)

NORA: What are you doing?

CHRIS: I've gotta Instagram that. Wow. I've never seen anything like it.

(JD enters.)

JD: What the hell are you two doing crawling on my newspaper?

(They jump up.)

CHRIS: Sorry, we were just in the neighborhood, and…

NORA: Not exactly "just in the neighborhood." Hi, I'm Nora, I'm from New York… and this is my friend Chris from California.

CHRIS: Silicon Valley. Hi.

NORA: And Chris here was visiting me and neither of us understand what just happened in our country, and we'd never seen a Trump supporter.

CHRIS: Except for that guy in the Sweatshop Café with the Make America Great hat.

NORA: Yeah, except for him, right. So we thought we should look. And we figured it would be easy to find people because the signs would still be up on the lawns but a lot of them are down already.

JD: Yeah, I haven't gotten around to that myself. The weather took some of them.

NORA: We're sorry to bother you. We just want to talk.

JD: You couldn't just talk to the guy in the hat?

NORA: No we really couldn't.

CHRIS: That might have been good if we had. It's my fault. I wanted to put a photo of him on twitter, you know hashtag "spotted in Brooklyn" but I didn't get his permission and he saw me and he got all serious and he said, "you can take my picture, you just have to ask," and then I pretended I wasn't taking a picture and I didn't know what he was talking about and then he got pretty annoyed. Just kept staring at me.

NORA: The guy was a jerk.

JD: You were a liar.

CHRIS: Yeah, I shouldn't have lied. I just didn't know what he was gonna do. But as badly as that went, it made me realize: we shouldn't be staring down these people or tweeting about them, we should be talking to them... but where are they?

NORA: So we decided to take a road trip!

JD: Road trip? So you just up and left your jobs?

CHRIS: I was already on vacation in New York when it all happened.

NORA: And at the office where I work, in Brooklyn, everyone was so depressed that they weren't functioning. Productivity was at an all-time low, so they gave the whole staff two days off to process the election results.

JD: *(amazed)* It's like another world there, huh?

    (They nod.)

NORA: We just started driving... We'd heard about this "Rust Belt" but we'd never been. You don't have to talk to us if you don't want to. We're just —— hoping to understand.

JD: What's to understand? What was your girl gonna do about all these issues?

    (He points to the newspaper on the ground.)

NORA: Um, about that: You get completely different news than we do!

JD: That so?

NORA: Sharia Law is not on the rise in the Midwest! D'you ever google, to check this stuff?

JD: I google. Same stuff. Islamism coming up. The sheer arrogance of a woman who puts classified information into unclassified emails. All the violent beatings of cops.

CHRIS: Beatings of *cops?*

JD: Policemen are under attack in this country.

NORA: —You've read that on Google?

JD: Maybe my Google's different than yours.

NORA: It can't be!

CHRIS: *(realizing)* You know what… it could be! Google customizes its results!

NORA: It does what?

CHRIS: Each person's Google is different… Based on what you searched and clicked on in the past. So if you've been looking at articles that attack a person, or an idea, it'll show you more just like that one. It predicts what you want. We think of it as all one thing, but there isn't just one Google. There's my Google, *(to Nora:)* and your Google, and his Google. I'm sorry, What's your name?

JD: J.D.

CHRIS: I bet J.D.'s Google is completely different from ours.

JD: Why the hell do they do that?

CHRIS: It's been a big technology trend for years: Customization. A world designed just for you. All your favorite sections of the paper, without the ones you don't read. All the recipes you like, without the things you're allergic to. It gives you everything you think you want. So you'll be happier. …And see more ads.

JD: Yeah, but they should go ahead and tell you there isn't one Google.

NORA: You're right *(to CHRIS:)* It's true, he's right.

(JD picks up the newspaper.)

JD: So you think you get better news than this?

NORA: Sure. More rigorous reporting.

JD: Uh huh. And who'd they tell you was gonna win?

NORA: Um.

JD: My news had that right. None of us were taken by surprise. Or needed two days off. God, that's rich.

(laughs)

None of us are having trouble understanding what happened. We know what happened. A guy so plainspoken that he's downright vulgar, talking right to the people. Taking positions. And not caring who he offends.

NORA: No, he certainly doesn't care. But don't you care who he offends?

JD: Lord, when did everyone get so easily offended? Tell you what. He came out here. She didn't. Her people thought she had it in the bag, right? …He got around. Noticed that life hasn't gotten so much better for a lot of folks.

CHRIS: You're a man of faith, aren't you?

JD: What makes you say that?

CHRIS: Er… You said "lord."

JD: What if I am?

CHRIS: Even if you liked what he was saying about jobs, from a moral standpoint didn't you find him — concerning? With all the wives and divorces and the crude comments about women and mocking the weak and the crippled and building gold-plated skyscrapers and casinos?

JD: Sure, brash guy, likes to provoke, and not care and not apologize. But you know what? That's because he's not a real politician. I'm sick of those professional bullshit artists who are so careful with every word apologizing every second about this word or that one, who won't say that anything's wrong with this mess, and who got us into this mess in the first place. You're not tired of that?

CHRIS: Okay, yeah. There's a lot of bullshitting happening. And professional politicians can be exasperating. But—

JD: Tell me the truth. You never found him refreshing at all?

CHRIS: No!

(JD looks at NORA.)

NORA: Just on his reality show.

CHRIS: What?

NORA: When *The Apprentice* was first on, I was completely addicted. I couldn't wait for it to be on. When someone would annoy me I would think to myself, you know what? "You're fired!" But that lasted about three episodes and then I was... he wasn't refreshing anymore. He was just more of the same.

JD: I never did see that show.

NORA: Okay, I see why you find him refreshing. But don't *you* see that he's a bully? He would say people needed to be beaten up at his rallies—

JD: Oh please! They were fake protesters. They got paid for demonstrating.

NORA: No, they were real. The news stories about them being paid were fake. That was all made up.

JD: It was?

CHRIS: Yes! It was all fake! Except... there was this one demonstrator in Arizona who admitted in an interview he did get paid $3500 to protest and also complained that the people of color getting paid to demonstrate earned less than him. And that one article made people doubt all the other protesters.

NORA: What are you talking about? That was fake news too!

CHRIS: But... I read it in San Francisco.

JD: Huh. Guess they got fake news in California now.

CHRIS: I saw it on ABC! Here... I saved it because I was supposed to go to a protest to protest the accusation that there were paid protesters but then I didn't go because I read that three of them *were* paid and it felt a little...

(CHRIS, clicking on his phone, finds it.)

Oh wow. This isn't ABCnews dot com. This is ABCnews dot com dot co. This was fake! I was taken in! I work in the industry! How could I get taken in by a fake URL?

JD: Well, this is what we're dealing with. We got different news, different Googles... and a very different idea of a vacation.

NORA: You never wanted to drive across America?

JD: Not in these conditions. I'd invite you in but you might be stuck for a few days. You kids know there's a blizzard coming in?

CHRIS: The weather report didn't mention that.

JD: You don't need a weather report when the sky is turning colors like that. Just look at it.

CHRIS: Wow.

JD: You better hit the road.

NORA: I guess we can try again when it melts.

> *(JD nods)*

JD: Drive safe.

> *(JD waves at them, then shakes his head.)*
>
> *The End*

Zombies R Us

Rhea MacCallum

Premiered as part of the Aloha Performing Arts Company 24th Annual Original Play Festival, August 16-19th, 2017, in Kealakekua, HI. Jerry Tracy, Artistic Director and Melissa Geiger, Managing Producer. Director: Robin O'Hara. Cast: Sally: Janemarie Singer; Eric the Zombie: Rich Mears; Nance: Shelene Grey. Email: info@ apachawaii.org

CHARACTERS

SALLY: late 20s and up

ERIC THE ZOMBIE: recently reanimated corpse, grunts periodically

NANCE: late 20s and up

SYNOPSIS

He cooks. He cleans. He's the perfect boyfriend. He's Eric the Zombie.

SETTING

Living room. Present day.

Living room. There is a couch and coffee table. ERIC THE ZOMBIE is wearing a large electronic collar and groans every now and again, as zombies do. Music plays as SALLY and ERIC THE ZOMBIE dance.

SALLY: And dip, cha cha, one two three. And twist, cha cha, one two three. You know you're surprisingly agile for a zombie. I wouldn't have thunk it but, and DIP, you're the best dance partner I've ever had.

(Change in music.)

Want to go again? What am I saying? Of course you do because I do and what I say goes. Alright now, put this hand here, this hand here.

(Eric the Zombie lowers hand to her derrière.)

Oh, now watch it with that hand, Eric, you sly zombie you.

(Doorbell chimes.)

You weren't expecting anyone, were you, Eric?

NANCE: *(Knocking.)*C'mon, Sally. Your car is in the driveway, I know you're in there.

SALLY: Great.

(Sally extracts herself while Eric the Zombie holds position.)

I'll be right back, don't move.

(Sally answers door.)

NANCE: *(Pushing her way into the room.)*So you are still alive?! I could kill you!

SALLY: Well, hello sis, great to see you, too.

NANCE: Where have you been? You haven't answered your phone or replied to my emails or texts in weeks.

SALLY: I've been busy.

NANCE: You shouldn't do that to me, you know how I worry… Ummm… am I interrupting something?

SALLY: No, not at all.

NANCE: Really? 'Cause it kinda looks like I am.

SALLY: Don't be ridiculous.

NANCE: Were you hugging this thing?

SALLY: We were dancing.

NANCE: Dancing?!

SALLY: Yes, I'm teaching him how to salsa and rumba.

NANCE: The rumba?!

SALLY: Well, he already knows how to tango.

NANCE: I bet he does.

SALLY: What's that supposed to mean?

NANCE: Ever since you got this... this... THING... you've been spending all of your free time with it.

SALLY: That's not true.

NANCE: Oh, really. Have you danced with anyone else since you got it?

SALLY: Well, I...

NANCE: I didn't think so.

SALLY: It takes time to train a zombie, ya know.

NANCE: No, it takes time to train a puppy. Zombies are mindless monsters that some freaky company is trying to capitalize on. They just do whatever you tell them to.

SALLY: That's not true.

NANCE: He doesn't do what you tell him to?

SALLY: No, no, he does. He does EVERYTHING. He's perfect.

NANCE: Perfectly dead. An animated corpse, no thoughts, no feelings, no soul.

SALLY: You wouldn't say that if you knew him like I do.

NANCE: He's a zombie. What's to know? You bought him. He's a paid for servant in your home.

SALLY: He treats me better than anyone I've ever known.

NANCE: He treats you the way you've programmed him to treat you, which, by the way, happens to be how we living humans function as well. And, these things aren't exactly safe. If that collar of his ever comes off or malfunctions he goes back to his previous state of being a brain-dead, flesh-eating zombie. He could kill you!

SALLY: Eric would never kill me.

NANCE: Eric?!?! You named your zombie, Eric? Really? As in your ex-boyfriend, Eric? The jackhole who dumped you after nine years together, that guy? And you don't get why I'm so worried about you spending all of your time with it? I don't think you are emotionally prepared to handle... having an addition to your household.

SALLY: I'm handling it just fine.

NANCE: Sally, this Zombie business is still all so very new. The Consumer Reports on these things... they say they're dangerous.

SALLY: The 'Zombies R Us' salesperson said they've never experienced a malfunction.

NANCE: What do you expect them to say? They aren't going to honestly tell you how many unexpected complications and deaths their product is responsible for.

SALLY: I bought the Deluxe Zombie 5000. He is a top of the line model. As you can see he's in pretty good shape, just a few bruises here and there, there's minimal grunting and thanks to the 'Zombies R Us' and Febreeze partnership he smells clean and fresh at all times. He's an intuitive model so doesn't require as much instruction anymore and he's fully house trained. Did you notice my garden? It's never looked so good and that's all Eric. He cooks, he cleans. Just watch.

(To Eric the Zombie.)

Eric, please dust the living room.

(Eric the Zombie immediately does so.)

Eric, please offer Nance a taste of what's for dinner.

(Eric the Zombie exits and returns with a spoon he offers to Nance, who reluctantly accepts.)

That's fresh marinara sauce made from the tomatoes and basil and herbs that Eric has been growing.

(Sally sits down.)

Eric, bring me my wine.

(Eric the Zombie exits and returns with a glass of wine, hands it to Sally.)

Eric is the best purchase I ever made.

(Eric removes her shoes and massages her feet.)

He does everything I could possibly want. Oh yes, right there. That's the spot. My house has never been so clean. Oh. Yes.

Yes! It's amazing how he just knows what to do. Right there. That's the spot. YYYEEESSS!!!

(Eric the Zombie puts a cigarette in her mouth and is about to light it.)

NANCE: Ahem. Need some privacy?

SALLY: I knew you wouldn't understand.

NANCE: Oh, I think I do.

SALLY: I was lonely.

NANCE: That's why people adopt pets.

SALLY: He does so much more than a pet ever could.

NANCE: And that might be okay if he was just doing the laundry and fixing your meals. But... it's like, your boyfriend.

SALLY: He does listen to me.

NANCE: Of course it does. It has no brain. There's nothing else for it to do. Which is a problem. It can't challenge you.

SALLY: Yes, he can! He's the best chess player I've ever played with. Including you!

NANCE: Don't you have to tell it where to move the pieces?

SALLY: So?

NANCE: So?! Aren't you really just playing yourself then!

SALLY: But... he...

NANCE: You've really lost it this time, sis. I'm worried about you.

SALLY: So... maybe I've bought into the fantasy too much. It's just, he's so perfect.

NANCE: Because he isn't real. This emotional attachment you have to him... it's just not healthy.

SALLY: *(Beat.)* You're right. You're right. You're always right. Maybe I have grown too attached to Eric. I should probably return him or something.

NANCE: That would be best.

SALLY: Did you want to stay for dinner?

NANCE: No, I gotta run. I'm glad you're finally coming to your senses, Sally. You really do need to get outta this house and live a little. You know, with other living, real people.

SALLY: Sure.

(Nance leaves, Sally embraces Eric.)

Eric, how could anyone think you aren't real? You're so lucky you don't have anyone telling you how to run your life. She doesn't know what she's talking about. I know you'd never hurt me. I can see it in your eyes and I was going to save this for a special occasion but...

(Presents a manila envelope with a few papers.)

I was doing some research. I know that 'Zombies R Us' advises not to and they say whoever you were before, ya know, you aren't them anymore, but I just had to know. And, see, here, I found this company that works like Ancestory.com or one of those 'find your birth mother' services, only this was for zombie owners to find out who their zombie used to be. With their help I found out that you used to be Evan Jessup, so I was close on the name. Evan, Eric, not too bad. And you were an architect. I actually work in one of the buildings you helped design, isn't that amazing? And see here. You lived just a few blocks over. We may have met before. We might have passed each other in the grocery store and just didn't know it. No wonder you seem so familiar.

(Pause.)

You did volunteer work for the Humane Society. I knew you were a good guy, Eric, Evan. You are a good guy, aren't you? You'd never hurt me.

(Pause. Pulls out a vile of green goo.)

I've been doing some other research as well. There's this experimental treatment available to de-zombify those who have succumbed to the plague. The success rate has been so-so and I'd have to remove your electric collar in order to administer it, but... I think it could work. I mean, you seem almost human now, so why wouldn't it work? You want to try it?

(Pause.)

You just have to promise me, promise me, Evan, that you'll behave. Just sit tight while I administer the treatment. Can you promise me that?

(He seems to nod as he grunts.)

Okay. Now hold still and be patient.

(She unhooks the collar and he jumps up.)

ERIC THE ZOMBIE: Thank, God! I've been waiting, hoping you'd figure it out.

SALLY: Eric? I mean, Evan?

ERIC THE ZOMBIE: Oh no, I have no idea who that guy is. Sounds like a stuffed shirt to me. No, my name's Jimmy and I definitely don't have nothing to do with designing no buildings. I'm, ahhh, kinda between jobs and did one of those medical experiments for pay. Well, I have a low pulse and somebody thought I was dead when I was probably just passed out. Next thing I know I wake up with this collar on me and I can't talk and there's something in my brain telling me what to do. Thank god you freed me from that mess. Damn, my throat is sore.

(Sits, puts his feet up on the coffee table.)

Say, you don't mind if I stay here a while, just 'til, ya know, I get myself together. Seems only fair after all the work I've done around here for you. And while you're up, could you grab me some beer.

SALLY: So, you're really not Evan Jessup?

ERIC THE ZOMBIE: No, Toots, now where's that beer? You know it isn't gonna fetch itself.

SALLY: Sure, coming right up.

(She exits and re-enters, hands him a can.)

ERIC THE ZOMBIE: Just one? Best keep 'em coming, doll face. I'm a thirsty man, and the way I see it, you owe me big. We're talkin' huge.

SALLY: Right, right. Why don't I get started with that?

ERIC THE ZOMBIE: How ya mean?

SALLY: *(Moves behind him and starts massaging his shoulders.)* How about a nice massage?

ERIC THE ZOMBIE: Oh yeah, now that's what I'm talking about. Full body massage, right?

SALLY: Sure thing.

(She clicks the collar back into place and he reverts back into a zombified state.)

Zombie?

(He grunts.)

I think I'll take the rest of that beer...

(He hands it to her.)

And tonight, I'd like you to run me a nice warm bubble bath, okay?

(He grunts.)

LIGHTS OUT.

494

PLAYS FOR THREE OR MORE ACTORS

TEN-MINUTE PLAY PRODUCERS

Actors Theatre of Louisville
www.actorstheatre.org
Amy Wegener
(awegener@actorstheatre.org)

Acts on the Edge, Santa Monica
mariannesawchuk@hotmail.com

American Globe Theatre Turnip Festival,
Gloria Falzer
gfalzer@verizon.net
.

Appetite Theatre Company
Bruschetta: An Evening of Short Plays
www.appetitetheatre.com

Artistic Home Theatre Co.
Cut to the Chase Festival
Kathy Scambiatterra, Artistic Director:
artistic.director@theartistichome.org

Artist's Exchange, Cranston RI
Rich Morra
(rich.morra@artists-exchange.org)

Artistic New Directions
Janice Goldberg - Co Artistic Director -
ANDJanice@aol.com
Kristine Niven - Co Artistic Director -
KNiven@aol.com
www.ArtisticNewDirections.org

The Arts Center, Carrboro NC
10x10 in the Triangle
Jeri Lynn Schulke, director
theatre@artscenterlive.org
www.artscenterlive.org/performance/
opportunities

A-Squared Theatre Workshop
My Asian Mom Festival
Joe Yau (jyauza@hotmail.com)

Association for Theatre in Higher Education New Play Development Workshop

Contact Person: Charlene A. Donaghy
Email address of theatre/contact person:
charlene@charleneadonaghy.com

Auburn Players Community Theatre Short
Play Festival
Bourke Kemmedy
email: bourkekennedy@gmail.com

The Barn Theatre
www.thebarnplayers.org/tenminute/

Barrington Stage Company
10X10 New Play Festival
Julianne Boyd is the Artistic Director
jboyd@barringtonstageco.org
www.barringtonstageco.org

Belhaven University, Jackson, MS
One Act Festival
Joseph Frost, Department Chair
theatre@belhaven.edu

Black Box Theatre
FIVES New Play Festival
Producer: Nancy Holaday
(719) 330-1798
nancy@blackboxdrama.com

Blue Slipper Theatre,
Livingston, Montana
Marc Beaudin, Festival Director
blueslipper10fest@gmail.com
www.blueslipper.com

Boston Theatre Marathon
Boston Playwrights Theatre
www.bostonplaywrights.org
Kate Snodgrass (ksnodgra@bu.edu)
(Plays by New England playwrights only)

Boulder Life Festival, Boulder, CO
Dawn Bower, Director of Theatrical
Program (dawn@boulderlifefestival.com)
www.boulderlifefestival.com

The Box Factory
Judith Sokolowski, President
boxfactory@sbcglobal.net
www.boxfactoryforthearts.org

The Brick Theater's "Tiny Theater Festival"
Michael Gardner, Artistic Director
mgardner@bricktheater.com
www.bricktheater.com

Broken Nose Theatre
Benjamin Brownson, Artistic Director
Bechdel Fest
www.brokennosetheatre.com/bechdel-fest-3
ben@brokennosetheatre.com

The Brooklyn Generator
Erin Mallon (contact)
brooklyngenerator@outlook.com
website: https://www.facebook.com/TheBrooklynGenerator/info

Camino Real Playhouse
www.caminorealplayhouse.org

Chalk Repertory Theatre Flash Festival
produced by Chalk Repertory Theatre
Contact person: Ruth McKee
ruthamckee@aol.com
www.chalkrep.com

Chameleon Theater Circle, Burnsville,
MN 55306
www.chameleontheatre.org
jim@chameleontheatre.org

Changing Scene Theatre Northwest
ATTN: Pavlina Morris
changingscenenorthwest@hotmail.com

Cherry Picking
cherrypickingnyc@gmail.com

Chicago Indie Boots Festival
www.indieboots.org

City Theatre
www.citytheatre.com
Susan Westfall (susan@citytheatre.com)

City Theatre of Independence
Annual Playwrights Festival
Powerhouse Theatre
www.citytheatreofindependence.org

The Collective New York
C10 Play Festival
www.thecollective-ny.org
thecollective9@gmail.com

Colonial Playhouse
Colonial Quickies
www.colonialplayhouse.net
colonialplayhousetheater@40yahoo.com

Company of Angels at the Alexandria
501 S. Spring Street, 3rd Floor
Los Angeles, CA 90013
(213) 489-3703 (main office)
armevan@sbcglobal.net

Core Arts Ensemble
coreartsensemble@gmail.com

Darkhorse Dramatists
www.darkhorsedramatists.com
darkhorsedramatists@gmail.com

Distilled Theatre Co.
submissions.dtc@gmail.com

Driftwood Players
www.driftwoodplayers.com
shortssubmissions@driftwoodplayers.com
tipsproductions@driftwoodplayers.com

Drilling Company
Hamilton Clancy
drillingcompany@aol.com

Driftwood Players
www.driftwoodplayers.com

Durango Arts Center 10-Minute Play
Festival
www.durangoarts.org
Theresa Carson
TenMinutePlayDirector@gmail.com

Eden Prairie Players
www.edenprairieplayers.com

Eastbound Theatre 10 minute Festival (in the summer: themed)
Contact Person: Tom Rushen
email: ZenRipple@yahoo.com

East Haddam Stage Company
Contact person: Kandie Carl
email: Kandie@ehsco.org

Eden Prairie Players
www.concordspace.com/2012/11/18/submit-concords-1010-play-festival/
Reed Schulke (reedschulke@yahoo.com)

Edward Hopper House (Two on the Aisle Playwriting Competition) Nyack, NY
Rachael Solomon
edwardhopper.house@verizon.net
www.edwardhopperhouse.org

Emerging Artists Theatre
Fall EATFest
www.emergingartiststheatre.org

En Avant Playwrights
Ten Lucky Festival
www.enavantplaywrights.yuku.com/topic/4212/Ten-Tucky-Festival-KY-deadline-10-1-no-fee#.UE5-nY5ZGQI

Ensemble Theatre of Chattanooga Short Attention Span Theatre Festival
Contact Person: Garry Posey (Artistic Director)
garryposey@gmail.com
www.ensembletheatreofchattanooga.com

Fell's Point Corner Theatre 10 x 10 Festival
Contact Person: Richard Dean Stover (rick@fpct.org)
Website of theatre: www.fpct.org

Fine Arts Association
Annual One Act Festival-Hot from the Oven Smorgasbord
ahedger@fineartsassociation.org

Firehouse Center for the Arts, Newburyport MA
New Works Festival

Kimm Wilkinson, Director
www.firehouse.org
Limited to New England playwrights

Fire Rose Productions
www.fireroseproductions.com
kazmatura@gmail.com

Flush Ink Productions
Asphalt Jungle Shorts Festival
www.flushink.net/AJS.html

The Fringe of Marin Festival
Contact Person: Annette Lust
email: jeanlust@aol.com

Fury Theatre
katie@furytheare.org

Fusion Theatre Co.
http://www.fusionabq.org
info@fusionabq.org

Future Ten
info@futuretenant.org

Gallery Players
Annual Black Box Festival
info@galleryplayers.com

Gaslight Theatre
www.gaslight-theatre.org
gaslighttheatre@gmail.com
GI60
Steve Ansell
screammedia@yahoo.com

Generic Theatre Co.
www.generictheatre.org
contact@generictheatre.org

The Gift Theater
TEN Festival
Contact: Michael Patrick Thornton
www.thegifttheatre.org

Good Works Theatre Festival
Good Acting Studio
www.goodactingstudio.com

The Greenhouse Ensemble
Ten-Minute Play Soiree
www.greenhouseensemble.com

Half Moon Theatre
www.halfmoontheatre.org

Heartland Theatre Company
Themed 10-Minute Play Festival Every
Year
Contact Person: Mike Dobbins (Artistic
Director)
boxoffice@heartlandtheatre.org
www.heartlandtheatre.org

Hella Fresh Fish
freshfish2submit@gmail.com

Hobo Junction Productions
Hobo Robo Festival
Spenser Davis, Literary Manager-
hobojunctionsubmissions@gmail.com
www.hobojunctionproductions.com

The Hovey Players, Waltham MA
Hovey Summer Shorts
www.hoveyplayers.com

Illustrious Theatre Co.
www.illustrioustheatre.org
illustrioustheatre@gmail.com

Image Theatre
Naughty Shorts
jbisantz@comcast.net

Independent Actors Theatre (Columbia,
MO)
Short Women's Play Festival
Emily Rollie, Artistic Director
e.rollie@iatheatre.org
www.iatheatre.org

Island Theatre 10-minute Play Festival
www.islandtheatre.org

Kings Theatre
www.kingstheatre.ca

Lake Shore Players
www.lakeshoreplayers.com

Joan Elwell
office@lakeshoreplayers.com

La Petite Morgue (Fresh Blood)
Kellie Powell at Lapetitemorgue@gmail.com
www.lapetitemorgue.blogspot.com

Lebanon Community Theatre Playwriting Contest
Plays must be at least 10 minutes and no
longer than 20 minutes.
www.lct.cc/PlayWriteContest.htm

Lee Street Theatre, Salisbury, NC (themed)
Original 10-Minute Play Festival
Justin Dionne, managing artistic director
info@leestreet.org
www.leestreet.org

Little Black Dress Ink
ATTN: Tiffany Antone.
Email: info@LittleBlackDressINK.org
www.LittleBlackDressINK.org

Live Girls Theatre
submissions@lgtheater.org

Little Fish Theatre
Pick of the Vine Festival
holly@littlefishtheatre.org
www.littlefishtheatre.org/wp/participate/
submit-a-script/

LiveWire Chicago VisionFest
livewirechicago@gmail.com
Artistic Director: Joel Ewing
joel.b.ewing@gmail.com
I think they do an annual festival of 10
minute plays with a specific theme

Lourdes University Drama Society One
Act Play Festival, Sylvania, Ohio
Keith Ramsdell, Drama Society Advisor
dramasociety@lourdes.edu
www.lourdes.edu/dramasociety.aspx

Luna Theater
Contact: Greg Campbell
Email: lunatheater@gmail.com
Website: www.lunatheater.org

500

Madlab Theatre
Theatre Roulette
Andy Batt (andy@madlab.net)
www.madlab.net/MadLab/Home.html

Magnolia Arts Center, Greenville, NC
Ten Minute Play Contest
info@magnoliaartscenter.com
www.magnoliaartscenter.com
Fee charged

Manhattan Repertory Theatre, New
York, NY
Ken Wolf
manhattanrep@yahoo.com
www.manhattanrep.com

McLean Drama Co.
www.mcleandramacompany.org
Rachel Bail (rachbail@yahoo.com)

Miami 1-Acts Festival (two sessions –
Winter (December) and Summer (July)
Contact: Steven A. Chambers, Literary Manager (schambers@new-theatre.org Ricky J. Martinez, Artistic Director (rjmartinez@new-theatre.org)
Website of theatre: www.new-theatre.org
Submission Requirements No more than 10-15 pages in length; subject is not specific, though plays can reflect life in South Florida and the tropics and the rich culture therein. Area playwrights are encouraged to submit, though the festival is open to national participation. Deadline for the Winter Session is October 15 of each year; deadline for the Summer Session is May 1 of each year.

Milburn Stone One Act Festival
www.milburnstone.org

Mildred's Umbrella
Museum of Dysfunction Festival
www.mildredsumbrella.com
e-mail: info@mildredsumbrella.com

Mill 6 Collaborative
John Edward O'Brien, Artistic Director
mill6theatre@gmail.com

Monkeyman Productions
The Simian Showcase
submissions@monkeymanproductions.com.
www.monkeymanproductions.com

Nantucket Short Play Competition
Jim Patrick
www.nantucketshortplayfestival.com
nantucketshortplay@comcast.net

Napa Valley Players
8 x 10: A Festival of 10 Minute Plays
www.napavalleyplayhouse.org

Newburgh Free Academy
tsandler@necsd.net

New American Theatre
www.newamericantheatre.com
Play Submissions: JoeBays44@earthlink.net

New Jersey Rep
Theatre Brut Festival
Submissions should be emailed to nejrep@njrep.org. Include the full script, a brief synopsis, character description, and playwright bio. In the subject line put "Theatre Brut submission."

New Urban Theatre Laboratory
5 & Dime
Jackie Davis, Artistic Director:
jackie.newurbantheatrelab@gmail.com

New Voices Original Short Play Festival
Kurtis Donnelly (kurtis@gvtheatre.org)

NFA New Play Festival
Newburgh Free Academy
201 Fullerton Ave, Newburgh, NY 12550
Terry Sandler (terrysandle@hotmail.com
(may not accept electronic submissions)

North Park Playwright Festival
New short plays (no more than 15 pages, less is fine) Submissions via mail to:
North Park Vaudeville and Candy Shoppe
2031 El Cajon Blvd.
San Diego, CA 92104
Attn: Summer Golden, Artistic Director.
www.northparkvaudeville.com

Northport One-Act Play Festival
Jo Ann Katz (joannkatz@gmail.com)
www.northportarts.org

The Now Collective
Sean McGrath
Sean@nowcollective@gmail.com

NYC Playwrights
Play of the Month Project
http://nycp.blogspot.com/p/play-of-month.html

Northwest 10 Festival of 10-Minute Plays
Sponsored by Oregon Contemporary
Theatre
www.octheatre.org/nw10-festival
Email: NW10Festival@gmail.com

Nylon Fusion
nylonsubmissions@gmail.com
www.nylonfusioncollective.org

Old Brick Theatre (Scranton, PA)
Diva Productions

Open Tent Theatre Co.
Ourglass 24 Hour Play Festival
opententtheater@gmail.com

Over Our Head Players, Racine WI
www.overourheadplayers.org/oohp15

Pan Theater, Oakland, CA
Anything Can Happen Festival
David Alger, pantheater@comcast.net
http://www.facebook.com/sanfrancisco-improv

Pandora Theatre, Houston, Texas
Vox Feminina
Melissa Mumper, Artistic Director
pandoratheatre@sbcglobal.net

Paw Paw Players One Act Festival
www.ppvp.org/oneacts.htm

Pegasus Theater Company (in Sonoma
County, north of San Francisco)
Tapas Short Plays Festival
www.pegasustheater.com/html/submissions.html

Contact: Lois Pearlman lois5@sonic.net

Philadelphia Theatre Company
PTC@Play New Work Festival
Contact: Jill Harrison
Email: jillian.harrison@gmail.com
Website:
www.philadelphiatheatrecompany.org

PianoFight Productions, L.A.
ShortLivedLA@gmail.com

Piney Fork Press Theater Play Festival
Johnny Culver, submissions@pineyfork-press.com
www.pineyforkpress.com

The Playgroup LLC
Boca Raton, FL
Email: theplaygroupllc@gmail.com
Website: www.theplaygroupllc.com

Playhouse Creatures
Page to Stage
newplays@playhousecreatures.org

Play on Words Productions
playonwordsproductions@gmail.com
Megan Kosmoski, Producing Artist
Director

Playmakers Spokane
Hit& Run
Sandra Hosking
playmakersspokane@gmail.com
www.sandrahosking.webs.com

Playpalooza
Backstage at SPTC (Santa Paula Theatre Co.)
John McKinley, Artistic Director
sptcbackstage@gmail.com

Playwrights' Arena
Flash Theater LA
Contact person: Jon Lawrence Rivera
email: jonlawrencerivera@gmail.com
Website: www.playwrightsarena.org

Playwrights' Round Table, Orlando, FL
Summer Shorts
Chuck Dent charlesrdent@hotmail.com
www.theprt.com

Playwrights Studio Theater
5210 W. Wisconsin Ave.
Milwaukee, WI 53208
Attn: Michael Neville, Artistic Dir.

Renaissance Guild
www.therenaissanceguild.org/article/aos-xv
actoneseries@therenaissanceguild.org

Renegade Theatre Festival
www.renegadetheatre.org

Ruckus Theatre
Allison Shoemaker
theruckus@theruckustheater.org
www.ruckustheater.org/home/contact.html

Salem Theatre Co.
Moments of Play
New England playwrights only
mop@salemtheatre.com

Salve Regina University
www.salvetheatreplayfestival.submishmash.com/submit

Santa Cruz Actor's Theatre
Eight Tens at Eight
Wilma Chandler, Artistic Director
onziob@email.com
http://www.sccat.org

Secret Room Theatre
Contact: Alex Dremann
Email: alexdremann@me.com
Website: www.secretroomtheatre.com

Secret Rose Theatre
www.secretrose.com
info@secretrose.com

Secret Theatre (Midsummer Night Festival), Queens, NY.
Odalis Hernandez, odalis.hernandez@gmail.com
www.secrettheatre.com/

She Speaks, Kitchener, Ontario.
Paddy Gillard-Bentley
(paddy@skyedragon.com)
Women playwrights

Shelterbelt Theatre, Omaha, NB
From Shelterbelt with Love
McClain Smouse, associate-artistic@shelterbelt.org
submissions@shelterbelt.org
www.shelterbelt.org

Shepparton Theatre Arts Group
"Ten in 10" is a performance of 10 plays each running for 10 minutes every year.
Email: info@stagtheatre.com
Website: www.stagtheatre.com

Short+Sweet
Literary Manager, Pete Malicki
Pete@shortandsweet.org
http://www.shortandsweet.org/shortsweet-theatre/submit-script

Silver Spring Stage, Silver Spring, MD
Jacy D'Aiutolo
oneacts2012.ssstage@gmail.com
www.ssstage.org

Sixth Street Theatre
Snowdance 10-Minute Comedy Festival
Rich Smith
Snowdance318@gmail.com

Six Women Play Festival
www.sixwomenplayfestival.com

Source Festival
jenny@culturaldc.org

Southern Repertory Theatre
6 x6
Aimee Hayes (literary@southernrep.com)
www.southernrep.com/

Stage Door Productions
Original One-Act Play Festival
www.stagedoorproductions.org

Stage Door Repertory Theatre
www.stagedoorrep.org
Stage Q
www.stageq.com

Stageworks/Hudson
Play by Play Festival

Laura Margolis is the Artistic Director
literary@stageworkshudson.org
www.stageworkshudson.org

Stonington Players
HVPanciera@aol.com

Stratton Summer Shorts
Stratton Players
President: Rachel D'onfro
www.strattonplayers.com
info@strattonplayers.com

Subversive Theatre Collective
Kurt Schneiderman, Artistic Director
www.subversivetheatre.org
info@subversivetheatre.org

Ten Minute Playhouse (Nashville)
Nate Eppler, Curator
newworksnashville@gmail.com
www.tenminuteplayhouse.com

Ten Minute Play Workshop
www.tenminuteplayworkshop.com

Ten Tuckey Festival
doug@thebardstown.com

The Theatre Lab
733 8th St., NW
Washington, DC 20001
https://www.theatrelab.org/
Contact: Buzz Mauro
(buzz@theatrelab.org, 202-824-0449)

Theatre Odyssey
Sarasota, Florida
Tom Aposporos Vice President
www.theatreodyssey.org

Theatre One Productions
theatreoneproductions@yahoo.com

Theatre Out, Santa Ana CA
David Carnevale david@theatreout.com
LGBT plays

Theatre Oxford 10 Minute Play Contest
http://www.theatreoxford.com
Alice Walker

10minuteplays@gmail.com
Theatre Roulette Play Festival
Madlab Theatre Co.
andyb@mablab.net

Theatre Three
www.theatrethree.com
Jeffrey Sanzel (jeffrey@theatrethree.com)

Theatre Westminster
Ten Minute New (And Nearly New) Play
Festival
ATTN: Terry Dana Jachimiak II
jachimtd@westminster.edu

Those Women Productions
www.thosewomenproductions.com

TouchMe Philly Productions
www.touchmephilly.wordpress.com
touchmephilly@gmail.com

Towne Street Theatre Ten-Minute Play
Festival info@townestreet.org

Underground Railway Theatre
www.undergroundrailwaytheatre.org
Debra Wise, Artistic Director
(debra@undergroundrailwaytheatre.org)

Unrenovated Play Festival
unrenovatedplayfest@gmail.com

Vivarium Theatre Co.
www.vivariumtheatre.com

Walking Fish Theatre
freshfish2submit@gmail.com

Weathervane Playhouse
8 X 10 Theatrefest
info@weathervaneplayhouse.com

Wide Eyed Productions
www.wideeyedproductions.com
playsubmissions@wideeyedproductions.com

Wild Claw Theatre:
Death Scribe 10 Minute Radio Horror
Festival
www.wildclawtheatre.com/index.html
literary@wildclawtheatre.com

Winston-Salem Writers
Annual 10 Minute Play Contest
www.wswriters.org
info@wswriters.org

Write Act
www.writeactrep.org
John Lant (j316tlc@pacbell.net)